Matthew Arnold Revisited

Twayne's English Authors Series

Herbert Sussman, Editor

Northeastern University

TEAS 560

MATTHEW ARNOLD
CORBIS/Hulton-Deutsch Collection

Matthew Arnold Revisited

Linda Ray Pratt

University of Nebraska–Lincoln

Twayne Publishers
New York

Twayne's English Authors Series No. 560

Matthew Arnold Revisited
Linda Ray Pratt

Twayne Publishers
1633 Broadway
New York, NY 10019

Library of Congress Cataloging-in-Publication Data
Pratt, Linda Ray.
    Matthew Arnold revisited / Linda Ray Pratt.
        p. cm.--(Twayne's English authors series ; TEAS 560)
    Includes bibliographical references (p.) and index.
    ISBN 0-8057-1698-X (alk. paper)
    1. Arnold, Matthew, 1822–1888—Criticism and interpretation. I. Title. II. Series.

    PR4024 .P73 2000
    821'.8—dc21   00-030247

This paper meets the requirements of ANSI/NISO Z3948-1992 (Permanence of Paper).

10 9 8 7 6 5 4 3 2 1

Printed in the United States of America

To Bill

Contents

Acknowledgments

I am grateful to the following publishers for permission to quote from copyrighted materials:

The Complete Prose Works of Matthew Arnold, vols. 1–11, ed. R. H. Super. Ann Arbor: University of Michigan Press, 1960–77. Reprinted with permission of University of Michigan Press.

The Letters of Matthew Arnold, vols. 1–3, by Cecil Lang, ed. 1996–1998. Reprinted with permission of the University Press of Virginia.

Culture and Anarchy by Matthew Arnold, ed. Samuel Lipman 1994. Reprinted with permission of Yale University Press.

A Life of Matthew Arnold, by Nicholas Murray. Copyright © 1996 by Nicholas Murray. Reprinted by permission of St. Martin's Press, LLC.

Victorian Poetry for permission to reprint sections from my essay "Empedocles, Suicide, and the Order of Things" 26: 1–2 (Spring-Summer) 1988.

On the Poetry of Matthew Arnold by William Buckler. New York University Press, 1982.

I would also like to thank my colleagues in the Department of English at the University of Nebraska–Lincoln whose joint efforts fund our sabbatical program of Faculty Development Fellowships. Special thanks go to Steve Hilliard who was willing to be acting chair while I took a semester from chair duties. Without Linda Rossiter's help in protecting my time the chair's duties would have invaded all my days. I would also like to thank Herbert Sussman, general editor of this series, who asked me to do this book, and for his prompt readings of the chapters. He offered the good editor's mix of helpful criticisms and encouraging comments. My assistants Mary Trauthen provided excellent editorial assistance, and Mary Johnson formatted the manuscript. Finally, I wish to thank my historian husband, Bill Pratt, for his interest in Arnold and our many hours of conversation about everything from Cromwell to contemporary liberalism.

Chronology

1822 Born December 24 at Laleham-on-Thames to Thomas and Mary Arnold.

1828 Arnold's family moves to Rugby with the appointment of his father as Headmaster of Rugby School.

1836 Studies at Winchester College for a year.

1837 Enrolls at Rugby School.

1840 Receives school award at Rugby for his poem "Alaric at Rome."

1841 Wins fellowship to Oxford's Balliol College, where he will become friends with Arthur Hugh Clough.

1842 Death of Thomas Arnold at the age of 46.

1845 Temporary appointment as assistant-master at Rugby School and, later, election as Fellow of Oxford's Oriel College.

1847 Becomes private secretary to the Marquis of Lansdowne.

1848 Journeys to Switzerland where he probably becomes romantically infatuated with a woman identified only as "Marguerite."

1849 Publishes his first volume of poetry, *The Strayed Reveller, and Other Poems*. Second and final meeting with "Marguerite" at Thun, Switzerland.

1851 Marries Frances Lucy Wightman, daughter of Sir William Wightman. Accepts appointment as Inspector of Schools.

1852 Publishes *Empedocles on Etna, and Other Poems*.

1853 Publishes *Poems, A New Edition*, a revision of previously printed verse.

1857 Elected Professor of Poetry at Oxford University.

1861 Publishes *On Translating Homer* and *The Popular Education of France*. Clough dies in Florence.

1865 Publishes *Essays in Criticism*.

1866   Publishes "Thyrsis," his verse elegy for Clough.

1868   Deaths of his infant son Basil, and eldest son, Thomas, at the age of 16.

1869   Publishes *Culture and Anarchy,* a collection of essays in cultural criticism.

1870   Publishes *St. Paul and Protestantism.*

1871   Publishes *Friendship's Garland,* a collection of essays previously printed in the *Pall Mall Gazette.*

1872   Death of his 18-year-old son, William Trevenen.

1873   Publishes his controversial *Literature and Dogma.*

1875   Publishes *God and the Bible,* a rebuttal of criticisms excited by *Literature and Dogma.*

1877   Publishes *Last Essays on Church and Religion.*

1884   Promoted to Chief Inspector of Schools.

1885   Publishes three-volume edition of *Collected Poetry.*

1887   Retires as Inspector of Schools.

1888   Sudden death from heart failure in Liverpool.

Chapter One

The Uncertain Legacy of
Arnoldian Culture:
Done, Undone, and Done Again

Why faintest thou? I wandered till I died.
Roam on! The light we sought is shining still.
Dost thou ask proof? Our tree yet crowns the hill,
Our Scholar travels yet the loved hill-side.
                    Matthew Arnold, "Thyrsis"

In 1880 the London *Times* called Matthew Arnold "at once the most formidable and the most temperate champion of the Humanities."[1] Arnold's ideas and emotions are so much a part of the modern way of thinking about the humanities that we often forget, transmute, or evade his presence in our midst. As both a poet of intellectual suffering and a critic whose ideas reflect the main line of cultural development, Arnold provides the model for the uncertain role of the modern artist and the authority of the modern critic. Assessing Arnold's thought is complicated by the tendency to divide his long and essentially coherent career into parts reflecting the range of his work in poetry, educational reform, social criticism, and religious commentary. Arnold's first volume of poetry appeared in 1849, and he published his last volume of prose, *Discourses in America,* in 1885. His most controversial work of social criticism, *Culture and Anarchy,* appeared in 1869 and his most controversial work of religious commentary, *Literature and Dogma,* in 1873. Although his conception of audience and the range of genres in which he worked varied across his career, Arnold carried out a related set of ideas that addressed how we were to live in the modern world.

Perhaps surprisingly after a hundred years of commentary, critical opinion of his work remains unsettled, and understanding of his career as a whole is more fragmented now than it was at any time in the past. Revisiting Matthew Arnold requires us to look at both the poet and critic, at both the commentator on culture and on religion. It also

1

requires us to look at the changes in critical perspective that have made Arnold's work a text that demands to be reread.

Perhaps more than any of his contemporary Victorian critics such as Thomas Carlyle, John Henry Newman, or John Stuart Mill, Arnold's influence will extend into the new millennium because the debate about his value for our time is still caught up in widely ranging contradictory positions. Some argue that his ideas are keenly appropriate for our time, and others argue that his solutions simply cannot work in the modern world. Arnold said with great foresight of his own poems, "My poems represent, on the whole, the main movement of mind of the last quarter of a century, and thus they will probably have their day as people become conscious to themselves of what that movement of mind is, and interested in the literary productions which reflect it."[2] The "main line of modern development" Arnold identified in his poetry came to consciousness as the modernist intellectual crisis assumed sharper outline in twentieth-century literature. In addition to the attention his own work still attracts, his influence on many important poets and critics of the twentieth century, such as Lionel Trilling and T. S. Eliot to name only two of the most prominent, comes down to us again refracted through their influence on us. Certainly, as Jonathan Arac has noted of our whole academic enterprise, "Arnold is everywhere—though rarely acknowledged."[3] His presence extends beyond the academy into the general intellectual life whenever questions of democracy, class, religion, and culture arise.

The New Critical Controversy

The first few decades of the twentieth century were too close to the Victorian era to see how early modernism evolved from Victorian and fin de siècle movements. The modern poets defiantly defined themselves against the grain of the earlier century, and Ezra Pound's modernist motto of "make it new" discouraged a disinterested assessment of the importance of a powerful critical and poetic tradition. Even though "Dover Beach" frequently appeared in poetry anthologies, Arnoldian poetry, like most Victorian poetry, was not the ideal organic form the "New Critics" of the 1940s and 1950s valorized. Victorian poems reflected inescapable connections to the culture and politics of nineteenth-century England, and cold-war era New Critics usually wanted—needed—to avoid the political and social dimensions of literature. Arnold's discursive poetry about the crisis of his age was largely pushed aside.

Arnold as critic of Victorian times in works such as *Culture and Anarchy* was safest in modern times when his definition of culture could be eased, incorrectly, into a defense of elite culture. His religious writings were not of compelling interest to an era of intellectuals not interested in religion. Prose works such as *Literature and Dogma* or *God and the Bible* actively sought to salvage religion in a way that many modern intellectuals no longer were concerned to do. It was only in the 1980s and 1990s when contemporary criticism was once more eager to engage the political context of literary production that Arnold's prose again became politically alive and again controversial.

In the early part of the twentieth century, the sanity of Arnold's defense of democracy and his pragmatic hope for public education unquestionably informed the thinking of early modern intellectuals such as John Dewey, but many others were trying to articulate the modernist experience of existential anxiety, Freudian psychology, and revolutionary chaos that most engaged modern minds. Some heard in Arnold's poetry what he labeled "the dialogue of the mind with itself" facing just such modern dilemmas, but rigidities of definition between what we called "Victorian" and "modern" obscured the continuum between the two eras. Others heard in Arnold's prose the ameliorizing prescriptions of a modern liberal, but Arnold troubled others by favoring a strong state over the individual's rights. Arnold's liberal ideas about education, for example, lacked the purity of Mill's individualist liberalism; his ideas about religion scorned the mystery of Newman's metaphysics. His praise of "culture" did not refer to any particular body of knowledge but to something as abstract as an ideal of perfection and an intellectual habit of mind.

Neither radically progressive nor reactionarily conservative, Arnold did not speak directly to either polarity in the political and cultural debates of the last 30 years. As Gertrude Himmelfarb observes, Arnold was "politically incorrect" for "the England of his day as much as the America of ours, and for conservatives as much as liberals."[4] Arnold's most noted work, *Culture and Anarchy,* went against the fashion: it began with culture as an inward state that he hoped would translate into the external forms of government that could control anarchy. Neither the scourge of Yeatsian "mere anarchy" nor the romance of anarchism was Arnold's subject, and his more deliberative voice was often lost amid the extremes of thinking fed by the nightmare of twentieth-century history. In the political and economic conflicts of the 1930s and 1940s, Arnold was not assignable to the left. In the cold-war conservatism of the 1950s he was not assignable to the right. It was, however, the ideological upheavals of the recent "culture wars" that created an Arnold who could be either dismissed as a stereotype or valorized as the eloquent proponent of a culture at risk. Some see him as the elite white man who used Western art and letters as the measuring stick against which all truth and beauty were to be gauged. His misfortune has been that those who cited Arnold to support their conservative agenda distorted his real positions as much as those who targeted him as apologist for all that is wrong in the West.

Paradoxically, our critical engagement with Arnold was renewed in the 1980s and 1990s when voices on both sides of the debate about theory read him to bolster or dismiss some of the central issues about the methods and function of criticism. Postmodern philosophy and poststructuralist criticism have deeply altered the canon and the values attached to the literary past, and the resulting conflicts became known as the "culture wars." Arac claims that contemporary criticism has "inverted the Arnoldian canon" (118), though Arnold himself maintained that we should read the best that had been thought and said wherever it appeared. If the revolution in the canon has not been quite as thorough as Arac suggests, criticism has at least opened the canon and occasioned a new evaluation of traditional authors to determine whether we still value what they have to say. Critical directions that had once focused on the organic structure of the text began to move in the 1970s toward an interest in the cultural and political contexts of literary production, however, and Victorian literature as a whole emerged as one of the primary areas for a new historical criticism and a new linguistic approach to understanding texts.

Arnold's political work has been dramatically and often pejoratively reassessed in recent decades. Some critics point to how his fear of violence between the classes led him to urge force to restrain dissent by the workers in the street. Raymond Williams, in *Culture and Society 1780–1950,* faults Arnold for missing the more conscientious ways in which British workers sought to advance their cause without general violence.[5] Arac characterizes Arnold's views of the Hyde Park "rioters" as "a privilege of domination" (136). Arnold's prominence makes him for some the symbol of British Imperial rule, the defender of Western colonialist culture that exploited and controlled its dominions while it claimed to cultivate and develop them. This Arnold is one of the colonialist elite who defended the British status quo on race, class, and gender.

Edward Said's work explores the way in which Victorian writers like Arnold identified with Britain and "British power virtually unchecked over the entire world."[6] "To speak of culture, ideas, taste, morality, the family, history, art, and education as they did . . . was perforce to recognize them on a world scale" (Said 1994, 105). An internationally powerful Britain "provided irresistible models to emulate" in all corners of the globe. These models included cultural nationalism, Said argues, and a critic of culture, such as Arnold, implicitly aims "first to distinguish the national canon, then to maintain its eminence, authority, and aesthetic autonomy" (Said 1994, 106, 316). Said recognizes that discussion of "our" culture always results in banishing the outsider, but he especially faults nineteenth-century European critics for doing so because their "imposing edifice of learning and culture was built, so to speak, in the face of actual outsiders (the colonies, the poor, the delinquent), whose role in the culture was to give definition to what *they* were constitutionally unsuited for."[7] Said's reading takes no note that Arnold's criticism of "our" national culture is scathingly harsh, and that his fear was that British middle-class culture would indeed take over the world. The idea of "culture" Arnold proposes instead is not tied to national identity or a particular body of literature but is intended to displace what he sees emerging as a self-righteous but narrow-minded materialist national culture.

Arnold, then, remains a figure not easily categorized, inescapable as an influence, and still the subject of controversy. If we could not get past Arnold, still, we could not easily get to him. A grudging T. S. Eliot remarked that it is not to charge that Arnold's work was in vain if one says that it is to be done again.[8] Arnold's work is being "done again" in the philosophical pragmatism and democratic structures of thinkers as diverse as Richard Rorty and Jürgen Habermas. Russell Jacoby, whose recent book, *The End of Utopia,* attacks contemporary skepticism from within the left, looks to Arnold both for a genuinely democratic criticism of mass culture and as a model of how critical thinking should be done.[9] Donald D. Stone's recent book, *Communications with the Future: Matthew Arnold in Dialogue,* "pays tribute" to Arnold's "dialogical temper" by examining his dialogic relationship to such major figures as Henry James, Friedrich Nietzsche, Hans-George Gadamer, Michel Foucault, and American pragmatists William James, Dewey, and Rorty.[10]

Arnold's poetry continues to attract readers, but his poetry has drawn less controversy than his prose. *Culture and Anarchy* has attracted the most fire of any of his writing because it is the major document in which he uses the value-laden word "culture" and the source of several of his most disturbing comments about working-class dissent and the use of force to oppose it. In 1995 a new edition of *Culture and Anarchy* appeared that brought the controversy into focus. Arnold's text was accompanied by essays from several points of view by critics such as Samuel Lipman, publisher of *The New Criterion* who edited the book, and distinguished scholars Maurice Cowling, Gerald Graff, and Steven Marcus, who provided additional commentaries. Though they vary in their assessment of how well Arnold's ideas work in the contemporary world, all of them agree on the inescapable importance his work continues to have.[11]

Revisions of Arnold's Biography

Revisions of our thinking about Arnold extend to our understanding of his life. Although Arnold's public intellectual life was well known in Victorian times, his private life was sketched primarily in terms of his father's influence and his personal geniality. The poems known as the "Switzerland" poems seemed to be about a powerful romantic attraction to a "Marguerite," about whom nothing was known beyond her characterization in the poems.[12] Cecil Y. Lang's multivolume edition of *The Letters of Matthew Arnold* (published from 1996 to 1998) opened up new resources for study that illustrate, among other things, Arnold's deep regard for his mother's opinion, details of his vocational life as an Inspector of Schools, and emotional accounts of his tenderness and sorrows as a father. The letters give us an Arnold who is much more than a compelling intellectual. The Arnold of the letters is an engagingly affectionate man whose essential sanity balances his equally intense emotional nature.

Lionel Trilling's 1939 study was a biography of the mind, but Park Honan's 1981 biography began a new and closer look at the specifics of Arnold's life. Honan's work was based on many unpublished sources and is an important revision of Arnold's private life. Honan excited much speculation and some controversy with his theory that the unknown woman in Arnold's "Marguerite" poems was his literary summer neighbor, Mary Claude. Nicholas Murray's 1996 *A Life of Matthew Arnold* is a solid and friendly treatment of his subject. The reviewer in the *Times Literary Supplement* perhaps best characterized this biography "as a 'safe' alternative to Honan: soundly equipped with well-documented archival evidence, and without the controversial view of 'Marguerite.' Unfortunately, it is also without the intellectual excitement."[13]

Biographers and critics of Arnold's life and work tend to separate his poetry from his prose, partly because of the obvious need to organize a long life, and partly because his poetry largely came to a close before he was in his forties and his prose continued until he was in his sixties. Ian Hamilton's recent biography drew the line more sharply than others had, and some critics rapped his biographer's knuckles for doing so. Titled *A Gift Imprisoned: The Poetic Life of Matthew Arnold,* Hamilton's study presents Arnold's life as full of sorrow and shame at failing his father's ideal. In time he stifled his poetry and imprisoned the poetic self that was expressed in those poems in order to attain a life that was more useful. Hamilton makes few connections between the interests of the poems and the later prose. Helen Vendler has countered Hamilton's "tragic" Arnold with a view of Arnold as having "an imaginatively successful life, in which a great critic, having trained his taste by the study of poetry and the practice of it 'from the inside,' decided to embark on a vigorous analysis of the state of his country."[14]

The nature of Arnold's life perhaps lies somewhere between Hamilton's tragic imprisonment and Vendler's imaginative success. Born into a happy home in 1822 at Laleham-on-Thames to a loving but dominant father and an affectionate and literary mother, Arnold was the second child in a rowdy family of nine siblings. His family all had affectionate nicknames, but his special designation of "Crab" or "Crabby" makes one wince when we know that for two years when a small boy he had to wear heavy leg irons that impeded his agility in walking. In 1828, free of leg irons and walking straighter, he moved with his parents to Rugby when his father became headmaster of the prestigious Rugby School. Thomas Arnold became the famous "Dr. Arnold" whose work as headmaster was known for generations through A. P. Stanley's biography of Thomas Arnold, and through the tales and memoirs of his many notable students.[15] In many ways Arnold's educated and affectionate family life was an ideal environment. As a boy he traveled to France with his parents, and from 1834 on they summered at Fox How, the residence Dr. Arnold built in the Lake District where Wordsworth was a neighbor and frequent visitor.

Aside from falls and burns and other such miscellaneous episodes, Matthew Arnold's childhood offers little to suggest the somber poems that were to come. His performance at Rugby School and Oxford University was always a mixed success. He won prizes for verse but never won plaudits for his diligence. When he should have been studying for the Balliol Scholarship, he went fishing for two weeks. His father candidly assessed his son as having little possibility of success in his exams, but Arnold did win the scholarship, and in the fall of 1841 he was enrolled at Oxford's Balliol College. Arnold counted his Oxford years among his happiest, and he formed important friendships with men such as Arthur Hugh Clough and listened to the lectures of preeminent scholars of the day such as John Henry Newman, later Cardinal Newman.

Thomas Arnold's sudden death at age 46 in 1842, of a heart condition that Matthew was told he could expect to inherit, was no doubt a watershed in the son's life. Biographers usually see this episode as allowing Arnold to begin to move out of the shadow of his father and at the same time, eventually become more like his father. Evidence in the letters suggest that his father's death also marked an intensifying of Arnold's relationship to his mother. All of Mary Penrose Arnold's children were exceptionally devoted to her, and in his adult years when he was away from her Arnold almost never let a week go by without writing. The steady stream of long and detailed letters to his mother is one of the best sources of understanding events of his daily life and his own assessments of his various kinds of work, both literary and vocational. His father was the famous parent, but taken in the whole of his life, his mother may have been the more influential.

Arnold completed a less than distinguished career at Oxford, despite having won the Newdigate prize for his poem "Cromwell" in 1843. His next steps were uncertain—a trip to France, a temporary position at Rugby, a new mode of poetry, and a pressing need for employment. In the polite Victorian parlance, Arnold was "without means" and "lacking in worldly prospects." His reputation for being a bit of a fop or at least a dandy was perhaps a cover for his insecurities, but such affectations did not improve his opportunities. In 1847 he was offered a position as private secretary to the Marquis of Lansdowne, a man known for his interest in "practical business."[16] Arnold and Lansdowne appeared to get along well and to have had a satisfactory relationship during the four and a half years of his employment. The practical-minded Lansdowne may have been a healthy counter to the melancholy young poet who was better known among his friends for his affectations than his effectiveness.

Prior to his courtship and marriage in 1851 to Frances Lucy Wightman, the major romantic episode in Arnold's life was with "Marguerite." We know nothing of Marguerite except what is represented in the poems, and it is possible but unlikely that Marguerite was no one real person. Arnold's most thorough biographers believe that she was a real person for whom Arnold felt, at least temporarily, an intense passion. The outlines of this mysterious romance apparently are that he met, or met up with,[17] Marguerite in Switzerland in 1848 and revisited her in the same town of Thun in Switzerland a year later in 1849. Speculation about who Marguerite was and the nature of her character and status has entertained Arnold scholars for years, but real information has never surfaced. Confronted with questions later in his life about the woman in his "Switzerland" poems, a much-married and properly discrete Arnold never confirmed her existence. Honan's biography identifies Marguerite as the German-born Mary Claude who sometimes summered in the Lake District, claiming that Arnold's sisters knew of his passion for her (Honan, 142). Other biographers have remained less than fully convinced by Honan's case, but no one has disproved it, either.

The brief episode of two visits to a woman with a lovely pair of blue eyes while traveling in Switzerland occasioned several of Arnold's most interesting poems. The "Switzerland" poems chart the familiar pattern of a lover's initial romantic infatuation, aching loneliness when the loved one is not attainable, disillusionment with love, and eventual irritation and anger that he had ever fallen for one so unworthy. The Arnoldian hero is not *gallant* about his former ladylove and shows little of the Tennysonian idea that it is better to have loved and lost, etc.[18] The poems portray the agonized lover as intellectual, but the portrait is often a less than flattering picture of Arnold or Marguerite. Part of the power of the poems is the recognizably ordinary way in which infatuation wanes and lovers delude themselves about what they once felt and what the lost lover was really like.

Whoever and whatever Marguerite was in Arnold's real life, he was soon preoccupied with his emerging reputation as a poet. His first volume of poems, *The Strayed Reveller, and Other Poems,* appeared in 1849, and soon after that he met Frances Lucy Wightman. Fanny Lucy (Arnold often called her "Flu") was accomplished and strong-minded about her Tory politics and High Church religion, but her successful papa had little use for the underemployed poet. His need for a better job if he was to marry Fanny Lucy motivated Arnold to take the post of Inspector of Schools, a position he was to have for the rest of his working life and that was to provide the experience for many books and essays on education. The wedding in 1851 began the long, happy marriage, even if the honeymoon had its well-recorded ups and downs.

The newlyweds honeymooned in France, visiting such places as the Grande Chartreuse—the monastery of the Carthusians—and crossing the channel at Dover Beach. Seldom has a honeymoon lived in literature as such a gloomy, despairing affair as that of the Arnolds![19] "Dover Beach" pictures the lovers looking out into the moonlight on the sea only to be overwhelmed by the moaning sound of eternal sadness and the despair of the ebbing Sea of Faith. At the monastery of the Carthusians, they have a cold, wet journey up the dark mountainside to visit silent monks whose very beds are said to become their coffins. Fanny Lucy slept alone that night while Matthew communed with the monks and the memory of his intellectual teachers who had ruined his faith. The actual honeymoon was, apparently, not so disastrous as the poetic musings that came out of it would suggest, but the poems that draw on this period are some of Arnold's best and most melancholy.

Real life in the Arnold household was soon taken up with the rigors of Arnold's exhausting new job, a steady procession of babies, some of them sickly, and an unsettled residence located in hotels and the home of in-laws. Arnold's school inspector post took him across England and kept him on the road much of the week. This exhausting job required Arnold to visit hundreds of elementary schools where he "inspected" the teachers, many of whom were young people who were pupils themselves. He had to report on their work, the nature of the facilities, the school's budget, and other items of school management. Most of these schools were desperately poor. The job was notoriously demanding on the health and energies of the inspectors, and apparently the home office was very inefficient in providing inspectors an accurate list of schools to inspect and other such information that might have made the job less frustrating.[20] A few times during his career Arnold took up other educational tasks, such as his travel to France to review their school system and make recommendations for the English schools. From this difficult work Arnold made a living but not a comfortable one, and it was many years before the family had settled into a home of their own.

In 1852 he published *Empedocles on Etna, and Other Poems,* but a year later he had retracted the title poem with a preface that aired the conflict he felt between what his poems expressed about his emotions and what he believed they should do for the reader. He wrote to Clough in November 1853, "I am glad you like the Gipsy Scholar—but what does it *do* for you? Homer *animates*—Shakespeare *animates*—in its poor way I think Sohrab & Rustum *animates*—the Gipsy Scholar at best awakens

a pleasing melancholy. But this is not what we want" (*Letters*, 1:282).
Arnold's belief that literature should animate and ennoble, not merely
portray a melancholy state of mind, was the measure he used in judging
his work throughout his career. Despite his own conflicts about his
poetry, by 1857 his reputation was sufficiently established as an important poet that he was elected Professor of Poetry at Oxford University.

The 1850s were a period in which Arnold wrote many of his best
poems and began publishing his essays on literature. His family settled
into a place of their own, and his career as a poet was secure. As Professor of Poetry at Oxford he began publishing some of his most famous
essays, such as "On the Modern Element in Literature." The 1850s were
a time in which he gained literary success and established domestic and
vocational stability, but the 1860s were years in which loss punctuated
that success. In 1861 his friend Clough died at Florence. Though
Arnold was not always generous in his assessments of Clough, his affection for him was deep and the loss of this closest of friends lingered in
Arnold's life for many years. His 1866 poem "Thyrsis," was an elegy for
Clough, though, like his friendship, not an unstinting one.

In 1868 in what was surely the most heartbroken year of his life,
Arnold lost two of his children, his infant son Basil and his oldest son,
Thomas. Arnold's habit of writing long personal letters to his mother
and sister Jane, known in the family as "K," provides us with an excep-
tional Victorian account of an affectionate father's grief at the death of
his child. He writes his sister on January 4 of how he sat up all night
with the baby as its life ebbed away: "I went to him, stroked his poor
twitching hand & kissed his soft warm cheek; & though he never slept
he seemed easy and hardly moaned at all" (*Letters*, 3:211). On January 6
he writes to his mother of little Basil's death and the photograph that,
like many Victorians, they had taken of the dead baby: "This morning
he was photographed—we should else have had no picture of him whatever, and now he lies in his little grey coffin, with his hands folded on his
breast and a little cross of double white primroses placed in them, looking sweeter and more touching than I can say" (*Letters*, 3:213). In
November of the same year his 16-year-old son, Tom, died after a lin-
gering illness. Arnold wrote many letters to friends and family about
"My poor little boy" as a way of expressing his grief. To his mother and
women friends such as Louisa, Lady de Rothschild, he describes the final
scene and last words; to male friends he writes shorter, more restrained
letters, but all the letters express an overwhelming sense of grief at the

loss of another "darling" boy. Tragically, Arnold would again face the death of a son just four years later when William Trevenen, then 18, also died.

Arnold's letters about the death of his little Basil provide important signposts of a shift of his interests from criticism of literature and culture to his preoccupation with the state of religious belief. In 1869 Arnold published *Culture and Anarchy*, his best known set of essays critiquing middle-class values and expressing his hope for "culture" to transform the moral life and democracy of his society. Many of his most important works on education and democracy had also appeared in the 1860s. The close of his January 4, 1868, letter to "K" indicates a change in perspective that we see extended in the preoccupation in the 1870s with issues of religion and righteousness. He writes to her:

> And so this loss comes to me just after my 45th birthday, with so much other 'suffering in the flesh,'—the departure of youth, cares of many kinds, an almost painful anxiety about public matters,—to remind me that *the time past of our life may suffice us!*—words which have haunted me for the last year or two;—and that we 'should no longer live the rest of our time in the flesh to the lusts of men, but to the will of God.'—However different the interpretation we put on much of the facts & history of Christianity, we may unite in the bond of this call, which is true for all of us, & for me, above all, how full of meaning & warning. (*Letters*, 3:211)

The death of his sons and the loss of Clough were reminders of his father's death and that his own life might follow this path to an early end. He wrote to his mother on December 24, 1868, that the tragic events of the year signaled "the beginning of a new time to me" and that "Tommy's death in particular was associated with several awakening and epoch marking things" (*Letters*, 3:305). Those awakenings resulted in part in Arnold's new awareness of the need for religion. Arnold's persistent sense that life and literature had meaning when it achieved something is here expressed as following "the will of God." His "interpretation" of Christianity was not in the mainstream, but he devoted much of his writing for the next 10 years to articulating a vision of Christianity as a "wonderful remedy for the great plain faults of human nature" (*Letters*, 3:463).

Although many scholars have pointed to what they see as a marked division in Arnold's career between the years in which he wrote poetry and those in which he wrote prose, perhaps the more significant transition was from the publication in 1869 of *Culture and Anarchy* to the publication in 1870 of *St. Paul and Protestantism.* He wrote his mother in January 23, 1869, "And now I have done with this social-political writing for some years, and shall let it work—" (*Letters,* 3:310). The essays in *Culture and Anarchy* were witty and biting in their characterizations of the classes. This kind of writing in advocacy of the state largely gave way to studious essays about the Bible and the meaning of Christianity as morals for living and not metaphysics. Arnold essentially rereads the Bible in light of scholarly and scientific study that was questioning the credibility of biblical accounts of history and miracle. Arnold was also convinced that Protestant movements away from the established Church of England of his day were distorting the essential truth of Christianity and that in time religion would collapse under the strain of dogmatic misreadings and scientific proof.

St. *Paul and Protestantism* was followed in 1873 with *Literature and Dogma,* a book that argued that the Bible must be read as literary language and that Jesus' life was the model for righteousness. Arnold's work on religion excited a good deal of controversy because he interpreted such central doctrines to Christianity as Incarnation as metaphors for living in the spirit of Jesus' life. In 1875 he published *God and the Bible,* which was primarily intended to be a rebuttal of criticisms to *Literature and Dogma.* In 1877 he published *Last Essays on Church and Religion.* Arnold's writing career lasted roughly another decade, and the essays in the 1880s were on a wide range of subjects, including literary figures, the state of liberalism and other political topics, and critical appraisals of the United States and Ireland. His essays continued to focus on a number of poets, and in 1885 his own three-volume collected poems appeared.

In 1887, Arnold retired from his position of Inspector of Schools. Less than two years later, the sudden heart failure that had killed his father struck the son. Arnold was in Liverpool to meet his daughter and her new baby on her return from the United States.[21] As he was walking briskly to catch a tram to go to the docks, he collapsed and died at age 66. He was buried at Laleham, the place of his birth.

Arnold's life was one of joy in his family, both in his childhood home and in his marriage to Fanny Lucy and their six children, and of tragedy in the deaths of his father, two brothers, three sons, and his best friend. His life was also one of grinding work and what we might recognize today as a commuter marriage of sorts. Out of the pressures of family and vocation, he made time to write one of the most substantial bodies of both poetry and prose in the Victorian era. As Murray says, "He produced, the hard way, a major body of work. He is the patron saint of those who have struggled to do serious intellectual work at the same time as holding down a conventional job" (125).

Reading Arnold

Arnold wrote prose for the educated public and frequently reminded his readers that he was a critic, not a philosopher. Many of his essays appeared originally in literary or intellectual journals of the day and contained many topical references that were designed to entertain as well as illuminate. He excited controversy with his style; courting controversy seemed to be one of his rhetorical strategies for making his readers think about what he was saying. Ideas drive the prose, but topical political anecdotes and representations from the media punctuate the argument with popular examples. Reading Arnold at this remove from his historical time often subdues the effect of the biting humor his original audiences would have caught in many of the references, but his tone still carries meaning even when the particulars of the public person or event may be obscure.

Arnold invented a critical vocabulary to express his ideas, and many of those words and phrases are so familiar now as to sound like clichés. Reading him well requires us to put aside the distorted popularizations of Arnold's terms and revisit his own definitions. His label for the materialist middle-class values as "Philistine" has lasted beyond his time, but his views of the middle class are complex and not at all wholly dismissive. Other terms, such as "sweetness and light" to suggest the qualities of beauty and the free play of informed thought, were less successful and subject to some ridicule by critics of the day. Other terms, such as political labels of liberal and conservative, have substantially changed their definition since Arnold's day. As Honan remarks, when readers neglect to understand Arnold's definition of culture, they "garble the book's meaning" (346). Reading Arnold calls on us to tease out his actual usages from the popular versions of them.

One of Arnold's most misunderstood concepts is "culture." In a tradition of thinking descending from Edmund Burke, Arnold believes that culture, and education, serve to cultivate our full human development, and he rejects the more narrow functionalism of the Utilitarians who looked at human action in terms of its social use. Culture was Arnold's counter to Philistine materialism and the demands that the national life serve industry and commerce. For Arnold culture is not the world of elite arts that later came to be called "cultural events." He consciously sought to free his concept of culture from a pedantic idea of the arts. Arnold frequently praised the power of poetry, but poetry is not "culture" because of its literary form. Poetry is part of culture because it animates and ennobles the mind. Arnold defines culture as a way of thinking in which reason and flexibility open the mind to critical thinking. Culture is the pursuit of perfection, and for Arnold that means thinking objectively, reading widely and analytically, connecting the whole, and learning "the best that has been thought and said"—by artists, philosophers, and critics of all ages and any civilization. The "best" was what could comfort and sustain us in its rational wisdom.

Arnold linked the word "culture" with "anarchy" in the title of his most famous book. In the twentieth century, in the wake of events such as the Russian Revolution and the Spanish Civil War, "anarchy" became a more ambiguous word than it had been in Arnold's time. For Arnold "anarchy" is the extreme embodiment of the nineteenth century's liberal view of sanctioning individual freedom as long as it does not harm others. Arnold fears an excessive indulgence of doing as one likes that can result in two kinds of harm: disorder in the streets that threatens established society, and diffusion and dispersal of the unity of values and institutions that make up the collective identity of a people. In *Culture and Anarchy* Arnold's concern about doing as one likes is a pervasive worry that individual will, unchecked by education and culture, can erode the collective identity of the state that depends on a common experience of values.

"Democracy," "equality," and "liberal" are three words that Arnold frequently uses that must be put in specific political and historical contexts before they have much meaning. Arnoldian democracy is more about the citizen's attitude toward government than it is about specifics of suffrage and representation. "Democracy," says Arnold, "is trying *to affirm its own essence;* to live, to enjoy, to possess the world, as aristocracy has tried, and successfully tried, before it."[22] In his many trips to France Arnold came to admire the quiet pride and self-possession he saw in the French. In his mind the kind of equality that the French common people feel results from being invested in the organization of France. Arnold praises France where the effects of democracy have been to give the common people "a self-respect, an enlargement of spirit, a consciousness of counting for something in their country's action, which has raised them in the scale of humanity" ("Democracy," 2:9). His concept of equality also stresses a relationship to the State, and not a change in class relations. Where equality of investment in the state is real, national identity is more important than class structures. Arnold argues that the strength of French national identity allows class distinctions to exist with less friction and less sense of oppression, since everyone is equally "French."

In France before the Revolution the aristocratic class was more disrespected than it was in England, where, according to Arnold, the aristocratic class was historically more in sympathy with the underclasses. British democracy evolved in a series of historical events that gradually limited the authority of the aristocracy. Feeling less oppressed and powerless before the aristocracy, the English middle and lower classes were disposed to act more individually and independently than in terms of class conflict ("Democracy," 2:13). As the English aristocracy wanes, the other classes seek to affirm themselves rather than to assault the aristocracy.

The actual degree of equality of the classes Arnold supports is not always clear. He dissects the weaknesses of each class in England and finds none that is ready to rule wisely. His hope is that democracy in government will provide the mechanism in which the best of each class will rule in partnership. Arnold was stung by criticism that he had contempt for the uneducated classes, but his comments about the populace indicate a deep distaste and distrust of many aspects of the working class. On the other hand, he opposed the laws that provided for the right of inheritance and would have ended inherited wealth if he had had his way. Such a measure would indeed constitute a radical strategy for leveling the power of the classes and redistributing the wealth.

Arnold thought no existing class was adequate to rule: the aristocracy was out of touch with new realities; the middle class was too materialistic and lacking in perspective; the working class was too uneducated and inexperienced with governing. For Arnold the solution was a democratic State in which all classes were invested, all participated, and the best of each class could contribute to the unity of the whole, which would become the powerful State. Arnold warned his fellow citizens not to let English democracy become "Americanized," by which he meant dominated by the will of the individual. His solution to a destructive individualism was the power of the State. In modern times the State has often been the vehicle for totalitarian rule, but Arnold's ideal of the State was meant to avoid the rule of one class over another. His conception resembles in many ways the contemporary liberal idea of the State in which government pursues policies to educate citizens, provides welfare to the needy, protects civil liberties, and plans for an enlightened and safe environment in which the pursuit of happiness is possible for all citizens.

One of the most important debates in England in which Arnold was an influential participant was the one about personal liberty and liberalism in government. On occasion Arnold identified himself as basically a liberal, but at other times he launched critical attacks on the liberals. He agreed with and admired John Stuart Mill's defense of liberty but differed with him about the power of the State over the individual. Mill's work focused on the limits of the rights of the State to impose on the individual; Arnold's work defined the State as the proper entity to exercise the collective will over that of the individual. Since he defined the State as the collective best self of all classes, he was less troubled than Mill about the tendency to authority such a State might have. The issue was an especially emotional one for the newly empowered middle class. As Trilling explains, "Liberalism means many things, but to a member of the British middle class of Arnold's time liberalism meant one thing primarily: a State that could not control him except when he indulged in common law crime, an activity which did not attract him."[23] For Arnold, the emphasis on individual freedom, like the economic theory of laissez-faire, was a form of social selfishness. Arnold's views of democracy as a unity among the classes and equality as equal investment in the making of the State were clearly progressive for the time and a challenge to the nature of British government, but they did not always conform to the dominant idea of liberalism in his time or in ours.

Many of Arnold's class labels are idiosyncratic to him and often satiric. Arnold labeled the smug materialist values of the middle class as "Philistine." The biblical Philistines were the perpetual warlike enemy of the people of Israel. They worshipped idols and were once so foolish as to steal the Ark of the Lord. Arnold's use of "Hebraism," also drawn from biblical associations, was connected with what he saw as Jewish culture. In *Culture and Anarchy* Arnold contrasts "Hebraism" with "Hellenism" to distinguish two influences that have the same goal, perfection or salvation, but through different teachings. Hebraism refers to conduct and obedience and Hellenism to seeing things clearly. Both Hebraism and Hellenism seek to fulfill the will of God. Hebraism is more concerned with sin and strictness of conscience, and Hellenism with beauty and spontaneity of conscience. Arnold viewed his time as too much influenced by Hebraism and in need of a Hellenic intellectual and critical development. Neither can be the law of human development, he argues, and the ideal society balances their equally important contributions.

Hebraism and Hellenism come together in Arnold's later writing on religion in the term "righteousness." Religion is about conduct, he asserts, and the Old Testament Hebraic evolution of moral conduct and obedience to God is a major source for his understanding of righteousness. The term also includes the qualities he tried to suggest in "sweetness and light" and "Hellenism." Thus, conduct becomes not merely obedience to religious law but a form of human development that is in harmony with the wholeness of life and the will of God. For Arnold the teachings of Jesus are the essence of religion—not just of Christianity—because they possess the deepest wisdom and moral beauty of any example he knows. Hebraism and Hellenism achieve the perfect balance in Christ, and Jesus' life translates that balance into the conduct of the righteous.

Arnold's long career is too often approached in its parts, too often valued or attacked for ideas that are isolated from the richness of their context, too often distorted to serve agendas he did not espouse. His work as both poet and critic is best seen in terms of an unfolding development that comes in stages rather than twists and turns at many intellectual junctions. Spurred by his father's example and his mother's expectations, he sought always to make his work *do* something in the service of his society and for the affirmation of humanity. His commitment was to the intelligible law of things in this world and the free play of mind in the search for beauty and knowledge. His inescapable and still unsettled legacy reaches into our future as the work of one of our sovereign educators.

Chapter Two

Duped Souls and Best Selves, 1840–1844

Say not such dreams are idle: for the man
Still toils to perfect what the child began.
Matthew Arnold, "Cromwell"

The educated world in which Arnold was born was one where intellectual life flourished and poets populated the neighborhood. It was not surprising that the children of Thomas Arnold might pass their time with books and poems, but when Matthew Arnold first started showing his friends and family the poetry he was writing in the early 1840s, they were surprised that it was so somber and melancholy. The young man they knew best was the dandy and "social lion" who dressed too fashionably and studied too erratically.[1] His two prize poems from school days, "Alaric at Rome" in May 1840, and "Cromwell" in February 1843, had seemed more dutiful than melancholy.[2] The other poems that were written in 1843–1844, however, were marked by questioning, resentment, and sadness. The social Arnold who liked to joke and fish clearly had something deeper on his mind than his outer manner had suggested.

The poems of this early period share Arnold's exploration of philosophical and metaphysical questions by dramatizing how the way a man may face his death grows out of how he lived his life. How to live would be one of the abiding questions of Arnold's long literary life. Arnold would struggle with this question on the personal level of being his venerated father's somewhat rebellious son and on the artistic level of being an aspiring poet in an age of aesthetic transition. For Victorians the old social and political world of the three classes under monarchy was impossibly archaic, but the grand dreams for the future of democracy embodied in the French Revolution had been compromised in the Napoleonic era that followed. The economic and class upheaval of industrialization had moved the poor people off the land and into the squalor of overcrowded cities. The middle class had prospered and reformed the government to accommodate their new power, but middle-class culture was vulgar and materialistic. The intellectual life of the universities belonged to an elite class whose education in the classics was not the education of the new ruling class. On the spiritual side, the loss of the Romantic vision and the nineteenth century's doubts that God was in his Heaven and all would be right with the world complicated the question of how to live.

Arnold's early poems often bluntly pose the most unsettling Victorian questions about the nature of God and the meaning of our lives in a world where God may not be a force for peace and harmony. The poems that appeared as *The Strayed Reveller, and Other Poems* in 1849 set the major directions of almost all of Arnold's future poems. The mature Arnold, as critic, gives us the best answers he has found to the question of how to live, and the poems are the site of the emotional, intellectual, and aesthetic struggles with that overriding question. Arnold explores these disturbing subjects in poems that frequently displace his own person and present by using ancient historical settings and characters from mythology or legend. Many of the poems are tentative, and some express contradictions that he cannot resolve. As a whole he asks more questions than he answers, and the mood of anxiety that many of the poems air measures the uncertainty Arnold felt about the poet's role and the poet's wisdom in his changing Victorian world.

In "To a Gipsy Child by the Sea-shore," written between August 1843 and 1844, Arnold countered Wordsworth's notion of the happy child by asking, "Who massed, round that slight brow, these clouds of doom?" (*Poems*, line 4). In "Mycerinus," composed between 1843 and 1844, he characterized the just men who think they do Heaven's work as "duped souls" victimized by careless gods. In "A Question," written in 1844, he tutors his sister on the illusion of joy since everything ends "in the grave." In this grim and sad Arnoldian world, neither Cromwell nor Wellington, Emerson nor Shakespeare will get their due or rise transcendent on their virtues or their actions. "In Utrumque Paratus," composed in 1846, poses two conflicting possibilities about the nature of the gods and then pursues how our assumptions about the alternative conditions will influence the kinds of choices we should make in life. "If" God is the first cause and all life "took then its all-seen way," then we wake on a world in which the pursuit of that original "pureness" should be life's goal. "If," however, there is "no birth / In divine seats," humanity is "monarch" but should not pride itself on a status built on nothing more than "self-exalted" consciousness (*Poems*, lines 7–39). As J. Hillis Miller notes, "There is no way to tell which theory is correct" except by endless testing.[3] Intellectually, one may be "prepared" to consider either alternative, but how can one find inner peace or a sense of selfhood if one must *live* as if either alternative might prevail?

Arnold is the child of a long religious tradition that says that God is the first cause and all flows from that purity, but before his career ended he would drastically revise his father's faith. Arnold is also the citizen of "iron times" when "Nature is cruel," humanity lives alone and full of doubt, the inward essence is "buried," and knowledge is of "what we feel." These polarities in received tradition and the "modern" sensibility formed by science and the city are familiar to students of Victorian literature as the "two voices" that structure the "Victorian frame of mind."[4] Contemporary criticism has taught us to be skeptical of seeing matters in binary oppositions, and Arnold's poetry does indeed need to be revisited, not only to listen for a more dialogic set of voices but also to see how Arnold's poetry embodies a method of exploring numerous alternatives to serve some end other than finding absolute answers. Arnold's poetry sometimes implies what the answer must be, but at other times it asserts that we cannot know, and occasionally, as in "Stanzas from the Grande Chartreuse," he declines to continue with the dialogue. The poetry and later the prose are less insistent about having answers than in setting the standards one should demand in an answer. The best, most enduring guidance for how one might find one's way is preserved in literature and culture. Arnold will later urge us to turn to literature when there is no clear path and no certain end.

Underlying Arnold's difficulty of knowing how to live one's life is the riddling uncertainty about the cosmic order, or even if there is one. "In Utrumque Paratus" poses the dark alternative that "the wild unfathered mass no birth / In divine seats hath known" (*Poems,* lines 22–23). Humanity and its dream of relationships to others and to nature are but an illusion if we do not share a common divine origin. The poem cannot get beyond the question to address how one might be prepared for such a possibility. Written between 1844 and 1847, "In Harmony with Nature" is fiercely declarative that "Nature and man can never be fast friends" (*Poems,* line 13) and that Nature has the lesser character because it is cruel, fickle, unforgiving, and stubborn. Among his earliest poems Arnold's bluntest questions about the nature of fate and the presence of human suffering are in "To a Gipsy Child by the Sea-shore." Looking into the somber eyes of a child on the pier at Douglas in the Isle of Man, Arnold asks:

Who taught this pleading to unpractised eyes?
Who hid such import in an infant's gloom?
Who lent thee, child, this meditative guise?
Who massed, round that slight brow, these clouds of doom?

(Poems, lines 1–4)

When read against the Wordsworthian notion of the child who comes
trailing clouds of glory from God who is our home, these questions seem
to revise the cosmos of "Ode: Intimations of Immortality." Later in the
poem Arnold refers to "The Guide of our dark steps," which seems in
this context to imply a grim cosmic force behind the human suffering
that the child intuits before the age of understanding.

The four questions that open "To a Gipsy Child by the Sea-shore" are
about agency—who is responsible for this grief and sadness? Arnold
does not actually assign responsibility to a cosmic force, and the poem
gives us other answers nearer home than the heavens. This is, first of all,
a gypsy child. By birth the child is poor and scorned by others in terms
of class and "race."[5] The "pleading" in the eyes recalls the tradition of
gypsy-begging and European hostility toward its importunate forms.
The "clouds of doom" that hang over the child may or may not be
divine, but they are most assuredly social. The alienation may go
beyond the social to the divine, but, again, estrangement begins with
his mother whose breast "knows not thee." We do not have to look to
the heavens to imagine the sources of gloom in this child—hunger, cold,
lack of affection and proper care, social ostracism, and the prospect of a
future full of more of the same. Arnold's gentle heart toward children
does not need to see some horrid cosmic force at work in the child's eyes
because he sees rather plainly the abuse and poverty that condition the
child's everyday life. He is especially saddened by the suffering and
weary acceptance of it in the child because Arnold's ideal of childhood is
that it should be Wordsworthian.

The infant eyes that already know too much of sorrow speak of the
"vanity of hope," a theme that structures the last few lines of the poem.
Arnold closes the poem by noting that the forces that often dull or dis-
tract our awareness of life's suffering cannot finally break the chains that
link us to grief. That grief is connected to the absence of a benign divin-
ity of cosmic order of justice and mercy. The sunshine that may "blind"
us to our fate is "blank," and the "Guide" throws a "triple veil" over us
so that we cannot fully fathom the reality—and thus, the meaning—of
our sorrowful end.

The gypsy child may forget the tragic knowledge that infant suffering has taught, but Arnold will not. Their eyes "converse," and whatever knowledge the child possesses or embodies is passed to the poet when "that soul-searching vision fell on me" (*Poems,* line 16). His vision moves him to think of the limits of both the heavens and the earth. The child, whose sex is never implied by a gendered pronoun, is an emblem of all humanity poised between "Earth and Ocean," the "swinging waters" of time and the "clustered pier" of ordinary human activity.

When the child chooses Arnold's eyes for communion of spirits, the poem offers us an anti-Romantic moment of poetic inspiration. Unlike the Wordsworthian child, Arnold's child does not speak from innocence or lift the poet's spirits to the essential harmony of the universe. Finally, the gypsy child has nothing to say, and its dark eyes that seem to express sorrow are an image of an abyss from which the dim signs convey more darkness than illumination. Victorian poets such as Arnold and Tennyson must face the "blank" heavens and explore the sadness, alienation, and anger that they feel in that disorienting and disheartening knowledge. Out of that knowledge they make poetry, but they cannot reside solely in the "palace of art." They also must find some way to act as moral agents in the unsheltered universe, to do something more than stoically endure. The first act of courage, which Arnold sees in the child, is to proceed to live, but to live as more than animals in the geological slime and better than the ignoble and cruel gods who mock human suffering. After the question of "who" comes the question of "what," and most of Arnold's writing will explore what one can or must do to sustain a humane and moral society.

Arnold's Surprising Prize Poems

According to Lionel Trilling, the first of Arnold's school poems, "Alaric at Rome," "despite its naivety and frequent triteness, is a real poem."[6] "Alaric at Rome" is a "saddening tale that tells of sorrow and decay" in much the same terms as the later poems. The end of Arnold's second prize-winning poem imagines the heroic Cromwell, like those who follow him, "stretched on that bed of death" and "nothing now." Neither Alaric, the Barbarian conqueror of Rome, nor Cromwell, the leader of the Puritan revolt against the king, seems a likely candidate to stir a young Victorian man's heroic fancy.[7] Certainly the "barbarian" and the "round head" appear at first to have little in common, and neither is the kind of heroic figure that inspires unambiguous regard. Cromwell was the assigned topic of the Newdigate Prize in 1843 (Honan, 69), but both figures reflect Arnold's avid interest in history. In the poems, they each have a moment of "vision" shortly before death that qualifies their own sense of success if not history's judgment. Their "glory passeth not away," but their lives are "a lesson to all eyes" (*Poems,* lines 7, 11). Like Rome itself, both had "a glorious manhood, yet a dim old age" (*Poems,* line 39). Even as Alaric surveys the city he has just conquered, he "perchance" has his own Arnoldian moment of lone sadness. Arnold imagines Alaric might have longing thoughts of home and sorrow for the shattered city, the "solemn sight" of which "might well" whisper to him " 'All earthly things must die' " (*Poems,* line 180).

On the other hand, Alaric might "perchance" imagine "new dreams of wide dominion" for further conquest and look on "that wondrous city" as "one voiceless blank," seeing the ruined people only as his "slaves" and the desolation of Rome as "but another step to climb to victory!" (*Poems,* lines 175–86). What the narrator knows from history and Alaric did not know on that triumphant morning was that death was hastening its way within the year.[8] Had Alaric, like the narrator, known how soon his life would pass, he might perchance have had an even more sobering thought of the bitterness of "each fairest dream" (*Poems,* line 211) that melts away in a world that is both beautiful and blank.

> A little while, alas, a little while,
> And the same world has tongue, and ear, and eye,
> The careless glance, the cold unmeaning smile,
> The thoughtless word, the lack of sympathy!
> Who would not turn him from the barren sea
> And rest his weary eyes on the green land and thee!
> (*Poems,* lines 217–22)

The poem illustrates Arnold's effort to see a thing whole by looking at it from different perspectives. First, the poem tells the story of the conquest of Rome, which exists as recorded in history. Arnold then imagines this event as experienced by the people of Rome and as Alaric's imagination might have configured it in sorrow, triumph, ambition, alienation, and metaphor. Alaric's story also becomes a poetic statement that draws on history but imaginatively goes beyond what it can tell us. The city is shattered, or beauteous, "one voiceless blank," "warm and bright," "cold and sad," "glorious" and decayed. Confronted with the ruin of the city and the subjection of its people, one wants to look on Rome, and to look away. A tale so full of contradictions and uncertainties, of power and "the nothingness of power," of personal triumph and the "crumbling clay" of mortality cannot be resolved by historical account. It "needs a minstrel of diviner might" than this poet can chant. The poet ends with a sense of his limitations that he cannot "harp aright" the whole of the tale of Alaric at Rome. Just what the "right" version of the tale might be is marked, of course, by where the poem's text ends and its interpretive life begins.

The creation in art of a poetic reality that the poet rhetorically claims he *would* invent if inspiration could lift him is a familiar Romantic trope. In Coleridge's "Kubla Khan" the speaker longs for the poetic inspiration that would allow him to build again those "sunny caves of ice," but both poet and reader know that they have already been "built" in the opening lines of the poem. This trope depends, however, on a belief in a divine source of poetic inspiration that moves the human imagination to a more exalted state from which creation flows. For a Victorian like Arnold, such a belief was not possible, and the absence of such confidence in poetic inspiration moves Arnold and other Victorian poets to a self-conscious examination of the poetic act. Thus, when Arnold expresses the need for a "diviner minstrel," it is not a rhetorical strategy but an assessment of artistic limitation.

Lacking an absolute vision, the poet's vision is speculative. Arnold gives us several versions of what Alaric might have thought and seen in the spectacle of the conquered Rome. As Grob notes, "the poetry of Arnold is far less predictable than its critics take it to be: rather than illustrating principles it explores options, momentary possibilities, which are divergent and even contradictory and which, at best, receive only a qualified and provisional assent."[9] At the end of the poem, neither poet nor reader "knows" any more about this moment than we did before reading the poem, but both poet and reader have imagined a wider range of possibilities in the story. In this youthful poem, "this feeble lay," Arnold casts the blank moment of history into literary form, and the artistic vision opens up a rich range of suggestions of how such a moment might be experienced. Perchance it was like this; perchance it was like that. Perchance he thought this; perchance he thought that. The poet himself does not say what he thinks and puts no pressure on the reader to conclude which version is most likely. In his later work Arnold will insist on the importance of seeing life whole in order to know its meaning. The speculative possibilities in "Alaric at Rome" represent an imagination willing to risk the complexity that history contains when it unfolds from more than one perspective.

What some perceive as Arnold's lack of resolution has often troubled readers, but today his open-endedness is an artistic and cultural virtue. What is certain is that the world seems many things and that there are many ways to experience it. Arnold will not find through poetry firmer ground for knowing than the ground of feelings, and feelings are changing responses to a changing world. Stripped of the Romantic's confidence in inspiration and skeptical of the "truth" of feelings, Arnold must bring intellect and imagination together to critique that which can be thought. Like other Victorians, Arnold fears the potential chaos and solipsism of a completely self-reflexive consciousness in which doing as one likes is the only law. Paradoxically, the imaginative construction of other possibilities serves to contain chaos because these imagined alternatives act as a dialogic commentary on each other. The criticism of the argument is built into its form. For Arnold it is imperative that our choices about culture and ethics reflect our best moral sense and intellectual understanding. Literature is the vehicle by which possibilities are envisioned, and criticism is the vehicle through which we can find the guidance necessary to make that best choice. The poetry of "diviner" minstrels sees life steadier and more whole, and literature and criticism can thus lead us toward the right through exploring and weighing the best possibilities that have been imagined.

Poems as early as "Alaric at Rome" and "Cromwell" begin the process whereby a richly discursive artistic intelligence addresses itself to thinking through how we should best live by imagining alternatives. The still controversial figure of Cromwell offers Arnold another excursion into the wonders of history in which the central figure is both hero and nothing. There is, as Arnold knew, "great fault" in this poem, but in other ways, it is also "fairly good."[10] Written in the traditional heroic couplet of the Newdigate poem, the poem draws on Arnold's reading of Carlyle's Cromwell. Cromwell's youth lacked the tradition of the heroic; the mountains and the waves "where Freedom's form abides enthroned" had "no sound" for Cromwell who lived in the fen country of Huntingdonshire. Yet among the swamps and plains of his native "dull waste" and "familiar field" Cromwell read "in common sights" of the local landscape "All Freedom's mystic language" (*Poems*, lines 17–34). Cromwell's destiny seems like something that easily might not have happened if his plan to emigrate to New England had gone forward. The poem cannot quite account for Cromwell's vision and revolutionary leadership, seeing only that "his heart awoke" and "his eye kindled" as the future, "like a kingly river," "rolled its tides along." The historical Cromwell could move statesman and soldier to courageous battle, and he walked "loftier than the steps of man," but Arnold's poem imagines him, not in his glory, but on his deathbed. Although Cromwell faces death with the same fears and regrets of ordinary men, at the last he sees his life clearly and sees it whole. Arnold pictures him as he delivers his famous dying prayer:

> Then from those whitening lips, as death drew near,
> The imprisoning chains fell off, and all was clear!
> Like lowering clouds, that at the close of day,
> Bathed in a blaze of sunset, melt away;
> And with its clear calm tones, that dying prayer
> Cheered all the failing hearts that sorrowed there!
>
> (*Poems,* lines 213–18)

Cromwell the ordinary man and Cromwell the hero remain in unresolved tension for Arnold. Unable to account for Cromwell's inner fire, Arnold views the hero in terms of historical accomplishments and "not as the life of man." Yet no sooner than Cromwell expires with his exalting prayer and is praised for a life that wrote his purpose in actions, not words, Arnold raises other, compromising issues.

If Cromwell had a daring hand and undaunted will, he also had "a heart that recked not of the countless dead, / That strewed the blood-stained path where Empire led" (*Poems,* line 225–26). Arnold's reference to the "blood-stained path" of Empire most likely refers to Cromwell's willingness to impose British rule on Ireland and Jamaica. It is unclear how aware Arnold was in 1842 when he was 20 years old of the nature of British rule in Jamaica, but his disapproval of English prejudice against the Irish appears in many comments throughout his career.[11] Cromwell led the expedition to Ireland in 1649 and directed the massacres at Drogheda and Wexford.[12] Arnold no doubt knew that Oxford had awarded Cromwell an honorary degree in the same year as the brutal campaign in Ireland. Later Cromwell pursued the "Western Design" in an effort to colonize Jamaica with Irish, Scots, and New Englanders as part of England's plan to reduce Spanish influence in the West Indies and make a profit from the slave trade (Hill, 152–53). Cromwell's role in Ireland and the slave trade would not have stirred Arnold's approval. In recalling the dark, imperialist side of the Lord Protector's capacity for action, Arnold foils the expectations one might hold for the national hero.

Arnold's interest in Cromwell goes beyond his use of the Puritan leader as a strategy to rebut the influence of Oxford Tractarians and

Catholicism. The paradox of Cromwell cannot be resolved and so it must be balanced carefully. Cromwell's life combines liberal greatness with bloody action, government by the people with the usurping of parliamentary interference with his will. The leader who brought constitutional democracy to England also killed the king and many others. His democratic legacy in expanding the rule of Parliament was compromised by his impatient assumption of tyrannical rule when Parliament did not carry out his will. He sought to have men decide their government by vote but rejected the Levellers' desire to extend it to those without property. His treatment of Ireland was harsh and intolerant. Yet Cromwell led the Glorious Revolution that broke the Divine Right of kings. Arnold associates him with "Freedom's lessons," and the poem is one of several in this period in which Arnold examines concepts of freedom, justice, and law.[13] The lessons are mixed, and Arnold seeks to weigh authoritarian rule against the excesses of the individual will in determining how such concepts work in the realities of lives and, thus, how we can find stability in that uncertain balance.

Mycerinus's Dilemma

After his father's death in 1842 of a heart attack at the age of 46, Arnold's own life was marked with a new level of personal sorrow. Many critics and biographers note that his father's death brought Arnold to the understanding that he could face a similar fate. "Mycerinus" has traditionally been read as a response to the injustice of his father's untimely death and his own confrontation with the possibility that the same injustice could befall him. There is little doubt that his father's death deepened Arnold's sense of a "tyrannous necessity" that usurped right, reason, and joy in human experience. There is not, however, so abrupt a shift as many critics assume from his "dutiful" prize poems to the somberness of "Mycerinus."

"Mycerinus" again draws on "historical" sources in the form of Herodotus's account of the Egyptian king whom the gods condemned to die after seven years on the throne. The distant legend of a little-known figure from ancient history offers Arnold a shield for his own questions—not about "the gods," but the concept of God taught by his father. The obscure story of a minor Egyptian king is touched throughout by emotions that are more contemporary than ancient. The poem openly questions the nature of the gods, but Arnold is also concerned with the implied issues of law and justice when Mycerinus puts aside his kingship and abandons his people. The poem raises unsettling meta-physical questions and challenges traditional ethical assumptions, but it also asks about the consequences for others of Mycerinus's choice. Myc-erinus ironically defines his crime as sitting obedient "at the feet of Law," in contrast to his father who had spurned justice, slain his people, and ravaged the altars and temples of the gods. Mycerinus's doom came on him because, in establishing a society of justice and law, he had acted contrary to fate, which called for Egypt to suffer affliction for 150 more years.[14]

This poem, as well as several others, questions the essential fairness of the gods, and critics have often focused their discussions on the meaning of Mycerinus's scorn of the gods. As David Riede notes, "The dutiful exercise of justice becomes meaningless when disconnected from any authority higher than man, when the notion that 'Man's justice from the all-just Gods was given' becomes a mockery."[15] Mycerinus no longer believes that the gods are all-just, and he must find a new rationale for his life. His comments are dramatic and disturbing, bitter and angry, but not, as Murray suggests, "almost atheistical" (56). The questions he asks about the gods grow out of the apparent failure of law and justice to be the divine order. The question embodies the intensity of a particu-lar life when injustice displaces the rule of law under such a king as Myc-erinus.

Mycerinus had chosen the love of good in the belief that "Man's jus-tice from the all-just Gods was given" (*Poems*, line 20) and that he was following the will of the gods in his just rule. Now he considers that he is a "duped soul," but bitterly acknowledges that he is a self-duped one whose vain dreams arose from what the heart wanted to believe. If the gods act out their own will, they are cruel and unworthy of praise. If this cruelty is the will of the gods, then his father's hated ways were in tune with divine order and his brutal rule was sanctioned. Either Mycerinus is duped by his beliefs, and must now bow to the lesser gods who punish him, or he is morally superior to the gods who deserve only his scorn. Another possibility, however, is that the gods themselves may not be free, that "some Force, too wise, too strong" even for them makes the gods themselves "slaves of a tyrannous necessity" (*Poems*, lines 37, 42). This possibility leaves Mycerinus no less helpless to change destiny, and it destroys the figure of authority and will against which he can mean-ingfully react. The gods become like him, and both are subject to an unknown and unnamed force. So abstract a first cause leaves one unable to deduce rational effect or a basis for law, even if one believes that in the mysterious force there may be reason. The third possibility is that the gods are unseeing and unaware of life on earth, and thus "careless of our doom." This possibility, one that Hardy will ponder in "Hap" and Frost in "Design," offers the least comfort because it makes the whole question of gods, or absolute authority, irrelevant to the matter. One is thrown back completely on one's own feelings and thoughts to define meaning in our actions and ethics.

The possibility that there is no meaning in the universe would become the central question for the moderns, but it was a terrifyingly unfamiliar one to the Victorians. For Arnold acts of extreme individuality, doing as one likes, were almost the moral equivalent of the godless universe. Speculation about the death of God is impossible if "duty" is an abiding social value. In all three versions that Mycerinus poses, justice is traduced and humanity is powerless to control fate. In the first, the gods are a source of injustice and wrong. In the second, the gods are neutralized as having no essential power of their own. In the third possibility, the gods are removed from the realm of will and knowledge where actions can have any inherent meaning. Arnold, unwilling to grant individual subjectivity such unrestrained play in the rule of society, will replace in his later work such incipient anarchy with the concept of the state in which the nation's collective best self holds ascendancy over the individual.

Although the "the will / Of the great Gods is plain" to Mycerinus, the meaning of the will of the gods is not. Grob describes Mycerinus's thinking as "relatively tentative and undogmatic" (Grob 1982, 4), but the level of bitterness undermines his ability to speculate disinterestedly. In the shadow of a death sentence, Mycerinus may not have the free play of mind to move beyond feelings. His imagination works in terms of irony. He refers to "my crime" but clearly does not believe he has committed one, and he refers to the "lips that cannot lie," but gods who make a mockery of justice do lie, either in their pretense of the power to set the moral order, or in their pretense that they act on what is right. His ironic turn of thought locks Mycerinus into the binary thinking that divides issues into contradictions. Good becomes bad, law becomes the source of injustice. The actions one may take in such an ironic world are limited to acceptance or scorn, not negotiation or amelioration. As Mycerinus prepares to leave his people, he tells them that "something would I say . . . yet what, I know not" (*Poems,* lines 68–69). In fact he proceeds to give them a powerful message designed to repudiate the authority of

the gods. He urges his people to abandon justice and morality and to
give mere obedience to the gods:

> " . . . and ye must bring
> Ill deeds, ill passions, zealous to fulfil
> Their pleasure, to their feet; and reap their praise,
> The praise of Gods, rich boon! and length of days."
>
> (*Poems,* lines 75–78)

In so counseling them, Mycerinus recommends a complete reversal of a
recognized moral order intended as an affront to the gods. His intent is
not to inspire ill deeds and passions, since it is justice and law he loves,
but to create an alienated people who will themselves mock the unjust
gods by an ironic obedience to a rule they cannot respect.

In a similarly ironic choice for himself, Mycerinus goes into the woods
to "give to joy" all he can through a life of hedonistic pleasures. In
choosing pleasure where circumstances might dictate tragic gloom,
Mycerinus manages a form of defiance.[16] The gods have proven themselves unmoved by "life's pleasant things" and seek to "cheat" him of his
joy in life. His revenge against such "dull Gods" is to enjoy "revels more
deep, joy keener than their own" (*Poems,* line 66). At the end of the
poem, two things are known for sure: Mycerinus did not outwardly
show any sign of inner conflict, and the revelry manifestly continued for
the six years. His ability to maintain his laughter and his intellect grows
out of his choice of revelry as an act of meaningful defiance. His
"smooth brow" and "clear laugh" may be sustained because his pleasure
is in finding a way of life that mocks the gods who condemned his superior beliefs. This choice is neither truly stoic nor truly hedonistic, nor is
it useful in terms of the social good. Although the choice of pleasure
over duty was always on the fringe of Victorian moral and esthetic
debates, only the Decadents of the fin de siècle would pretend to
embrace pleasure over duty. Even the most desultory and dandified face
of Arnold's youthful mask resisted sexual attractions and the distrac-
tions of involvement with women who might deter him from his serious
critical and poetic work.[17]

The suggestions in the poem that we may not know the will of the
gods and that Mycerinus may not have always felt content with his
choice are indications that Arnold may not have agreed with his character. Mycerinus's rebellious will, like that of the later Empedocles, may

reveal courage and fidelity to his creed, but he perishes as a force for a better society. He is not Cromwell, a type of heroic force in the world in whom the social good outweighs error and limitation. Arnold imagines a divided Mycerinus who sometimes shrinks "half startled, like a guilty man / Who wrestles with his dream" (*Poems,* lines 102–3). His metaphysical pondering is too unresolved to sustain clarity about the gods. Anger and scorn cloud his mind. Mycerinus cannot achieve stoic dignity since he responds to the will of the gods with anger and scorn, and he cannot be a hedonist since his embrace of revelry is a strategy for defiance rather than for pleasure. The restless speculation of Alaric's "perchance" has been replaced by "it may be" in this poem, and so "it may be" that Mycerinus shrank from his own laughter "like a guilty man," or "it may be" that his outward seeming had little to do with the inner man. It may be that he found an inner calm and was comforted and sustained, or it may be that he was often afraid in the shadow of death and found his only comfort in "the lifted bowl" of more wine.

Mycerinus is concerned with the absolute authority of the cruel gods and how to usurp it. Riede argues that Arnold is primarily concerned "with the oracle itself, the voice of an absolute authority" (46), but Arnold's deeper concern is the lack of an absolute authority on which one can determine how to live in an uncertain and perhaps cruel universe. One's responses to such gods might range from hatred and fear to rebellion, indifference, arrogance, alienation, stoicism, or even pity. Mycerinus must think within the context of the legend, which says that the gods pronounced his sentence. In that context, defiance and scorn may be an ethical response in which the moral power of the human will is posed against that of immoral gods. Arnold as poet is not bound in his commentary by the understanding of Mycerinus nor limited to the issues the character casts in the metaphysics of the classical world. The issues in the poem as a whole are more complex than those posed by its central character within the limits of his world.

Arnold's speculations go one step beyond his character's in that he considers the metaphysical and ethical issues from the possibility that there are no gods and no "will," just or unjust, directing fate. Mycerinus's debate is about the appropriate response to a troubling authority, and Arnold's debate is about how to respond if there is none. The difference in these questions open up the poem in ways we cannot resolve from the example of Mycerinus. A number of critics see the poem as maintaining a more open ending that rejects a "fixed creed" (Riede, 48) or a "dogmatic rigidity."[18] Perhaps Mycerinus does feel that "the aspiration of human speech to divine truth is an empty mockery" (Riede, 47), but this is a better statement of Arnold's starting place than his conclusion in the poem. No "diviner minstrel" appears in this poem, nor in any other Arnold will write, to solve this inadequacy of art by producing a revelation of divine wisdom. Arnold would later say that poetry will come to replace what passes for religion, but he attributes to poetry a criticism of life, not omen or vision. Arnold's writing, including his praise for the best that has been thought and said, anchors the power of poetry in what it tells us about human life, not about the nature of God. In his commentary on religion, he will speak of an eternal force for righteousness but debunk metaphysics and miracle. In "The Study of Poetry" Arnold praises poetry for interpreting life for us in such a way as can console and sustain us in this life; its "truth" is in the substance of its knowledge of human life. The high seriousness he accords to the best art is an embodiment of its beauty and the wisdom about life. In its most practical sense, as Arnold observes in "Literature and Science," literature offers experience that we may relate "to man's instinct for conduct, his instinct for beauty."[19]

The end of "Mycerinus" provides yet another context for interpreting his choice. Although most of "Mycerinus" is given over to the angry speech against the gods, the poem begins and ends with relating Mycerinus's fate to his society and its people. Grob calls the groves, the site of revelry, the "imaginative center" of the poem (Grob 1982, 16), but the center of judgment on Mycerinus as king is the city. The opening lines locate the offense to the gods in Mycerinus's social policies as ruler. In his final address to his people before leaving behind the rule of the kingdom, he counsels them to address their conduct toward the gods. At the close of the poem, the "echoes" of his mirth sound in the capitol "to tell his wondering people of their king" (*Poems,* line 125). These echoes cross "the steaming flats" and mix with "the murmur of the moving Nile" (*Poems,* lines 126–27). The people, the "steaming flats" of the fields, and the implicit site of government hint at the ongoing toil, daily life, and administration of law that continue in the king's absence. The "moving Nile" is more than "a moving image of eternity, the figurative embodiment of an irresistible cosmic will" (Grob 1982, 17). The river is a natural force, a majestic symbol of Egyptian society, a source of agrarian fertility, and the central transport for trade and international relations. Like the river, the lives and work of the people proceed, touched but unaided or enlightened by the conduct of their king. In the expanse of Egyptian history, the life of Mycerinus is a lost moment.

In "Literature and Science" Arnold will make clear the importance he attaches to work and education. Contempt for the daily lives of working people, which in the essay he associates with Plato, is "of a primitive and obsolete order of things, when the warrior caste and the priestly caste were alone in honour, and the humble work of the world was done by slaves" ("Science," 10:54). Mycerinus possesses a king's luxury of withdrawing, but the people he leaves behind are never far from Arnold's awareness in the poem. In fact, the fate of the people is an issue just below the surface of "Alaric at Rome," "Cromwell," and "Mycerinus," though the concern with government and society is secondary to the focus on the legendary historical figures. In the "Preface" to the 1853 volume of his poetry, Arnold criticizes his own *Empedocles on Etna* for not offering the reader more than a dialogue of the mind with itself. Poetry must find some "vent" in action that can translate anger and unhappiness into something constructive. The action Mycerinus takes cannot do that for his people, nor, it appears, for himself.

Alaric, Cromwell, and Mycerinus are all imagined to be in a dialogue of the mind, and all find in action a semblance of something heroic but limited. In each case, their actions are divided against some better part of the self. If Alaric can imagine the suffering of Rome when he inflicts it, if Cromwell undoes in Ireland the standards he protects in England, if Mycerinus deserts his people when his devotion was to law and justice, each man's life replicates in ambiguous actions the unresolved dialogue their imaginations engaged in the poems. Arnold's poetry as a whole illustrates that actions are no more likely to be efficacious than are words that turn in on themselves in inner turmoil. If the Victorian's inheritance is words from no divine source and deeds of a flawed and mortal humanity, then finding our best self and leading a worthy life become profoundly difficult.

Arnold frequently raises in the poetry through personas his own metaphysical questions about the nature of the gods—or the disappearance of his Victorian God—and psychological questions about the integration of the self. His concern typically comes back to the social and ethical effects of our response to such questions. The nature of the gods is judged by how much good or harm they do to humanity, and the confusions about self are related to how they affect what the individual can effectively do in society or in relationships with others. Mycerinus, for example, speaks of his "crime," not his sin, and of "Law," not kingship. Despite the remoteness of the classical and historical settings of the poems, Arnold's treatment of his themes reflect the broader ethical issues of his time. The justice of law and the role of the state were increasingly important public topics in Victorian England and openly important in Arnold's later work. More people from both the working and middle classes in the cities fell under the rule of law on matters ranging from participation in government to the regulation of work hours. The press played up crime and trial stories to increase sales in the competitive market of cities such as London. Newspaper accounts of crime and justice frequently made their way into Arnold's prose. Fiction tended to domesticate crime by bringing it into the plots of middle-class life. Charles Dickens's widely read novels frequently brought criminals and law-abiding good people within the same sphere. In Dickens's treatment of crime, however, good always prevails and criminals either drown, hang, kill each other, or emigrate. Even the unsentimental Trollope brings punishment down on his capitalist crooks and corrupt politicians. Arnold's treatment, like his thoughts on education, never left the quotidian stage of real life.

The ideology of democracy requires belief that law works and that justice can be wrought. In a world in which cause and effect were linked, the imposing of a death penalty would have its root in crime. The plight of Mycerinus is an appropriately unsettling lesson for a middle-class democracy, because his harsh fate usurps the relationship between law and justice. His choice of withdrawing from his people is equally troubling since he abandons in action the principles of law and justice that gave meaning to his life. Arnold treats Mycerinus with sympathy, but he also sets in the poem's frame both the personal and public consequences of his choice. Arnold refrains from judging Mycerinus, but he provides the perspectives within the poem to make more than one kind of interpretation of his life. Arnold's view of Mycerinus recalls that of Tennyson's King Arthur who tells his knights as they set out in search of the Holy Grail that the "chance of noble deeds will come and go / Unchallenged" while they follow wandering fires in search of their souls.[20] The conflicting claims of the self and society forge the sharpest of Victorian dilemmas.

Years later, Arnold would talk in *Culture and Anarchy* about the need to find our best selves, a concept that unites his definition of God with his definition of conduct. The best of his poems, as well as the later prose, combine the values of both self and society. These poems are a form of mediation through which our dilemma may be understood and perhaps resolved. In weighing examples such as Mycerinus or Cromwell, Arnold's poetry sifts the alternative ways one might organize one's life and seeks the standard by which to recognize our best selves. Cromwell found at times his best self, though apparently no one holds it equally steady at all moments. Mycerinus thought that six years of defiant revelry expressed his best self, but Arnold's concern for his "wondering people" suggests that Mycerinus selfishly sacrificed them. Mycerinus does not consider spending his six years in faithful pursuit of law and justice, an act that would have been even more effectively defiant of the gods than outstripping them in pleasure. His people's wonder is bewilderment, not admiration, and the "murmur of the moving Nile" sounds the rhythm of life that absorbs the loudest mirth of an idle king.

Arnold finds more fullness of the best self in Shakespeare, Emerson, and the Duke of Wellington, each the subject of a sonnet praising their triumphant virtues. Like the poem on Cromwell, the sonnet to Shakespeare owes a footnote to Carlyle's interpretation in *Heroes and Hero-Worship*. Shakespeare is an example of one who knew "All pains the immortal spirit must endure, / All weakness which impairs, all griefs which bow" (*Poems,* lines 12–13). Unlike Mycerinus who is given to defiant and immature reaction, Shakespeare was "Self-schooled, self-scanned, self-honoured, self-secure" (*Poems,* line 10). Knowing himself dispassionately, Shakespeare can know humanity. Further, he can write about humanity instead of dwelling narrowly on the self. Shakespeare's "victorious brow" surpasses Mycerinus's "smooth brow" because it is not a mask concealing inner doubt or anger at the gods. His "victorious brow," where might be laid the acanthus wreath in triumph, signals a wholeness of vision that is the genius in his work.

One danger to the Arnoldian poetic hero is always to be pulled by the many conflicting currents and beliefs of a contemporary world that has lost its focus and purpose. A man who is not secure within himself and his own vision will be befuddled by the times and lose himself in the muddy torrents of an unsettled society. "To the Duke of Wellington," most likely composed in 1844, gives us another counter example to Mycerinus. Wellington is a force as both a man who believes and one who labors in pursuit of the "general law." His "genius" is found in the strife of a life of principle accommodating the "chafing torrents" of politics and history. Wellington is not reduced to enervation and doubt by the "fretful foam / Of vehement actions without scope or term" (*Poems,* lines 11–12). He tracks steadily toward those understandings and purposes that structure his life, but not stupidly or dogmatically. The poem's subtitle, "On Hearing Him Mispraised," rejects the view of Wellington as a man who thought he possessed the "one thing needful" and would not recognize change. Instead, his genius was the ability to follow his vision as it existed in the tumult of historical movement. If Wellington is mispraised by the public, Emerson is ignored. Arnold declares in "Written in Emerson's Essays" (1844) that in Emerson we hear the oracular voice of a true hero. Unfortunately, Emerson goes unheeded by a world that seems dead to his genius. Despite what seems to be the hopeless condition of man's indifference in this "monstrous" and "unprofitable world," Emerson's example actually gives back a belief in the majesty of the human soul. In his kinship with humanity Emerson teaches us that "the will is free; / Strong is the soul, and wise, and beautiful" (*Poems,* lines 10–11). The transcendental soul contains the "seeds of godlike power" and reveals that "Gods are we, bards, saints, heroes, if we will!" (*Poems,* lines 12–13). Transcendental optimism will be replaced with a more balanced sense of the difficulties of finding a heroic self, but in these early poems the lessons of Emerson are important affirmations that the dead world may yet live and that literature offers words that can strengthen the will.

Despite their awkward poetic forms and stilted language, Arnold's early poems from his Oxford days pose fundamental issues of morality and ethics that will guide his writing for the rest of his life. The gods he imagines, like his Victorian one, are either dead or irrelevant to what humanity needs and can accomplish. Shakespeare, Wellington, and Emerson are hortatory examples that the heroic is still possible, but Mycerinus and Cromwell remind us of how difficult it is to find one's way and how qualified that heroic life may be. None of the figures Arnold imagines in these poems is fully satisfying; those who are most richly drawn are the most ambiguous. The figures in the three sonnets embody the wise and heroic, but they are not imagined in any complexity. We have to take the praise of Shakespeare, Wellington, and Emerson at face value; in contrast, the portraits of Mycerinus and Cromwell are deep enough to reveal the limits and confusion of heroic will. No one answer arises out of this array of possibilities to show us where we need to go and what we need to do. Yet, collectively, they expand our understanding and raise questions about the balance we must find on questions of law, justice, cosmic order, and the individual. If they do not embody that "best self" that inspires faith and affords a principle of authority, they are at least shadows of what it might be. In one form or another Arnold addresses throughout his career, first in the poetry and then in the prose, the struggle to know and judge wisely our own lives and relationships to society.

Chapter Three

To Be or Not to Be: The Question of Poetic Vocation in the Poetry of 1844–1852

Ah! two desires toss about
The poet's feverish blood.
One drives him to the world without,
And one to solitude.
Matthew Arnold, "Stanzas in Memory of the Author of 'Obermann' "

A young man who had won the top prize for poetry at Rugby and Oxford had reason to think he was a poet. Arnold did not put on the laurel with ease, however, and he did not wear the poet's wreath for a lifetime. His poetry between 1844 and 1852 is preoccupied with the power of poetry and his own vocation as poet. He wrestled for several years about what poetry should do for society, whether it could be effective, who its audience was, and whether social, personal, and aesthetic values could be unified in a poet of Victorian times. The poems of this period suggest that, although he wrote a handful of the most memorable poems of the age, Arnold could not convince himself that being a poet was being his best self. From the mid-1840s to the mid-1850s he interrogated the function of the poet and the costs of poetic vision. He also measured himself harshly against his own standards, and his letters are full of comments that reflect his dissatisfactions with his work. In 1853 he retracted his most impressive poem as failing to meet the requirements of good poetry. By 1866 he was essentially through as a poet except for a few occasional verses on topics such as the death of family pets. In 1857 he had been elected Professor of Poetry at Oxford, but in later years he twice declined to be re-nominated for this prestigious post. Arnold's turn from poetry grew out of the limits he found in the question of poetic vocation that these early poems explore.

Students and scholars have for many generations puzzled over the phenomenon of a talented poet so restless with his vocation and so critical of his art that he would seemingly abandon poetry at the height of his career.[1] The "Preface" to the 1853 volume in which he explains his rejection of *Empedocles on Etna* publicly airs the ambivalence he felt about the ability of his work to be effective, to *do* something for the reader. The poems before *Empedocles on Etna* in 1852 also fretted about the nature of the poet. Arnold did not resolve his questions about his own poetry with the "Preface," and some of his finest poems, such as "Stanzas from the Grande Chartreuse" in 1855 and "Thyrsis" in 1866, follow the 1853 "Preface." Clearly, however, Arnold drew away from poetry after he entered his mid-thirties. Married in 1851, he also began his job as a school inspector and was soon the father of a weak and disabled son. Distant from his beloved sister and quarrelsome with his dear friend Clough, Arnold perhaps felt with a new intensity that he was seeing neither deep nor wide into the mysteries of the human soul. The travel and contacts with pupils and teachers also influenced his social vision, liberalizing his political positions and deepening his compassion for the severity of the common lives he saw around him. According to Park Honan, "he could feel the poems were 'all wrong' in view of what he now saw" in the urban slums and industrial towns (271). His many new and difficult experiences no doubt dampened his confidence in his poetry and moved him to write with a more concrete social and moral intent, but the questions about himself as poet that perhaps overwhelmed his gift in his forties were incipient in his twenties.

One might argue that the surprising twist is that Arnold published as much poetry as he did, not that he stopped doing so. When Arnold's first book of poems appeared in 1849, many of his friends and family members were startled by the somber tone and high seriousness of his poems.[2] Still others were surprised that there was any poetry in the family at all![3] Between 1843 when his "Cromwell" had won the Newdigate Prize and 1849 when *The Strayed Reveller, and Other Poems* was published, only a small inner circle of friends really knew what Arnold was writing. When the book appeared to mixed reviews, neither the response of some of the critics nor some of his friends was the sort to boost his confidence. In time he distanced himself emotionally from the book and the ambitions he might have had for it. His life as poet was shaping up with the same diffidence his verse expressed about the function of poetry. The themes of the identity of the poet and the uses of poetry were central to *The Strayed Reveller,* and the themes of the 1849 volume continued to be reflected in his later definitions of culture.

For Arnold, the role of the poet was connected to the demands of the world. The ancient king Mycerinus had retreated from the rule of justice and law for a life of pleasure. "The New Sirens," which according to Allott was probably written between 1846 and 1847, carried the subtitle, "A Palinode," or retraction.[4] Although some critics debate just which poem "The New Sirens" was meant to retract, the nature of the seductions of the new sirens would indicate that the subtitle was aimed at "Mycerinus."[5] The habits of the new sirens are a more sexual variation on Mycerinus's hedonistic pleasure, and both the new sirens and Mycerinus serve as metaphoric comments about the nature of poetry. As G. Robert Stange notes of the poem, "Its real subject is the attitudes we must take toward experience, toward art, and toward the world."[6] The new sirens are flush with love, argue for pleasure, and demean all knowledge except that which arises from feelings. The speaker, identified in Arnold's elaborate synopsis of the poem as "one of a band of poets," is not impervious to their charms, but he is never in real danger of being seduced.[7] Indeed, his critical commentary throughout verges on a puritanical condemnation of sensuous experience, such as Arnold associated with Romantic poets like Keats. Since these are "new" sirens, they are, in style and rhetoric, a kinder, gentler version of the deadly ones that tempted Ulysses and his men. Instead of luring men to their death, these sirens lure them into pleasures that enervate the will through "fits of joy and fits of pain" (*Poems*, line 206). Their fount of wisdom is restricted to "what we feel, we know," a vulgar rewriting of Romanticism that Arnold condemns. Mirth and mad delight are their remedies for a weary and disordered world where "opinion trembles, / Judgment shifts, convictions go; / Life dries up" (*Poems*, lines 81–83).

The new sirens are associated with the "pensive Graces" and the Muse, and their seductive domain is an Arnoldian "palace of art." In 1832 Tennyson had published his poem, "The Palace of Art," an allegory of the aesthetic soul who builds the "pleasure-house" of ideal artistic beauty but finds that living in the palace, isolated from the common life of the world, is a form of madness. Like the Arnoldian poet, Tennyson's poet wants to "Reign thou apart" with the quiet cool of a god who contemplates all creeds but is committed to none. Unlike Arnold's wary poet who quickly takes over the poem to critique the failings of the new sirens, Tennyson's poet unhesitatingly embraces the pleasures of the palace. Soon, though, its corners fill with dark, uncertain shapes, and beauty is replaced by nightmare. At the climactic moment of revelation in Tennyson's poem, the poet's soul "shrieked," " 'No voice, . . . / No voice breaks through the stillness of this world: / One deep, deep silence all!' " (Tennyson, 417).

Arnold has picked up Tennyson's theme, but his more conservative poet is unwilling to run similar risks and, consequently, does not gain a saving wisdom. Arnold's poet has only momentarily "strolled and sang" in the train of the new sirens. By "noon" he has heard "sounds of warning" in the "hoarse boughs" that labor in the wind, and he has identified the sirens as "ye false ones" (*Poems*, line 39) who lack even the conviction of the earnestly evil old sirens. Four stanzas follow in which he rehearses the claims of the new sirens in a series of verses introduced by "you say." Their banal wisdom boils down to something like struggle is vain, time is lame, the soul is faint, and life dries up, so better to invest the moments with emotions and love-potions. Even so, the Arnoldian poet has trouble asserting a richer alternative. "I am dumb," he says, though he believes that "at God's tribunal / Some large answer you shall hear" (*Poems*, lines 89–92). His counter is to point out the limits of their solution, not propose one himself. Their morning gladness cannot last through afternoon, and the recollection of their joy cannot sustain the times when long hours drag on and thoughts need to be fed. Then even the new sirens weep and doubt themselves. The poet ends his critique with the injunction to "dusk the hall" with funeral greens of yew and cypress because a loveless dawn is coming.

No Lovelace nor Marvell, this poet hectors the hapless new sirens now that he is awake to their dangers. His warnings are tinged with a sense of betrayal since he had earlier given "what we had" to them by way of "frank faith which passion breeds" (*Poems*, line 230). Now he longs for a more rightly balanced life:

> Mirth to-day and vine-bound tresses,
> And to-morrow—folded palms;
> Is this all? this balanced measure?
> Could life run no happier way?
> Joyous, at the height of pleasure,
> Passive at the nadir of dismay?
>   (*Poems*, lines 197–202)

Readers need no more assume that this poet is Arnold than to assume that Prufrock is T. S. Eliot. Yet Arnold's poet resembles Eliot's in some interesting ways. "The New Sirens" gives us two versions of the poet Arnold does not want to be but recognizes as emotionally tempting. One clearly is the poet devoted to the new sirens who has given himself to their rhythm of pleasure and pain. The other is the poet who has nothing more to give than a resentful exposé of the limits of emotional gratification. Though he is ready to condemn the "fits" of passionate excess that reduce the new sirens to weary sadness, he is not far from a pattern of "fits" himself. He positions himself as a watcher "for a purer fire," but his vision of "the closing" sees only shame, regret, and decay. If what is sought can only be scorned, then neither lover nor poet should pursue it:

> —Shall I seek, that I may scorn her,
> Her I loved at eventide?
> Shall I ask, what faded mourner
> Stands, at daybreak, weeping by my side?
> (*Poems,* lines 271–74)

"Shall I say," Prufrock asks about what to do, and "Would it have been worth it, after all," he concludes in his self-justifying rationale for not trying. Arnold's poet sounds very much like his modern counterpart. At the end of Eliot's poem, Prufrock turns aside from the mermaids who presumably continue singing each to each and maybe to some others; Arnold's poet is more stringent: he would shut these new sirens down, silence even their unheard voices and dispel their power to attract.

The new sirens and their unsettled poet are not models for the Victorian poet Arnold would proclaim. They are too much given to passion without morals and beauty without purpose. For Arnold, emotion, even recollected in tranquility as Wordsworth defined poetry, was not an adequate basis for an art that should ennoble the spirit. Unlike Walter Pater, whose theory that the moments of passionate beauty make the successful life, Arnold wanted poetry to affect life in some comforting and morally sustaining way. The question is whether the poem offers anything other than hanging up the laurels, heaping the throne with myrtles, or dusking the halls with yew—that is, giving up poetry, embracing passionate emotions, or sorrowing in shame. Arnold's poet declares himself an exile, but he remembers the place from which he came with a different geography:

> From the dragon-wardered fountains
> Where the springs of knowledge are,
> From the watchers on the mountains,
> And the bright and morning star;
> We are exiles, we are falling,
> We have lost them at your call—
> (*Poems,* lines 33–38)

The Arnoldian exile, like many Victorian poetic personas, was caught between the lost world of youthful Romanticism and the future of bourgeoisie materialism. The poet in "The New Sirens" does not return to the mountain top or the springs of knowledge, but such sites are presumably where a poet not in exile might have another kind of vision. This lost land is Arnold's classical world where a hero like Ulysses might test himself against the old sirens, and a poet such as Homer would put into poetry the epic human drama. Like Yeats's heroic Maud Gonne, absorbed in the pettiness of modern Ireland, the Victorian poet found himself with no second Troy to burn. The poet of the purer fire "is not natural in an age like this, / Being high and solitary and most stern."[8] Even Arnold's poetic idols—Wordsworth, Byron, Goethe, Heine—are subdued and lost in his modern age.

Arnold did not think very well of Tennyson, the poet of his time most "high and solitary and most stern." A comparison of "The New Sirens" and Tennyson's "Palace of Art" points to some key differences in the ways these two poets defined the nature of the poet. Arnold's poet is exiled from a land of lost poetic pleasures to which he cannot morally return. He can neither reside with the new sirens of physical seduction nor build a more utilitarian kind of palace. Tennyson's poet builds a palace of idealized beauty and leaves it recognizing that art without humankind is not enough. The palace is left standing, however, with the dream that someday the poet can return "with others." Tennyson believed that "the Godlike life is with man and for man,"[9] a belief not unlike that of the mature Arnold. Tennyson's palace is built for his soul, which is figured throughout as female. Although the Tennysonian soul undergoes a development from pleasure to ennui to nightmare that is similar to the change of the new sirens, the poet in the poem and the poet writing the poem do not turn on her. The female soul turns her false pride on herself and sees what is wrong (" 'No voice,' she shrieked") and throws away her robes to reenter the world of ordinary life.

Tennyson perhaps allegorized his emotional and artistic temperament in the female soul. Arnold focuses on the male poet and assigns the female role to the new sirens, a gender conflict that sets up scorn and division between the sexes and within his own artistic self. Tennyson's female soul punishes herself but then seeks penance and unity with others, a metaphor that finally completes the Tennysonian artist. Arnold's poet rejects the sirens and would punish the women for their seductiveness. Both the soul and the new sirens are metaphors, but once the poets gender the metaphors, attitudes toward gender begin to lead the meaning. For Arnold at this point in his life, a unity with his "siren" self is not

an acceptable poetic path. His resistance to emotions and to his own
attractions to women becomes one with his resistance to himself and the
emotive poetry that slipped from his pen.[10] "The New Sirens" does little
to help Arnold settle his poetic identity because it divides his personality
too acutely. In later years Arnold would resolve these conflicts by finding a more valued expression of self in prose. His happy marriage
afforded him a secure emotional intimacy with women, and his knowledge of the people in the school inspector's world deepened his compassion. The mature Arnold combines his aesthetic, passionate, and activist
sides in social criticism of high literary merit. He rarely returned to
poetry as the voice of either his heart or his intellect.

Arnold's effort to distinguish the ideal from the poet we see in "The
New Sirens" is clearer in "The Strayed Reveller." Unlike the poet in
"The New Sirens," who had at least been lured by the Graces' joyful
songs of the morning, the strayed reveller comes in search of Circe, who
seems mildly amused at his foolishness. He wears the fawn skin of a fol-
lower of Bacchus, and his disheveled clothes "half untied, / Smeared
with red wine-stains" indicate a youth who is undone by his excess
(*Poems,* lines 89–90). His weakness is even more disheartening because
he has in fact been taught by a wise mentor and knows what the task of
the poet is. The strayed reveller evades his poetic calling because he does
not want to pay the price of poetic vision, which is "to become what we
sing" (*Poems,* line 234).

Arnold sets up the poem as a stage scene, a structure that allows him
to introduce Circe and Ulysses as speakers who help the reader judge the
shortcomings of the reveller. Circe indulgently patronizes the "foolish
boy," who needs little urging from her to drink himself blind. The gen-
erous-hearted Ulysses tries to evoke in the reveller his best poetic self,
telling him his "voice is sweet" and suggesting that he must have been
taught by "some divine bard." The youth recognizes him as "the wise
Ulysses," and Ulysses' presence is a reminder of heroic life. As Buckler
notes, "When Ulysses comes on stage, his strong sense of identity will
counterpoint the reveller's personal anonymity, just as, by extension, the
moral imperative at the center of the age of the heroes will define the
human role in an entirely new way and lodge man's identity, not in raw,
sensual nature, but in moral values" (Buckler, 29). If, Ulysses says, the
youth is one who has learned the songs of a divine bard, he will honor
and welcome him. According to Ulysses, divine poets sing "Of Gods and
Heroes, / Of war and arts, / And peopled cities" (*Poems,* lines 124–26).
The preponderance of the poem is the reveller's response to Ulysses'

inquiry. His speech confirms that he does know the subject of divine songs but also reveals his reluctance to sing them himself. The vision of divine bards that the reveller has learned is Arnold's most successful early poetic statement about the poet's art. Poets may see gods and heroes, but they also must see the reality of human life in its struggle, toil, and sorrow in this world. Arnold enumerates the sights of "earth and men" that divine vision must embrace. These include the tragic knowledge of Tiresias, who can affect nothing with his vision; the naturalistic sensuality of the Centaurs rearing proudly in the glen or maddened with wine; the hard work of the Indian cultivating his melons and cucumbers, perhaps only to lose them to the gnawing worm; the Scythian who bakes his bread on the embers and furrows the parched soil, eking out existence on the wintry steppes; the workers on the ferry-boat struggling to move the cargo and stay afloat; and the merchants pale with fear that their holdings will be lost to robbers or tax-hungry kings. The many tasks indexed here perhaps mirror the Victorian sense that modern art must address the needs of a modern industrial society. These scenes embody both labor and pain, "groping blindness," "dark foreboding"—indeed, all the emotions that are part of a vision of human experience where happiness is tempered with bitter dissatisfaction, a life where even the heroes must "feel the biting spears."

The unusual "pictorial vividness" that some critics have noticed in "The Strayed Reveller"[11] has a critical function in the poem and, indeed, in Arnold's ideal of divine bards. If poetry is to help us know ourselves and understand life, it must reflect the reality of how one lives in a world of suffering and toil. Mycerinus had turned from the life of everyday rule and left his people to fend with the movement of the Nile and its ever-changing claims on life. Shakespeare, in contrast, had translated into divine art the reality of human pain and labor. This reveller, "strayed" perhaps from the true poetic identity that will most surely reclaim him when the wine wears off, is already too enmeshed in his vision to put it aside and take up his moral obligations to society. His poetic account of leaving the "rough fir-planks" of his hut in the "white dawn" and his journey over "the wet turf" following "the wood-cutters' cart-track" indicates an imagination that takes its strength from the particulars of human life. Reluctantly, but nonetheless, he has already felt the pain and labor of the people that the true poet knows. He notes the "strangely smiling Goddess," who perhaps also knows that he makes a poor Bacchant, and the "much enduring" Ulysses whom he honors. Although he desperately calls again for the cup and pleads, "Faster,

faster . . . Let the wild, thronging train . . . Sweep through my soul"
(*Poems,* lines 292–97), the Bacchanalian "bright" forms will not long
subdue the tragic vision he has already seen. Even the reveller seems to
half know this when he laments, "Who can stand still?" (*Poems,* line
289). To drink Circe's wine is to stand still, and Arnold's reveller is
already moving away from the hopes he had for ease when he entered
her empty palace.

"The New Sirens" and "The Strayed Reveller" emphasize the snares of
flesh and temperament that tempt the poet and that must be avoided,
and they identify the poet's subject as the essential human condition.
These poems have not yet, however, yielded an acceptable characterization of the modern kind of bard whom Arnold needed to find. Arnold
was not one to view himself, his friends, or his times as heroic. Even his
letters to his dear friend Clough were filled with sharp-tongued, injurious
criticism of his poetry. He was neither an aesthete nor a Bohemian artist,
and he believed that literature must serve the general happiness of the
world. He did not criticize his father, but he did not follow his more conventional footsteps, striking out for progressive ground in his ideas on
education and religion. The emotional poets who had meant the most to
him became subjects for critical appraisal. In later prose, his stinging
analysis of the "Philistine" culture of the nineteenth century would stick
as a permanent, pejorative label. In short, Ulysses' bardic poet was an
impossibility for Arnold given his acerbic tongue and critical intelligence
and the commercial age in which he lived. In such a world, action was
marked with uncertainty, compromise, and growing futility. Arnold's
poetic dilemma was that he was unwilling simply to hover over life and
reluctant to enter the confused eddies of a troubled time.

"Resignation," composed some time after his 1843 walk with his sister and the 1848 date of preparation for the 1849 volume, is another
effort to define the poet in the modern age. A similar vision of labor and
pain that the strayed reveller narrated for Ulysses is sketched in "Resignation," but this time Arnold will try to define what the poet must be in
relation to his subject. Arnold drops the classical setting and mythologi-
cal characters for the present time. The personae are the poet and his sister, presumably Arnold and Jane since the poem is based on a second
mountain walk they took together in the lake country in 1843, some 10
years after the first one. Heroic action itself is dismissed as "self-
ordained" labor of those enthralled by their own ambitions to leave their
mark on the world. Such people—warriors, pilgrims, zealots of every
cause—have no use for the past: "to stand again / Where they stood

once, to them were pain" (*Poems,* lines 18–19). Even the present counts only as the point from which to move forward into the imagined future. In contrast, the poet stands above the fray and looks down, subduing his energy to the discipline of vision and escaping the narrowness of time and the consuming flame of what he calls the furnace of contemporary society.

In this conception the poet attains vision without becoming what he sings, a possibility the reveller did not imagine and one that Arnold will not often be able to embrace himself. In "Resignation" the ideal poet possesses the serenity of a mild and free nature schooled in his mind and resigned to the vagaries of time and tide because he knows that is the way of life. He is, in short, a stoic. He sees the people, the leaders, all history unfold before him without desire to be part of it or to share its triumphs. Such a poet does not even say, "*I am alone,*" though he is transparently so in his serene position above the "eternal mundane spectacle" of life. His "sad lucidity of soul" is gift enough to provide the "peace" that comes to one who "bears" rather than seeks to triumph or enjoy. His stoic acceptance grows out of his view of an enduring nature in which the specifics of any given era in time are subsumed in the continuity of all time.

A number of critics find this poem a richly satisfying statement about the ideal poet, but several aspects of the poem tend to undermine its exemplary lesson.[12] Arnold's sister, called "Fausta" in the poem because she seems to want too much to enter the hurried race of the vain world, is not persuaded by the sudden wisdom of her unsettled brother. The poet-speaker overstates his case, teaching the poet's possession of a calm she knows he does not possess. At its worst, the speaker's description of calm disengagement may turn classic stoicism into an incipient nihilism. In "Tintern Abbey," which serves as a model for this poem, Wordsworth intends to offer real comfort to his sister, Dorothy, by urging on her the ways that nature can sustain us. Arnold's intentions toward his sister are more measured, since a young woman making no claim to being a divine bard can hardly be comforted by so slight a promise as Arnoldian resignation affords. Addressing her as "Fausta" is also patronizing and even slightly insulting, since any version of Faust suggests one who is unwisely willful or ambitious.

The speaker turns to the unchanging countryside to bolster his lesson about the continuity of nature, but the narrative structure of the repeated walk undermines the lesson the speaker wants to teach Fausta. Sounding philosophical about the road of life and what we must learn

from it is easier when the road has already been traveled. Arnold's mind
is free to philosophize because someone else has taught him this path.
The speaker recalls the first trip when they were under the guidance of
"our leader" who stands on a high bank and "reviews and ranks his mot-
ley bands" (*Poems,* line 44–45). The leader "makes clear our goal to
every eye— / The valley's western boundary" (*Poems,* lines 46–47). The
second trip is made apparently only by the poet and his sister, but the
walk is possible because they had been this way before, learning the
path from a man of action who would, perhaps, die or attain the goal.[13]
The "familiar whole" of this second journey conveys the sense that there
is an unchanging sameness about life that vindicates the poet's disengagement with the "fierce work" of those foolish enough to think that
they will change things. If life does unroll a "placid and continuous
whole" over the "murmur of a thousand years," then there is no cause to
"blame" the poet who stands above human cares and illusions:

> Blame thou not, therefore, him who dares
> Judge vain beforehand human cares;
> Whose natural insight can discern
> What through experience others learn;
> Who needs not love and power, to know
> Love transient, power an unreal show;
> Who treads at ease life's uncheered ways—
> Him blame not, Fausta, rather praise!
>   (*Poems,* lines 231–38)

One who claims to be able to judge "vain beforehand," understand
without experience, and measure love and power without knowing
either may convince himself, but he is not likely to sway others. The
rhetoric of this passage brings us back to the self-deluding, world-weary
pose of Prufrock, who has, he claims, known them all already. Prufrock
also wants a blameless peace from struggle and commitment, but Eliot
leaves little doubt that his "conclusion" is a moral and spiritual failure
papered over with a self-justifying pretense of knowing resignation.
Arnold does not judge his ideal poet as negatively as Eliot does, but the
ways of the world that intrude on the poem's "quiet" batter the credibility of the Arnoldian poet's possession of peace in his nineteenth-century
waste land.
    The speaker in "Resignation" deduces his insights from the meta-
phors associated with the sameness of the walk that reminds him of the

changeless pattern of human experience. Other metaphors point to the power of change to alter the meaning of experience. The poem never quite admits that the second walk is only possible because of what he learned from the first and that, though the physical landscape may appear the same, the poet and his sister, now fatherless, are most certainly changed. The gypsies are another sign that, though things seem not to change, they do in ways one might better notice. Their rambling lives "rubbed through yesterday / In their hereditary way, / And they will rub through, if they can, / To-morrow on the self-same plan" (*Poems*, lines 138–41). Unlike the more heroic quest of Arnold's later poems about the "scholar-gipsy," these gypsies blindly persist, but the changes in the landscape that threaten their way of life illustrate the new developments that will disrupt that continuity. The "crowded and keen" countryside and the stronger force of law bear down on them, and "signs are not wanting," which suggest the end of the gypsy way of life. They, however, do not read the signs or recognize the meaning of the change. Oblivious to change, they are passing from the landscape. They do not take up the law and enter the fray where they might pursue a goal so mundane as local ordinances to protect their way of life. The plight of the gypsies divides the poem's logic between the case for the poet observing from above the common life and the case for the "leaders" whose "fierce work" may be "vain" in the eternal perspective but may change laws or even organize a hike in the temporal world of historical time.

The function of Fausta in "Resignation" further clouds the meaning and the view of the poet-speaker. She never speaks, but her brother, who believes she is in need of tutoring, assigns her a set of ideas ("so your thoughts I scan") that carry their own weight. She, like the reader, must listen to the speaker's perhaps grandiose claims, but her "wandering smile" indicates that she has not been persuaded by the lecture. In an effort to correct her false thinking, the speaker extrapolates what he assumes she is thinking in order to answer her. Yet her view is an equally compelling—and familiar—one of the poet as one who feels life more deeply than ordinary humanity and is able to transcend the "*iron round*" of the "*common life of men.*" "*Not deep the poet sees, but wide,*" she concludes. Although the syntactical structure sets up Fausta's thoughts as opposed to the speaker's, we find Arnold giving Clough this same advice in a February 1849 letter: " 'Not deep the Poet sees, but wide':—think of this as you gaze from the Cumner Hill toward Cirencester & Cheltenham" (*Letters*, 1:131).

It is possible to read this letter as Arnold's patronizing advice to a friend who has nothing of the true poet in him and so counsels him to settle for the lesser gift. The more generous interpretation of the letter might be that careful attention to forms, details, and human experience is the avenue to the "natural" and "beautiful" in poetry. The letter advises Clough to "consider" whether he is attaining the beautiful and ends by averring that Arnold is "always prepared myself to give up the attempt, on conviction: & so, I know, are you" (*Letters*, 1:131).

Fausta's views on the poet may be more subtle than we have yet honored. Instead of a counter to the speaker's views from one who would rush into the world, Fausta seems to give us a deflated view of her brother's sublime poet. His poet is implicitly "more" than man because of his vision, and she puts in more banal terms his own view of the gypsies. If he is not "*bound*" by the "*iron round*" of the social fray, then he does leave his kind, "*o'erleaps their pen, / And flees the common life of men*" (*Poems*, lines 211–12). The speaker's poet "from some high station . . . looks down," but Fausta rephrases this from the point of view of the one who is poetic object: "*He escapes thence, but we abide— / Not deep the poet sees, but wide*" (*Poems*, lines 213–14). One definition of not deep but wide is "shallow." Rather than posing a different kind of poet, Fausta seems to be critiquing the one her brother has been describing.

The speaker's response to Fausta in "Resignation" is to paint life as even more grim and unsatisfying than before. In a litany of things that will not last that rivals the closing lines of "Dover Beach," he concludes that the world, "in some sense, Fausta, outlasts death" (*Poems*, line 230). He then asks, in his most pompous voice, that she "blame not" his poet for judging "vain beforehand" what he does not need to experience in order to know. In his most patronizing advice, he urges her to seek something better than "to amuse" herself:

> Rather thyself for some aim pray
> Nobler than this, to fill the day;
> Rather that heart, which burns in thee,
> Ask, not to amuse, but to set free;
> Be passionate hopes not ill resigned
> For quiet, and a fearless mind.
>   (*Poems*, lines 239–44)

The speaker's language in the next section indicates that he knows he has lost the argument with Fausta. "And though," "Yet," "believe me," "yet not," "not yet," lace almost every line in a section that argues defensively that his ideal poet is, "I might reply, / Not foolish, Fausta, in His eye" (*Poems,* lines 255–56). The evocation of "His eye" in a poem that has not mentioned God is the last resort of a failed argument. Unable to persuade the smiling Fausta, he cuts off the discussion with "Enough." In the last lines the speaker, lacking assurances that Fausta accepts his argument, diminishes the scope of his vision and lets go of his stoic philosophy. Pointing to the turf, the hills and stream, the "lonely sky," he suggests, "If I might lend their life a voice," that they seem "to bear rather than rejoice" (*Poems,* line 269–70). This "voice" of enduring what we cannot change is more Arnoldian than divine and less than the "sad lucidity of soul" of the ideal poet. His final justification for staying out of the action is that it cannot make milder "the something that infects the world" (*Poems,* line 278), a position Arnold eventually reverses as a critic who writes specifically to affect his times and influence change. In the poetry, issues and settings are often remote from Arnold's Victorian world, but in the prose the historical world will emerge in all its topical detail. What the poet cannot change in its abstract and metaphorical presentation the critic can analyze in its particulars and influence with arguments about the issues.

In these poems Arnold's personas seem to take a stoic position, but their postures are not those of classical stoicism. The stoic's position is calm acceptance of the flow of events based on the belief in the wholeness of life in which both birth and death are part of a continuum where nothing is ever lost or vain. For a stoic, the world is not sick nor evil nor without cause for rejoicing. A stoic might reject action in the world because, in time, it would not be needed since things right themselves in the overall balance. A stoic world is not "infected" with disharmony and without discernable logic. In contrast, Arnold's speaker resists action because of the effect it will have on his ability to recollect the causes of evil and disorder. He rejects action because he cannot affect change, not because he does not believe that things need to be righted. In this sense, the speaker's position winds up more closely allied with modern nihilism than classical stoicism.

"Resignation" is a complicated poem, and in the context of other poems by Arnold, interpretation becomes even more problematical.[14] If "Resignation" defines an ideal poet that neither Clough nor Arnold nor any contemporary Arnold can name can become, the poem has only deepened the problem of poetic identity. Arnold's letter to Clough concluded that they lived in a "deeply *unpoetical* age," but if they live in an age in which harmony and beauty are "infected" by some terrible disorder that robs the ideal poet of stoic lucidity, then the "resignation" of the ideal poet also becomes inappropriate. Arnold's 1849 volume has taught him that he cannot live in the palace of art, in the fray, or above its troubles in peace. He can withdraw from action but not be content in doing so because the changing misery of the world does indeed trouble and dismay him deeply.

Wordsworth's death in 1850 signals the change in poetic generations that will be reflected in new directions in Arnold's career. Arnold's "Memorial Verses" gives a fond farewell to Romanticism and Wordsworth's "soothing voice" that had "loosed our heart in tears" and laid us "on the cool flowery lap of earth" (*Poems,* lines 47, 49). The deaths of Byron and Goethe marked the end of "Titanic" force of will and the clarity of "causes of things" by the "physician of the iron age." Goethe sounds like the ideal poet of "Resignation," but Arnold is too much indebted to Wordsworthian and Byronic feelings to be like Goethe. In the fall of 1849, after the lukewarm reception of *The Strayed Reveller, and Other Poems,* Arnold charted a new path for himself as poet in "Stanzas in Memory of the Author of 'Obermann.' " The author of *Obermann* was the less well known Senancour, a figure in part attractive to Arnold because he was "the least attitudinising," but also because his work captured the currents of "modern life" that Arnold, too, had felt.[15]

"Stanzas in Memory of the Author of 'Obermann' " is Arnold's most openly heart-broken farewell to the Romanticism he could not make work in his Victorian world of science, democracy, and industrialism. The poem ends in a near sob of farewell that puts to rest any image of Arnold as the serene poet who looks on life with disinterested calm. Senancour's pages "feign" calm but burn with the fever of the wounded human spirit. Like Arnold, Senancour's Obermann speaks to an age that lacked the tranquil world of Wordsworth's and Goethe's youth. His advice, however, is just short of an injunction to suicide: "I hear thee saying now: / *Greater by far than thou are dead; / Strive not! die also thou!"* (*Poems,* lines 90–92). Obermann's command takes to its logical end the movement away from the life of the world and pushes Arnold to a crisis in deciding between entering the world and removing himself from it.

The position of the poet he had tried to articulate successfully in "The New Sirens," "The Strayed Reveller," and "Resignation" appears now to be an impossibility. The Arnoldian poet is "tossed" by two desires that cannot be resolved: "One drives him to the world without, / And one to solitude" (*Poems,* lines 95–96). The hope that in solitude one finds peace is shattered by Obermann's case when solitude becomes a form of misery and "icy" despair. For the modern poet there is no calm in which to arrive at peace. In a stunning metaphor of children drowning, Arnold characterizes the modern poet's lack of shelter:

> Like children bathing on the shore,
> Buried a wave beneath,
> The second wave succeeds, before
> We have had time to breathe.
>
> (*Poems*, lines 73–76)

Metaphors of being powerlessly in the grip of an overwhelming force continue when "some unknown Power's employ" drives him on so that he cannot be what he might will himself to be.

> We, in some unknown Power's employ,
> Move on a rigorous line;
> Can neither, when we will, enjoy,
> Nor, when we will, resign.
>
> (*Poems*, lines 133–36)

Arnold uses the word "will" twice in these four lines, each time acknowledging how powerless it is. He is concerned that his poetic mentors not "condemn me, nor upbraid" for letting go the ideal of the divine bard. The metaphors consistently stress his helplessness to do other than to live in the world. As "fate drives" him in "a rigorous line" he can only say farewell to the dreams that have proven in his day to be illusions. His guides are "gone away from the earth," "transfigured," "unspotted by the world." Left alone, metaphorically he must live in the world or die.

The poem's closing lines are a farewell to the poetic masters of his youth, such as Wordsworth, Goethe, and Senancour, whose ways he cannot pursue. "I in the world must live," but the parting from his ideal poetic self breaks his spirit and his poise:

> Farewell! Under the sky we part,
> In this stern Alpine dell.
> O unstrung will! O broken heart!
> A last, a last farewell!
>
> (*Poems*, lines 181–84)

This poem, with none of the masks of mythic characters and long ago times, is poignantly personal in its sense of failure to obtain the vocation of the true poet.

It is difficult to account biographically for the intensity of grief and failure that Arnold felt in his mid-twenties. His father's death when he

was 20 may have left him more adrift than it appeared. By the time of
this poem he had met and known disappointment with "Marguerite."
Since scholars have never settled on who she was, we cannot adequately
assess the relationship, though it seems highly likely that there was a
relationship that went beyond a pair of blue eyes encountered a few
times in a hotel in Switzerland.[16] His 1849 volume did not meet raves
about his genius, but neither was it bludgeoned. The "logic" of these
apparent causes probably has little to do with the emotional intensity
Arnold attached to some hopeless dream or image of himself that as he
matured he knew he would not attain. If his destiny was not to be the
true poet, he had to rethink his vocational identity as writer. The experience he had as poet did not necessarily prepare him to be the critic he
eventually became. Arnold may well have seen one cherished aspect of
his life failing without being able to see how a new one would open up.

Late in 1849 or early 1850 Arnold wrote "Self-Dependence," a poem
that begins, "Weary of myself, and sick of asking / What I am, and what
I ought to be" (*Poems*, lines 1–2). He looks to the stars and the sea to
"calm" and "compose" him to the end, but they give back a stern answer:

"Wouldst thou *be* as these are? *Live* as they.

"Unaffrighted by the silence round them,
Undistracted by the sights they see,
These demand not that the things without them
Yield them love, amusement, sympathy."
                    (*Poems*, lines 16–20)

In response the poet resolves "to be thyself." This is more a declaration
of courage to try to be than a definition of self. The poems about poetic
vocation were not successful in establishing what the modern poet could
be that was worthy. Too often they brought clarity only to what should
be "condemned" or "upbraided." The calm and peace of the ideal poet is
never realized by the speakers, and the "unstrung" "Farewell" to that
illusion brings to the surface the underlying doubt and despair that
drive these poems.

The story of Arnold's life from 1849 on, and especially after 1852, is
increasingly one of involvement with the world. The mask of the calm
sublime of the ideal poet is put aside for the public voice of the social
and moral critic. On subjects as diverse as education, religion, and the
arts he will write to analyze and advise in the interest of alleviating the
economic, emotional, and spiritual misery of his "unpoetical" age.

Chapter Four

Empedocles and the Bondage of Mind

Ask what most helps when known . . .
Matthew Arnold, *Empedocles on Etna*

The poems in Arnold's 1849 volume explored several visions of the poet ranging from the ecstatic reveller to the resigned sage. None of these efforts arrived at a satisfactory resolution for Arnold of what posture the poet should take in the "modern" age. Hovering alternatively between stoicism and rebellion, the speakers in the poems collectively constitute a dialogue about how to live and how to write when the assurances of traditional truths are withdrawn or dead. In his next major poem, *Empedocles on Etna,* the tension between how to live and whether to live at all breaks into an open dialogue, both between the characters in the poem, which is in the form of a verse play, and between the author and his public in the form of the preface Arnold would write to explain why he was withdrawing from future publication this extraordinarily rich poem.

As early as 1849 Arnold began his verse drama, *Empedocles on Etna,* which was completed and published in 1852. The dialogic nature of the discourse among the poems in the 1849 volume is drawn together in this poem of the ancient Greek philosopher who commits suicide. The poem's speakers have different perspectives on the malady afflicting Empedocles, and they also offer prescriptions about how to live. Empedocles' alienation and emptiness as an exile from his culture and his fellow human beings are greater than his stoic philosophy can heal. Though the mind can analyze and teach, intellect cannot cure the wounded spirit of the man. The poem was quickly associated with Arnold's own frame of mind and said to reveal the "drapery" of his own thought.[1] Arnold denied such a direct connection, but readers of the 1849 volume will recognize in the speeches of Empedocles and the lyric singer Callicles who tries to comfort him a continuity with the artistic, emotional, and intellectual uncertainties of the earlier work.

The sublimated suicidal implications of many of his poems rise to the surface in the action of *Empedocles on Etna*.[2] The state of mind of alienation and withdrawal presented in *Empedocles on Etna* would have been disturbing to Victorians who believed in action to improve society, but the poem was even more troubling because Empedocles seeks to resolve his misery through suicide. Some hint of an emotional and artistic death hangs in the shadows of many of Arnold's poems, but elsewhere it is not acted out as a literal suicide. Metaphorically many of his poems portray characters suffering from some inescapable doom such as that imposed on Mycerinus or Tristram. Other speakers retreat from a living community, such as we see at the end of "Stanzas from the Grand Chartreuse" or even in the more domestic "Lines Written in Kensington Gardens." Between the characters who die by their own hand or another's and those who withdraw from society, Arnold's poetry is preoccupied with a sense of retreat and withdrawal from life, one version of which is suicide. Empedocles reasons his way into jumping into the crater of Etna in a conscious decision to die. The association of Arnold's thought with that of Empedocles suggests the depth of the emotional and artistic problems that Arnold was trying to work through in his poetry.

The place of *Empedocles on Etna* in Arnold's body of work and its significance to him as an artistic and philosophical statement became central to our understanding of Arnold as poet when he removed the poem from his 1853 volume of *Poems*. Withdrawing *Empedocles* made it the most discussed poem of his career.[3] Arnold wrote the "Preface" to the 1853 volume to explain why he was withdrawing what was clearly a major poem. He thought the poem had fallen short of doing what poetry ought to do for the reader, and he was unwilling to reprint it. Arnold explained that *Empedocles on Etna* was a "dialogue of the mind with itself" offering "no vent in action; in which a continuous state of mental distress is prolonged, unrelieved by incident, hope, or resistance; in which there is everything to be endured, nothing to be done."[4] Arnold believed that literature had to do something positive, that it was not enough to present a state of mind. Measuring his own poem by what it effected, Arnold judged that the internal turmoil of Empedocles, ending as it did in suicide, offered no appropriate outlet in action for the brooding presentation of his mind. Of course, as J. Hillis Miller notes, "Empedocles does after all perform a decisive act."[5] Arnold's use of the word "action" refers to the aesthetic qualities of the poem. As a work of art it offered no vent in action that could "*animate* and *ennoble*" (*Letters,* 1:282), two characteristics Arnold felt necessary to the role of art.

Arnold believed that the poet should see life in its wholeness and express in the work an understanding of human experience. Poetry offered a criticism of life in the sense that it gave us the essence of human experience and revealed its meaning in ways that allowed us to see more deeply into our own and others' lives. In a fundamental sense *Empedocles on Etna* failed to meet Arnold's most basic criterion for poetry: "that poetry is at bottom a criticism of life; that the greatness of a poet lies in his powerful and beautiful application of ideas to life,—to the question: How to live."[6]

In the following year when *Poems* was reprinted, Arnold added another preface that further complicates the issue of assessing what the poem represents in terms of Arnold's theories about the nature and function of poetry. In 1853 Arnold had argued that the moderns had lost "the calm, the cheerfulness, the disinterested objectivity" of classical artists; that the Greeks regarded the whole of the work of art, while the moderns were concerned only with the parts; and that in Greek art, action dominates expression, whereas for the moderns expression dominates action ("Preface" 1853, 1:1).

In 1854 Arnold shifts the terms of his argument. Instead of "disinterested objectivity," Arnold argued that the choice of a subject from ancient times was not a barrier for modern literature since the effectiveness of any character lies in our "capacity for imagining him, irrespective of his times, solely according to a law of personal sympathy."[7] By this criterion *Empedocles* was successful since its presentation of character had undoubtedly struck a note of personal sympathy in many readers, as it had in Arnold. Empedocles' emotional despair was easier to imagine and more relevant to readers than the calm, cheerful disinterestedness that Arnold had attributed to the ancient Greeks and that was represented in the poems by the songs of Callicles. In 1854 Arnold rephrased his argument so that instead of disinterestedness the "great virtue of the ancient literature" was its "sanity." Lack of sanity was the "great defect of the modern" ("Preface" 1854, 1:17), and Empedocles' suicide raised the question of his soundness of mind.

Arnold does not define "sanity," but the two prefaces link the word to Empedocles and suggest that "sanity" is connected to the ability to live without enervating emotional or intellectual torment. As a work of art *Empedocles on Etna* fails to rise to the level of its classical models because its intemperate central character and his concluding action cannot show us how to live. In its original conception the act of suicide that concludes Empedocles' deliberations was apparently intended as a kind of heroic action. Empedocles chooses to die while still in command of his mind as a way to defeat the deadening alienation that separates him from the rest of humanity. Empedocles' own overwrought state and the concern for his emotional frame of mind from friends Callicles and Pausanias suggest, however, that Empedocles is losing his sanity and that his suicide is less a matter of free choice than an emotional necessity.

The arguments within the poem and the prefaces create an unresolved dialogue about the adequacy of the poem and about the nature of Empedocles' state of mind. The poem contains a contrast in that it teaches the stoic vision of acceptance of universal law but illustrates the heroic rebellion against it. In his misery, Empedocles is unable to address objectively the ethical and philosophical confusions that grow out of the contrast. Arnold's own judgments about the merits of the poem in first publishing and then withdrawing it,[8] and the shifting arguments in the prefaces confuse the critical premises for judging the poem. Empedocles describes a universe in which the conception of self as a unified whole distracted by the world is a delusion but asserts the triumph of self over that world. He tells Pausanias that there is no moral order and then teaches the stoic way of thinking, which is premised on a moral order. The idea of self Arnold pursues is "buried," an ambiguity that allows him to acknowledge the self's unrealizable nature while asserting its ultimate reality. Perhaps the most important point about the Greeks and their art that Arnold makes in the "Preface" to the 1853 *Poems* is that "they, at any rate, knew what they wanted in Art, and we do not." *Empedocles on Etna* is one of the poems in which Arnold seems not to know what he wanted. He speaks of "the uncertainty as to what is really to be aimed at which makes our difficulty," and his poetry eventually collapses under the burden of that uncertainty.

Since Walter Houghton's essay in 1958, critics have generally agreed that *Empedocles* charts a crisis produced by the "social dislocation" of "modern" times (Houghton, 321). Empedocles hopes that suicide can preserve the integrity of self and soul against the corrosive complexity of modern society, but the intruding "modern" world has changed the context in which suicide can be the rational act of will it often was in the eighteenth century. Romantic models of a self-affirming suicide with which Arnold was familiar included heroes from Byron and Goethe, but Empedocles suffers from a malaise that is related to "something that infects the world." Today, we would probably say he suffered from clinical depression, but even in the pre-psychoanalytic world of Victorian psychology, Empedocles' state of mind would have been viewed more as mental disturbance than heroic will.

Empedocles justifies his suicide as a last attempt to preserve the integrity of the self—to die before the pressure of living destroys the sense of life. Romantic suicides defied cruel and unjust fates by taking their lives, and the stoic suicide of the ancients might be the final courageous act of complete acceptance of the law of the universe. Stoics such as Epictetus saw the natural order as divine, and Marcus Aurelius thought it rational and intelligent. Stoic "apathy" depends on the assumption that the natural order is eternal and rational. In "Spinoza and the Bible" Arnold labels as stoic the belief that "God directs nature, according [to] the universal laws of nature" and that "our desire" is that "we obey nature."[9] Questions about the universal laws of nature reshaped the most basic assumptions of nineteenth-century values. The "natural" order taking shape for the Victorians was an evolutionary and scientific one that might be only physiological, not moral or intelligent, perhaps not orderly, and possibly not even protective of humanity's survival.

Several influential medical and sociological studies of suicide were published in England and Europe in the nineteenth century, culminating in 1897 with Emile Durkheim's classic study, *Suicide*. Victorian medical and sociological attitudes viewed suicide as something between insanity and abrogation of one's public duty. Popular moral judgments were even harsher. The medical and cultural understanding of suicide changed after the French Revolution. Earlier literary heroes such as Goethe's Werther and Byron's Manfred represented the possibility of a justified suicide that, while touched with nervous agitation, remained a rational and heroic act. Empedocles' mid-century suicide does not quite fit either the classical or Romantic models.

In general, nineteenth-century medical researchers considered suicides to stem from physiological causes, a diagnosis that ruled out the possibility of suicide as strictly a moral or philosophical decision. The stress of modern life increasingly became identified as a common cause of discontent, depression, and alienation, especially among artists and intellectuals. By 1810 medical publications associated "public health" with social conditions, specifically linking mental illness with the social upheaval of such events as the French Revolution.[10] In England the works of Sir Andrew Halliday and George Burrows, both appearing in 1828, linked intellect, society, and "derangement" in a special relationship. Burrows identified moments of rapid social change such as revolutions as sources of mental disorder. He also associated "intellectual" derangement with "civilized" society.[11] Similar arguments followed in the wake of the 1848 revolutions, especially by continental scientists. Although intellectuals who chose suicide on a rational basis were often considered false suicides, the influence of society in such a decision made it something less than a free choice. After mid-century, suicide was often linked with the Darwinian idea of the survival of the fittest. Popular attitudes viewed suicide as a family "disgrace,"[12] and the traditional Christian judgment was that suicide was a sin. Within these frames of thought, any Victorian suicide would be an ambiguous act open to negative medical, social, moral, and religious interpretations.

The condemnation of suicide as immoral or mad was linked with the growth of what Emile Durkheim called "the religion of humanity." In this context suicide weakens the human community because it undermines the common value of life itself.[13] Arnold's judgment that *Empedocles on Etna* fails to meet the standards of art may reflect his sense that the poem's "action" ultimately attacks the most fundamental values of the human community. For Arnold, one important reason the dialogue of the mind failed was that it was only "with itself." An ideal poetic dialogue should reflect the harmony in "the life of life," the "flow" that finally connects all "enisled" things. "The Buried Life" describes moments when a "bolt is shot back" and "the heart lies plain, / And what we mean, we say, and what we would, we know'" (*Poems,* lines 84–87). The theory of such moments of unity is idealized in Arnold's poetry, but such moments are seldom captured. As Miller notes, Arnold believes in this fundamental unity, even when the force of experience denies it: "Certainly Arnold rejects the division of *man's* nature into multiple faculties. Against this modern psychological theory he sets his notion that each man is inwardly and secretly one, as coral islands, separate on the surface, are joined in the deeps" (Miller 1965, 225). Metaphorically, the Arnoldian self is mainly buried or "enisled" in the sea that divides the self from others. This sense of loss is more poignant in Arnold because he idealizes a Romantic sense of ultimate attachment that seems particularly lost to his generation.

Empedocles' emotional and philosophical strategies in defining the self revert to a belief in a timeless "genuine self" "hidden" from us by alienating external forces that "infect" the world. Instead of wholeness, Empedocles metaphorically describes the soul as "like a mirror, hung," which "hither and thither spins . . . A thousand glimpses wins, / And never sees a whole" (*Poems,* 1.2.80–85). This image implies an inner self that changes with the changing and fragmented images of the world. "The Buried Life" asks, "Whence our lives come and where they go." The lesson Empedocles implicitly teaches is one that the poem does not fully acknowledge: that our lives come and go in history and that the "self" is an obscure composition drawn from historical time, actions not in our control, and influences beyond our power to resist or even recognize. For Arnold, the inability to find harmony of self undoes the connections between intellect and emotion, art and the world. The psychological product of this lack of harmony is modern alienation. "The disease of the present age is divorce from self," Arnold wrote (*Poems*, 149n). The "divorce from self" is another Arnoldian metaphor similar to the "buried self" or the self "enisled" that capture his sense of the essential self as a unity that the age has somehow fractured. When the self loses this harmony, the consequences are a profound loneliness and emptiness. The divorce within self results for Arnold in the dispossession of soul and the failure of intellect. Thoughts that do not flow freely are "congested," a word Arnold once used to describe his intellectual affinity with Empedocles' problem: "yes—*congestion of the brain* is what we suffer from—I always feel it and say it—and cry for air like my own Empedocles," he writes to Clough in 1853 (*Letters*, 1:254). When functioning without a sense of the unified self, the mind cripples the ability of intellect to affect emotions. Mind becomes for Arnold an oppressing force instead of a liberating one, and the end of thought that cannot unify is either delusion or sophistry.

The dialogic nature of the poem is evident in the distinct discourses it contains about the cosmic order and the power of the mind. All three of the characters, Empedocles the philosopher, Callicles the poet, and Pausanias the disciple, put forward their views. The arguments in the poem go in several directions. The poet Callicles sings about the cosmic order. His lyrics tell the stories of Cadmus and Harmonia, the rebel Typho, and the faun who challenged Apollo. Empedocles overhears these songs but interprets them differently than Callicles apparently intended. Pausanias seeks to know the secrets of Empedocles' magic, but Empedocles scorns such magic as offering any recourse for life. When Empedocles delivers a philosophical lecture instead of giving out magic secrets, Pausanias reminds his mentor of earlier comments and contradictions to what Empedocles now says. The poem's most fully developed arguments are in the long speeches of Empedocles. Empedocles himself runs two distinct discourses, one in the form of a lesson to Pausanias that mainly urges the stoic virtues of acceptance of universal law, and one in the form of a soliloquy that expresses his inner emotional torment of profound alienation and despair.

The poem's contradictions are built around two opposing views of mind. One says, "Mind is the spell which governs earth and heaven . . . /

Know that, and help thyself!" and the other says, "Mind is a light which the Gods mock us with, / To lead those false who trust it" (*Poems,* 1.2.27–33). Mind, in the context of a unified sense of self, has the ability to influence emotions and actions and thus govern self and society. Mind divorced from the unified self cannot be trusted, and its "light" is a mockery since mind divorced from emotion lacks power to govern the self. This separation of mind from self explains why Empedocles' lesson on stoic acceptance and moderate bliss to Pausanias cannot help him with his own state of mind. Empedocles tells Pausanias to "ask what most helps when known" (*Poems,* 1.2.111) but ridicules the notion that spells and magic can "stay" the hand of the gods and allow us "to live free from terror" (*Poems,* 1.2.25–26). His philosophy, however, brings him no emotional comfort.

All the speakers in the poem address the issue of "how to live," but the poem also makes the case for why is it not worth trying to live in such an infected world. Some critics have viewed Empedocles' lecture to Pausanias on "how to live" as merely a practical prescription for those without his intelligence (Culler, 164), but his speech contains many of the contradictions we have seen in earlier poems such as "Mycerinus" and "Resignation." Contradictions occur even within Empedocles' lesson to Pausanias. He advises Pausanias to "read thy own breast" for enlightenment, but then questions if one can trust the mistaken heart. The heart thirsts for "bliss" but errs to think the world exists to provide it. We are "Born into life," a metaphor that locates the self in the world rather than suggesting its timeless essence.

"Born into life" is the refrain throughout Empedocles' lesson to Pausanias, and "life" here seems to mean both the conditions of place and time as well as the process of living in the world. "Life must be our mould" acknowledges that the powers that define us lie beyond self and must be accommodated. The "I" can neither define itself nor resist the definitions of the world: "To tunes we did not call our being must keep chime" (*Poems,* 1.2.196). Experience effaces will; the world will take its own course, not ours; and "other existences" clash with ours and may darken our lives. Empedocles admits the sovereignty of history when he says that it is the person who is new and the world that is old. The rule of history is the temporal parallel with the rule of universal law, and the individual has no power to control either.

In this lesson about "life" Empedocles defines an essentially godless universe in which human need invents the idea of gods. His speeches are rhetorically dramatizing, a stylistic mode that raises the question of whether Empedocles actually believes what he says or is trying to convince himself to believe his own rhetoric. Such a universe contains no inherent order of right or justice. In order to articulate our misery we invent gods, either to blame or lean on. The invention of the gods, Empedocles explains, is an effort to claim the power over "life" humanity lacks by setting up surrogate powers who may be addressed as the will demands. Because such gods are accorded will and reside beyond history, they can be seen as sources of good and evil, right and wrong, which are the kinds of ethical judgments humanity must make about the "empirical clutter"[14] if one believes that history reflects universal law.

Empedocles proceeds to quarrel with himself. He admits that everything except the human will argues that the historical world is the one reality:

> Fools! That in man's brief term
> He cannot all things view,
> Affords no ground to affirm
> That there are Gods who do;
> Nor does being weary prove that he has where to rest.
> *(Poems,* 1.2.347–51)

Gods and fates are merely dreams, and Empedocles finds nothing "clear" but a vision of "year posting after year" (*Poems,* 1.2.364). Through Empedocles' discourse, Arnold is exploring the implications of his own religious skepticism. In his notes for the poem Arnold had written of Empedocles, "He sees things as they are—the world as it is— God as he is: in their stern simplicity. . . . His mind is overtasked by the effort to hold fast so great and severe a truth in solitude" (*Poems,* 154–55nn). Empedocles begins by arguing only that there are no grounds on which to assume that there are gods. By the end of this speech, however, he no longer makes even rhetorical references to "the Gods" or "the Powers" that he uses in the earlier sections. The sources of bliss he outlines for Pausanias belong solely to the domain of the physical world and the authentic possibilities in human action:

> Is it so small a thing
> To have enjoyed the sun,
> To have lived light in the spring,
> To have loved, to have thought, to have done;
> To have advanced true friends, and beat down baffling foes—
> *(Poems,* 1.2.397–401)

This passage is the poem's fullest embrace of the law of the natural world and the richness of the human community as the source of joy. Rhetorically, though, the poem rejects this wisdom with its modulations of the definition of "bliss." Empedocles makes the stoic argument for the life of "moderate" bliss but cannot attain moderation. His stoicism, with its mix of desire for bliss and heroic defiance, is, as Miller observes, the opposite of stoicism (Miller 1985, 34).

The nature of "bliss" becomes a testing ground for what is real and sustaining. Empedocles had initially taught that humanity could experience "moderate bliss," but this concept is immediately altered from "moderate" to "true bliss." "True bliss" evokes the ideal of perfect happiness, which is not within the range of human experience. Underlying the debate between "true" and "moderate" bliss is the Romantic dream of perfect bliss. Rhetorically, "moderate bliss" is an oxymoron since "bliss" itself implies a level of pleasure that exceeds the "moderate." "True bliss" could mean the richest state one can experience, "true" because it can be real. Some kind of bliss may come to those "who know / Themselves" and accept "what they cannot break." Empedocles further undermines the strength of his argument for moderate bliss by taking as his example "the village churl." "Moderate bliss" may suffice for those so lowly in life as to have no exalted expectations, but it cannot satisfy those like Empedocles, and perhaps Arnold, whose imaginations have fed on the poetry of Romantic ecstasy.

The example of the village churl also suggests that bliss belongs to those who do not ask philosophical questions or fret about the "buried life." Those for whom the question of identity is lost in the details of everyday living do not, the argument suggests, suffer the angst of the intellectual. It also attaches the stoic model of acceptance to a social and intellectual lower class. When Empedocles abandons the lesson of the Golden Mean, that there is scope for human effort between despair and extravagant hope, he implies that heroic figures such as himself have no place in a world governed by the stoic's universal law.

Culler says that Empedocles' speech on bliss is "harsh, crabbed . . . aridly intellectual and uncouth" (163), but the poetry has an eloquence that rises above the philosophical confusions. The tone is passionate with bitterness, betrayal, and outrage. Arnold resorts to italicized words to bear the stress of emotion: the epithet "Fools," which includes Pausanias and himself, appears again and again. At the end anger is moderated to melancholy as Empedocles recognizes that he has lost "all our present state" dreaming of a "doubtful future date" (*Poems*, 1.2.403–5).

The underlying tone of grief and farewell implicitly acknowledges that the failure of Empedocles to be able to think how one can embrace the life of the world is a form of death.

Readers who interpret the lecture to Pausanias as Empedocles' philosophy of how things "are" use it to condemn the Romantic rationale for suicide. Others, like Culler, reject the stoic lecture as Empedocles' philosophy and see it only as a view of the world that is more suitable for lesser spirits like Pausanias (164). These interpretations are not in conflict since the speech is what intellect tells Empedocles, but at the level of emotion the spirit is unable to accept such cold truth. His mind pursues one discourse and his heart another, and his tragedy is that he can find no way to reconcile them. So extreme a disjunction means that Empedocles can neither live successfully in his society as a public figure nor find comfort in an inner life sequestered from the world and devoted to his art. This was one version of the plight Arnold would articulate in "Stanzas from the Grande Chartreuse" as wandering between two worlds with nowhere to rest his head. So profound a sense of alienation in time reduces the self to nothingness, a condition in which either death or madness seems inevitable.

The multivocal nature of the poem allows Arnold openly to argue a view and then criticize it within the poem. The dramatic poem with several speakers becomes a much more complex form than the dramatic monologue because of the number of speakers, the range of circumstances in which they speak, and their commentary on each other's songs and speeches. Empedocles, for example, admits the absence of gods and the absorption of self in history, but his rhetorical strategies continue to try to assert the arguments his philosophical musings defeat. Empedocles again places humanity at the center of meaning in the universe when he argues that his suicide preserves the living spirit and successfully defies the cosmic order. In contrast, the songs of Callicles reassert the supremacy of the Gods and that happiness lies in accepting the universal law. The final lyric from Callicles that ends the poem composes a stately procession of divine order that is indifferent to the sufferings or suicide of Empedocles. Callicles himself, however, seems very young and untouched by human suffering. His lyrics teach classical wisdom but sound hollow as authentic knowledge about how to live. Empedocles also puts aside his poetry as powerless to save him, but Callicles defends the power of art to teach and soothe. Callicles' chilling account of how Apollo flayed Marsyas is an object lesson in the brutalities of the gods. The incident diminishes the Apollonian ideal and pities

the poor faun who had dared to challenge him. All of these contradictions remain open to interpretation as the poem continues, and the ending, despite its "decisive act," settles none of the problems that have driven the poem.

Empedocles on Etna is a difficult poem in part because the classical philosophy cannot adequately address the Victorian problems that underlie
the spiritual crisis in the poem. Arnold's poetry writes many diagnoses
for the illness of the Victorian temper: the ebbing Sea of Faith; the
"buried" life; beliefs that are out of fashion; "rigorous teachers" who
purge faith; the "gradual furnace of the world," which curls the spirit
with its hot air; isolation from others ("enisled"); the fragmentation of
knowledge and identity; the frustration of desire; a hero like Achilles in
his tent; too much passion or too little passion; and too much action or
too much thought. Empedocles, and Arnold, too, see in this poem many
things "as they are," but the poem is more successful in presenting the
confusion of life than any resolution of the whole.

Arnold assigns to Empedocles' speeches imagery that reflects the
growing body of scientific evidence for evolution and the geophysical
universe. As Empedocles notes, "We map the starry sky, / We mine this
earthen ball, / We measure the sea-tides, we number the sea-sands"
(*Poems,* 1.2.319–21), but all we find is "dead" and "void." The "Fools,"
says Empedocles, are forced to redefine science in order to restore belief
in gods: "True science," they argue, abides within an "immeasurable All"
that the measures of mind and "the world's immense design" do not
contain. The classical Empedocles might well be seen as at strife with
cruel gods, but the Victorian Empedocles is in spiritual and intellectual
crisis because he cannot believe in the reality of the gods. Empedocles
has moved past what Miller describes as "the disappearance of God" to
glimpse Nietzsche's vision of the death of God and its consequence, the
"end of man" (Foucault, 385).

Although the controversy about evolution and geology focused on
the question of human origins and its conflict with biblical accounts, the
deeper cause for concern was less the question of origins than of our end.
If humanity evolved over time, there was no assurance that it would not
pass out of existence in time, a logical conclusion that Tennyson con-
fronts in *In Memoriam.* The fossil evidence suggests that humanity itself
might one day be "seal'd within the iron hills" like other once-living
things that became extinct (*In Memoriam,* 56.20). Tennyson grasped
with great clarity what evolutionary nature was saying: "A thousand
types are gone; I care for nothing, all shall go" (*In Memoriam,* 56.3–4).

Perhaps no argument was more devastating to the Victorian's sense of alienation and despair than the dawning realization that humanity might have no special status in the universe. Empedocles' definition of self depends on being godlike or heroically in defiance of the gods. His argument for stoic acceptance depends on belief in the ultimate moral design of the universal law. Victorian science, however, implied the meaningless place of humanity in a cosmos that was empty space.

In the absence of a faith in humanity's place in the universe, Arnold's typical question about the self is "Who or what am I that I am here," a question that places the self in history. From Alaric to Cromwell to Mycerinus and the strayed reveller, the place of the self in history and as part of a community was the context in which action could have meaning and be judged. The ideal of the poet as being somehow above history and the ideal of art that was timeless were never coherently articulated in Arnold's poetry. The specifics of history and the claims of the community cannot be put aside without guilt and grave doubt. Despite the belief that each one has a "buried life," the self is defined in history and attenuated over time. The image of the self as a mirror whirling in the wind is the reality of the "self" in a post-Romantic social and scientific order.

The postures of the speakers in the poems of 1849 and 1852 were often those of retreat, withdrawal, or death. Arnold's reluctance to project himself into any future time perhaps measures his dissatisfaction with the directions of his poetry as lessons in how to live. Arnold wanted an "intellectual deliverance," not the solitude and strain of holding "fast so great and severe a truth" as seemed to loom before Empedocles. The despair of humanity in the wake of the death of God was not a subject that could attain the standards of art; it could not teach us "how to live." With neither gods to create truth nor inspired poets to reveal it, the function of art would have to be redefined, and Arnold was clear that the dialogue of the mind with itself was not a sufficient subject. The ancients "knew what they wanted in art" because they knew what they believed. "Sanity" was a clarity of purpose and value possible only in the midst of a clear and powerful order, and Arnold was unable through his poetry to work his way to that ground.

Arnold's comments on Lucretius in 1857 may shed an indirect light on his understanding of figures such as Empedocles. Lucretius is another example of the "predominance of thought . . . in the unsound . . . overtasked . . . over-sensitive" individual. The result is "the feeling of depression, the feeling of *ennui*."[15] Arnold raises the critical question about whether such a literary example is "adequate" as a guide or teacher to address how we are to live. Both Lucretius and Empedocles are "overstrained, gloom-weighted, morbid; and he who is morbid is no adequate interpreter of his age" ("Modern," 1:34). Intellectuals such as Lucretius or Empedocles may have seen "the nature of things," but they are not "in sympathy" with the modern world. Arnold questions, "how can a man adequately interpret the activity of his age when he is not in sympathy with it" ("Modern," 1:33). Since the modern world is fragmented, to see it clearly is not the same as to see life steadily and see it whole because "the world in its fulness and movement is too exciting a spectacle for his discomposed brain" ("Modern," 1:33).

Arnold's contrasts between modern literature and the classical ideal strengthen the sense of alienation from his own time. If, he thinks, he cannot be in sympathy with the times, he cannot write poetry "adequate" to meet the standards he sets for the best literature. Arnold wrote to Clough on September 23, 1849:

> these are damned times—everything is against one—the height to which knowledge is come, the spread of luxury, our physical enervation, the absence of great *natures,* the unavoidable contact with millions of small ones, newspapers, cities, light profligate friends, moral desperadoes like Carlyle, our own selves, and the sickening consciousness of our difficulties. (*Letters,* 1:156)

The sentiments in this passage illustrate why the charge that Empedocles represents the drapery of Arnold's own thought persisted despite his denials. The belief that "everything" is "against one" places Arnold in the role of Lucretius and Empedocles.

Arnold hoped that to know and appreciate "the best that has been thought and said" could restore the continuity of history and unify the psyche. In his essay "On the Modern Element in Literature," he discusses the need for "an intellectual deliverance" ("Modern," 1:19). In a description of the problem of the modern intellectual that may remind us of our own contemporary sense of "information overload," Arnold describes his age as one in which the individual is confronted with "a vast multitude of facts awaiting and inviting his comprehension" ("Modern," 1:20). His "deliverance" from this spectacle is "perfect when we have acquired that harmonious acquiescence of mind which we feel in contemplating a grand spectacle that is intelligible to us; when we have lost that impatient irritation of mind which we feel in presence of an immense, moving, confused spectacle which, while it perpetually excites our curiosity, perpetually baffles our comprehension" ("Modern," 1:20). The "impatient irritation of mind" prods Empedocles into impulsive words and acts. He fails to achieve an "intellectual deliverance," and the "confused spectacle" of his own situation never becomes wholly intelligible to him or, judging from the mass of critical commentary, to the critics.

Arnold's poems deepen his estrangement and dismay with the "modern element" in literature. Miller sees this poetry as a futile "attempt to escape from himself" (Miller 1965, 268), but this is only partially true since Arnold was a complex man who found an ease within himself as cultural critic. Once literature was required to serve as a model for how to live, literature that "exhibits the lassitude, the incurable tedium" of modern depression and ennui, is, no matter how powerful, not adequate to the age ("Modern," 1:32). In response to arguments that the use of moral ideas in poetry was a limitation, Arnold insisted that moral ideas are central to human life. A dialogic poem such as *Empedocles on Etna* introduces a variety of moral ideas without settling them for the reader. For twentieth-century readers who are apprehensive in the presence of a monologic idea of moral ideas, the openness of such a poem is a critical virtue. Arnold's poetic misfortune was to so completely misjudge the power of literature, which mirrors the modern state of mind and unsettles the traditional definitions of truth. He confuses the portrait of modern angst with a literature that was itself tedious and without wisdom. Readers of modern literature, however, have found self-knowledge in fragmented and alienated sensibilities such as Arnold's and his Empedocles. Arnold's poems have been critical in the process of self-realization that many modern readers pursued through the very literature that Arnold cautioned against.

Arnold saw the world as a multitudinous spectacle that could reveal meaning only if one looked from "the true point of view" ("Modern," 1:20); one "must begin with an Idea of the world in order not to be prevailed over by the world's multitudinousness: or if they cannot get that, at least with isolated ideas" (*Letters,* 1:128). To begin with an idea of the world was to begin in ideology or doctrine, but poetry is not the best venue for polemics. When Arnold could not make his poetry fulfill his ideology of culture, he turned his attention to criticism that could. The purpose of criticism could be to direct, and the critic was free to interpret from a "true" point of view. Arnold's poetry interpreted the age, but in such a way as to open up chaos, emptiness, and suffering. His poetic world did not sustain sanity, but his prose could.

Arnold's ideal of art as healing and calming would be in sharp contrast to the art of the moderns, who saw art as a way to shock and unsettle a culture, to transgress accepted values, to create a new culture and dispose of a corrupt one. Arnold's critical designs were less revolutionary, and his hope was to sustain his culture's ties to its traditions as a means of guiding it into a stable future of familiar values. His instinct to sustain the future on the foundations of the past resulted in the subversion of his own poetic career and placed him in the role of the critic of culture whose ideas have been used to repress as well as sustain the movements in art that followed the Victorians.

In the work after 1853 Arnold tried his hand at some poems more classical, and hence, he thought, more sane. "Rugby Chapel," "Sohrab and Rustum," and "Thyrsis" are among the few poems in which the voice of depression and ennui is suppressed. His success with such poems was, however, limited, and grimmer poems such as "Dover Beach" and "Stanzas from the Grande Chartreuse" continued to punctuate his efforts to make a poetry that would fit his critical principles.

Chapter Five

The Fairest Resting Place: Poetry after 1852

> It is almost too much to expect of poor human nature, that a man capable of producing some effect in one line of literature, should, for the greater good of society, voluntarily doom himself to impotence and obscurity in another.
>
> Matthew Arnold, "The Function of Criticism at the Present Time"

The poems Matthew Arnold wrote after 1852 and the retraction of *Empedocles on Etna* in 1853 dramatically reveal the conflict between the emotional expression of the poems and his ideology about what poems should be if they were to meet the standards of literature. The 1853 "Preface" had explained that a poem could not be only a dialogue of the mind with itself, that literary genius demanded something that would ennoble and elevate the mind and spirit. A poem should be in some way a positive good for the moral and cultural life of a society, and to do that, it could not be too personal nor too subjective.

Between 1852 and 1867 Arnold published a dwindling number of poems. Some of these poems, such as "Tristram and Iseult" and "Dover Beach," had their origins in the period between 1849 and 1852 when his melancholy mood dominated his writing. Others, such as "Sohrab and Rustum" and "The Scholar-Gipsy," came after the disappointment of 1852 and reflect his efforts to write poems that did not sink under the sadness and ennui that marred his *Empedocles on Etna*. Thematically, Arnold is often able in these poems to wrest an uplifting conclusion from the borders of despair. Today's reader may view these poems as his most hackneyed and complacent paeans to Victorian optimism and elite British culture. Aesthetically, the poems that find their ennobling lesson often lose their poetic power, and the poems that continue to interest modern critics are those in which the power of language creates a new and modernist rhetorical order.

The contrast of poems written to fulfill Arnold's aesthetic standards and those that express his emotional turmoil dramatically illustrates the tension in his work between argument and metaphor. His narratives typically seek an ideological end; his metaphors create new spaces where meaning is unsettled and open for interpretation. Arnold relies heavily on narrative to lift the poems into the realm of the useful and good. The poems tell a story that embodies an adequate moral. His imagistic and metaphoric imagination, however, moves in a non-narrative way to make vivid his emotional state of mind. In these poems language creates the world in which expressing sadness and alienation is itself an act of order and meaning that redefines the world. Taking classical examples of narrative poetry as his standard, he nevertheless invested his keenest poetic sensibilities in memorable images and metaphors that remain hauntingly modernist. Advocating the moral lesson of an exemplum, he vivified the moment of grief and despair. Arnold was deeply conscious of the contradiction between his aesthetic ideology and the emotions that dominated his poems, but he seems often unaware of how his poetic techniques were themselves in a conflict that no thematic unity could overcome.

Arnold continued in 1852 and 1853 to write letters to Clough that sought to clarify his poetic practice. Having earlier praised the Greeks for knowing what they wanted in art, Arnold feels that he, too, now knows: "I feel immensely—more and more clearly—what I *want*—what I have (I believe) lost and choked by my treatment of myself and the studies to which I have addicted myself. But what ought I to have done in preference to what I have done? there is the question" (*Letters*, 1:264). His new poem in the first half of 1853, "Sohrab and Rustum," "pleases me better than anything I have yet done" (*Letters*, 1:264), he writes. The poem, which he lauded to his mother in another letter, was, he thought, "the best thing I have yet done," because "the story is a very noble and excellent one" (*Letters*, 1:266). Such poems allowed Arnold to believe that he was getting past complaint to animate and ennoble his readers. His confidence was not great enough, however, to temper his criticism when Clough was uncertain of his enthusiasm for the poem.

> You certainly do not seem to me sufficiently to desire and earnestly strive towards—assured knowledge—activity—happiness.
> You are too content to *fluctuate*—to be ever learning, never coming to the knowledge of the truth. This is why, with you, I feel it necessary to stiffen myself—and hold fast my rudder. (*Letters*, 1:282)

The poetic "rudder" that assured him "Sohrab and Rustum" was the best thing he had done did not steer Arnold into deeper, smoother channels of poetry. A year later in December of 1854 Arnold's enthusiasm about his new poems and his confident pleasure in the volume had waned. The book would, he assessed, leave his reputation as poet "pretty much at the point where the last left me—not advance me and not pull me down from it" (*Letters*, 1:300). The book "was worth publishing" because "I shall probably make something by the poems in their present shape, whereas if I had left them as they were, I should have continued to make nothing." He admits, though, that he regards the collection "with less interest than I should have thought possible" (*Letters*, 1:300). To his sister Jane he wrote at the end of 1854, "I daresay the book will dribble away in a year's time or so" (*Letters*, 1:301).

The two poems in which Arnold most self-consciously tries to solve his poetic problems are "Tristram and Iseult" (1852) and "Sohrab and Rustum" (1853). Both look to the world of legend for their content. In the tragic tale of Tristram and the two Iseults, Arnold's only resolutions are in artistic representations that we must then imperfectly interpret. In the tragic tale of "Sohrab and Rustum," in which father unknowingly kills son, the resolution is driven by the Greek model. The tragic recognition when knowledge is revealed illustrates that fate is inescapable and human understanding limited.

"Tristram and Iseult"

Despite its sources in Malory, Arnold's "Tristram and Iseult" is a romantic tale in which the Byronic elements have been sapped of their health and energy. All three main characters have been ground down by the sorrow of their fate. Tristram's bloom is gone, and he lies dying. Iseult of Ireland has withered under the stress of concealing a private passion amid a public life. Iseult of Brittany (of the White Hands) is a pale and bloodless woman whose sadness is not grief and whose love is not passion. Her children are cherubs innocent of the death and infidelity that have destroyed their father and eviscerated their mother. Rather than players in a tragic drama, Tristram and the two Iseults are objects of a charmed gaze that looks but does not touch except through the aestheticized image. The poem's artistic power lies not in their fates, but in the almost decadent images of their emotional waste. The pathos of these three lives is an object to be looked on or made into a tale, not to be felt as human experience. Through the complex narrative technique that Arnold devises for this powerful but static poem, he succeeds in distancing himself by creating a narrator whose focus is on how the artist might picture the details of a compelling scene.[1]

The deathbed reunion of Tristram and Iseult of Ireland might have been high drama, just as the tale of a love potion that ruins lives might have been intriguing narrative. Arnold's "Tristram and Iseult" is neither, but its mixed nature illustrates the poetic problems of form that Victorian and later modern poets had to resolve. When the narrative frame yields to human drama as an image to be composed and interpreted, Arnold is able to impose an aesthetic distance that controls the tendency to despairing emotions that overwhelms many of his other poems.

The poem begins with a dying Tristram awaiting the belated arrival of a faded and worn Iseult of Ireland. By his bedside sits a quiet and sad Iseult of Brittany whose presence at her husband's deathbed seems almost extraneous to the drama. The poem ends a year after the deaths with the still subdued Iseult of Brittany telling her children of the snare of Merlin by a wily Vivian who was "passing weary of his love." A typical Arnoldian passage tells us that it is neither suffering nor sorrow that robs us of all delight so much as it is "the gradual furnace of the world, / In whose hot air our spirits are upcurled / . . . Which kills us in the bloom" (*Poems*, 3.119–22). This insight seems, however, to have little to do with the these star-crossed lovers from a bygone time. They were victims of "some tyrannous single thought, some fit / Of passion" that subdues the soul, but their hapless mismatch tells us less about the genuine tyranny of mind in modern times than Arnold portrayed in characters such as Empedocles. Their madness is the result of a misdirected love potion, not the product of a misguided will or intellectual alienation. The poem evades Arnold's attempts to spell out its meaning, and his efforts to do so seem intrusive and irrelevant to the memorable pictures he gives us.

The poem is divided into three scenes that are named for the three lovers. Despite this structure around the characters, the narrator is the central intelligence in the poem.[2] He takes the outline of the legend and invents the characters, directing and controlling throughout the shape of their story and our possible responses to it. The narrator speaks more often than the characters, and at the two critical turns in the tale, the deaths of Tristram and the first Iseult and the conclusion of the story a year later, the narrator deflects the narrative away from the characters and action to provide us with an aesthetic construct that represents the narrator's interpretation. In Part III, "Iseult of Brittany," the narrator is the only speaker, and the account of Iseult's life with her children after Tristram's death is wholly in his voice. He ends his account by retelling a story Iseult presumably told her children on one particular day that the narrator seems to take as emblematic of her life. The story she tells of Merlin and Vivian has only a glancing parallel in plot (a man is made a fool of by indulging his passion for a beautiful woman). The narrator's choice to end the poem with this tale, however, forces the reader into attempting to create a structural and thematic conclusion for which the story of Merlin's fate is an appropriate "ending."

From the beginning of the poem the narrator shows a keen interest in arranging the picturesque details and inflating the emotional drama of the scene. One of his devices is the rhetorical question: "What Knight is this so weak and pale," or "What Lady is this, whose silk attire / Gleams so rich in the light of the fire?" (*Poems*, 1.9, 24–25). "But where / Is that other Iseult fair," he asks, wondering if her young heart is already so injured that she is "sunk and pale" (*Poems*, 1.48, 56–57). When the narrator has painted the drama sufficiently for his own emotional engagement, he proceeds in the next section to direct us about how to let the story go forward. He tells us, "let him dream!" "Let her have her youth again." In the next section he returns to an imagined scenario of their youthful passion and its effects on their inner lives. Having created them as endlessly anguished with frustrated passion that no action can displace, the narrator concludes that "only death can balm thy woe" (*Poems*, 1.289).

In the second scene, "Iseult of Ireland," the narrator stays out of the drama for 100 lines as the two principals trade accusations and protestations of love in the deathbed reunion. Just at the point that Tristram is about to expire, the narrator interjects, "You see them clear—" (*Poems*, 2.101). No further action about this moment is narrated, including how Iseult of Ireland manages to die with Tristram, but we are given an elaborate sense of how the scene appears. First the narrator places Iseult at the aesthetic center of the scene:

> "She sinks upon the ground; her hood
> Had fallen back; her arms outspread
> Still hold her lover's hand; her head
> Is bowed, half-buried, on the bed.
> O'er the blanched sheet her raven hair
> Lies in disordered streams; and there,
>
> Strung like white stars, the pearls still are,
> And the golden bracelets, heavy and rare,
> Flash on her white arms still."
>   (*Poems*, 2.103–11)

The narrator knows that, "though the bed-clothes hide her face," her expression, could we but see it, "would charm the gazer," as he clearly is charmed by the imagination of her beauty. Unlike Prufrock, this narrator has not "known them all already," but his image of the bracelets on her white arms may remind us of an essentially voyeuristic intrigue with women's sexuality and male-centered suffering. As if to verify his narrative credibility, the narrator turns to the "figure in the carpet,"[3] the huntsman in the tapestry, to also react to the scene. The huntsman's imagined disquiet at the scene parallels that of the narrator in Scene I, including a similar use of rhetorical questions designed to create drama. He, too, is an embarrassed gazer who asks, "What place is this, and who are they?" just as the narrator had suggested a context for interpretation out of the fabric of his questions.

The last scene tells of Iseult of Brittany's desexualized life as a widowed mother of angelic children. She is "dying in a mask of youth" in which life and joy have passed her by. Her beauty is "fatigued" and sunken; her voice (which is silenced in the poem) is "infantine," but it is the last reminder of her youth. Her love extends to her family, the women serving her, the dog, and the folktales she learned when a child. If her joy in storytelling seems unexpected, we should recall that she, too, made her husband and the first Iseult objects of her gaze when Tristram was dying. Instead of personalizing her sorrow, "Her look was like a sad embrace; / The gaze of one who can divine / A grief, and sympathise" (*Poems*, 1.322–24). She is thus like the huntsman in the tapestry and the narrator who is composing a picture. The price of such rarified compassion is the vitality of life, and Iseult's distancing eye substitutes the story of passion for the experience of passion.[4]

Arnold was not content with his use of the tale of Merlin and Vivian to end the poem. He had encountered the story of Tristram at Thun in Switzerland and pursued it on his return to England. He wrote to Herbert Hill that he brought in the Merlin legend "to relieve the poem which would else I thought have ended too sadly" (*Letters*, 1:247). Several critics have associated the story of Tristram and the two Iseults with Arnold's own unhappy romance with "Marguerite,"[5] an association that does little to explain the poem. Iseult of Brittany's tale of Merlin and Vivian is often interpreted as part of her life of fantasy that reveals her attitude about her husband and the first Iseult.[6] Underneath the still hands and passive eye is an imagination that may want to make a moral tale of her husband's philandering. The death-sleep of the foolish old man who lusted after the manipulative young seductress might symbolize Tristram's just rewards. Vivian's character then comments to condemn Iseult of Ireland as a vixen who snared Tristram. Iseult of Ireland's compassionate gaze on the dying Tristram suggests a deeper and more objectified understanding. The tale of Merlin and Vivian may be less a fantasy about her life than Iseult's alternative to her real life. This tale of passion and sexual desire especially appeals to her because she has observed firsthand another tale of sexual passion and wasteful death. She tells her children, and herself, the story of Merlin and Vivian so that she does not have to tell the story of her ruined life. To tell her own story would be to enter the drama that she only watches from a sheltered distance.

The poem throughout has many images of sheltered circles and crevices from which one can safely dream and gaze, or spin tales. Icy winds and rains howl throughout the first two sections of the poem, but Iseult watches from the fireside or bedside. The narrator objectifies this sense of protective distance when he elaborately describes the sleeping children "like helpless birds in a warm nest" despite the storm that rages even in the "park-glade" where they play and that brings the doomed Iseult of Ireland to their father's arms. The huntsman in the arras eyes the lovers from the safety of "the free green wood." Iseult of Brittany's children play "in a green circular hollow in the heath," and in the shelter of the holly-clumps, "warm in their mantles wrapped," she begins her story. Hers is a narrative within a narrative (the narrator's) within a narrative (Arnold's poem) about a narrative (Malory's) that was already folktale and legend when first written. Even within her own account Iseult is retelling a folktale learned in childhood in the peasant huts along the coastline. The narrative reference at the end of Scene II reminds us that these lovers have been dead 1,000 years, and what remains of human experience in the tale is the artistic interpretation of meaning rather than the raw emotion of actual life.

In "Tristram and Iseult" Arnold contains emotional extravagance through narrative technique, but he seems not to have fully appreciated how this poem potentially solved some of the problems of Victorian poets. Arnold's objectifying of Tristram and Iseult as figures in a tapestry was one way, to quote Pound's dictum for the modernists, to "make it new." Ruth apRoberts has argued that we may describe Arnold's "theory and practice as being in the symbolist mode even if he did not use the term."[7] Instead of "thinking aloud," he wanted his poetry to make something. His narrator in this poem and Iseult are both makers of something, but the price for making is distance from experience. In the

poem, Tristram seeks the "solitudes of the green wood" in order to tell
his pain to the forest, but unlike his wife or the huntsman who find
comfort in the green wood, he finds only another tormenting image of
Iseult of Ireland. He is unable to make anything of his suffering or find
any shelter from his passion. Like Empedocles, or Arnold himself in
many other poems, he cannot escape the immediacy of his passion or
translate it into metaphor, into poetry worthy of the name of literature.
In "Tristram and Iseult" Arnold both makes and illustrates the process
of making. "No fairer resting-place a man could find," the narrator says
of the daisied circle where Merlin sleeps,[8] and the same is true of Tristram and Iseult as memorable images captured in art.

"Sohrab and Rustum"

A comparison of "Tristram and Iseult" with "Sohrab and Rustum"
points out the artistic strengths of the first poem and the weaknesses of
the second. Arnold had found in "Tristram and Iseult" a narrative structure that permitted intense passion but was not engulfed by it, that
allowed him to use ancient stories but make them fresh, that allowed for
subjective comment within an objectifying frame, but he did not use
these techniques in the next long poem he wrote. Arnold's wrongheaded
misjudgment that "Sohrab and Rustum" was "better than anything I
have yet done" (*Letters*, 1:264) has not persuaded his critics. The story
was "a very noble and excellent one," he wrote to his mother and
believed that she, his wife, and his favorite sister would be "delighted
with it" (*Letters*, 1:266). The poem, taken from a Persian legend and
incorporating some Homeric parallels, is a straightforward narrative
account of the battle between a father and his unidentified son. The
father is a great and venerated warrior and his son a great and noble
young leader. The son dies knowing he has found his father at last, and
the father lives with the anguish of knowing he has slain his only son.
The legend is old and has many variations (Yeats's Cuchulain in *On
Baile's Strand* is a modern version) and draws on the economic and cultural importance of the son in patriarchal culture. Its emotional power
depends on the sense of tragedy that a great man will have no worthy
male descendent to inherit his legacy of name, fortune, and glory.

Arnold's telling of the story is simple and eloquent. The father and
son are measured for their sensitivity as well as their courage in battle.
The death scene is sentimental but not bathetic, and the moral is that
fate is poised like a "huge wave" that "hangs uncertain to which side to

fall" (*Poems*, lines 391–92). The story lacks complexity or ambiguity, and the familiar pattern leaves the reader disengaged and lacking in suspense. In contrast, the story of Tristram and Iseult may be interpreted as a lesson about fate, immorality, or a combination of both. We can quarrel over which Iseult is more tragic and who shares blame. The account of Tristram's affair with Iseult in Tennyson's telling is a court scandal that helps bring down the Round Table. Arnold's version is more open and ambiguous. Tristram may be a victim or a perpetrator, self-scourging or self-satisfied. The story may be sexualized or exemplary. Arnold's structure preserves the openness of the story and invites interpretation. In one sense "Tristram and Iseult" is about reading, about how subjective a reading can be and the ways in which artistic design enables it. The author and his narrator invite us to "see clearly," but we see only what must be interpreted. Arnold sexualizes this story of star-crossed lovers through the reminder of children and the tale of Vivian and Merlin. The children are the sign of the moral harm done, even if the love was undeniable. His form is like that thorny bush in the closing scenes that surrounds the daisied circle of fairest rest. The sexual story can only be "read" through the tropes, and the "moral" depends on one's interpretation of a complex set of suggestions.

In contrast, "Sohrab and Rustum" is about instruction and the sorrow of life. The poem reminds us that great men and things are broken by time and fate and that pride is a kind of blindness that trips us into disaster. Modern critics may find little of interest in "Sohrab and Rustum." Its appropriation of the myths of another culture leads it afoul of postcolonial critics, and its implicit gender values represent a singularly male perspective. Even for close readers of texts, the poem offers no "thorny" passages that lead us into the profundity of art.

"Dover Beach"

The poetic qualities lacking in "Sohrab and Rustum" are richly present in Arnold's best known poem, "Dover Beach." This poem, one of the most frequently anthologized poems in British literature, is generally considered Arnold's finest. Apparently inspired by a visit to Dover on his 1851 honeymoon, the poem reveals just how powerful a poet Arnold can be when he listens to the logic of his metaphoric language instead of resisting it with ideological intentions. Many readers have complained about a lack of logical consistency between the metaphors and the argument in Arnold's poems, yet clearly the poems are often emotionally convincing even when we question the logic.[9] "Dover Beach" illustrates how metaphoric structure may develop a logic of emotional experience different from the meaning traced through the grammar of argument. The poem upends our expectations of metaphor by beginning with a seemingly literal description of the cliffs that turns out to be the delusion and ending with apocalyptic metaphors of the darkling plain that are the poem's ultimate reality. Both landscapes are mental constructs that hold their authority only so long as language can sustain them. Perhaps like the opening lines that hide a broken sonnet structure,[10] the descriptive language, not troped on its surface, conceals its metaphoric context. The description of the sea as "calm" and the tide "full," both of which are relatively literal and even scientifically measurable, soon yields to the moon as "fair," an adjective that makes of the moon something more than an orbiting object and something less than a beautiful face.

The language of "gleams," "glimmering," "tranquil," "sweet," and "moon-blanched" is metaphorically contextualized through numerous figures of speech and literary allusions.[11] The cliffs are a physical object, but "the cliffs of England stand, / Glimmering and vast" is a mental experience with emotional value (*Poems,* lines 4–5). Ruth Pitman reads them as both the patriotic and geological symbol of the changing times. The cliffs are composed in landscape fit for Romantic poetry where the cadence whispers from Wordsworth, Keats, and Coleridge. Before our attention is drawn down to the shoreline, one might almost expect to hear the voice of a nightingale or a woman wailing for her demon lover, or see Coleridge's moon "overspread with phantom light." If the Romantic world that Wordsworth brought to life has vanished, then the landscape before Arnold, which depends on a particular kind of poetic language to sustain it, may prove as vulnerable to time as one's belief in the transforming power of Wordsworth's verse. The discursive thought will connect the failure of Arnold's genial spirits to the retreat of Faith, but long before we get to that point, the metaphoric subtext has brought to mind the loss of Romantic belief. Perhaps equally important to the retreat of religion is the retreat of aesthetic possibilities. The "cliffs of England" are eroded geologically as objects and poetically as mental realities when framed in a dying Romantic language.

The speaker tells us he hears "the grating roar / Of pebbles," but the rhythmic echo of iambic waves dominates the next few lines. The metaphoric subtext of the poem surfaces when the "tremulous cadence" of "begin, and cease, and then again begin" brings "the eternal note of sadness in" (*Poems,* lines 9–10, 12–14). The metaphoric eternal note

overwhelms the literal sound of the sea that yields at least two notes—
begin and end—and the monotone of meter drowns the possibilities of
language. The production of sound in the tremulous cadence of iambic
beats becomes an immemorial rhythm obliterating the distinctions of
history and human understanding. This moment is lost in the loss of
other past moments. If the sea's message is that all language is silenced,
then all mental realities must go, too. The immediate casualty is the
Romantic moment of the Dover night where nature was recreated in
tranquility. As the meter of "begin, and cease, and then again begin"
concludes the stanza, poetic language yields its power to create meaning
to rhythm's power to obliterate it. Poetry itself erodes as the verbal
ground on which "the cliffs of England" stand.

On the level of the poem's argument the reference to Sophocles on
the Aegean connects sadness to human tragedy and may help to explain
why we need faith, but on the level of metaphor it connects the vulnera-
bility of language to the force of time. Sophocles "long ago" heard the
sound that is not language in the washing of the Aegean and wrote to
fill the night with meaning. The sound of the tide brought to his mind
the cycle of human misery, but what he wrote represents a higher order
of experience. He made of turbid human misery the transfiguring order
of tragic drama. The strophe-antistrophe of the choral performance are
brought to "cata-strophe" as the artist translates the ebb and flow of
human misery into dramatic form.

The parallel of our speaker, at one level identifiable with Arnold as
poet, looking toward the coast of France and thinking in tropes, with
Sophocles, the classical dramatist, listening to the same sound and
singing the tragic chorus, reminds us that both are artists. The poet's
eye has been arranging the order of landscape through the order of
metaphors. Wallace Stevens in "The Idea of Order at Key West" calls it
the "Blessed rage for order . . . / The maker's rage to order words of the
sea." In "Dover Beach," Arnold's confidence in the power of poetry is
shattered by the numbing sound of the sea. Instead of arranging the
night, his words create the moment in which language will cease to
sound as words and linger only in confused alarms.

By the time the speaker introduces the "The Sea of Faith," the metaphoric logic in the poem is essentially in place. Romantic and classical
language has failed, and the poet's belief in poetry has been shaken.
"The Sea of Faith" enters the poem, overtly directing the argument to
its contemporary causality and implicitly illustrating the problematic
nature of contemporary poetic language. As metaphor we must read

both sea and faith back into our understanding of "The Sea of Faith"—
that is, it has ebbed, eroding the base on which civilization stands. As a
congruence of both sea and faith, "The Sea of Faith" as trope creates a
new meaning, one that is self-consciously metaphoric. When Arnold
introduces "The Sea of Faith," he notes that it was once *too* at the full,
but the implied comparison may include faiths other than religious
ones. Also once at the full was a classical sublime and a Romantic comfort, but they, too, are gone.

"The Sea of Faith" intrudes on the poem proclaiming the thematic
weight it is to carry. Then in one of the most awkward and obscure
images in his poetry, Arnold metaphorizes his metaphor when he adds
that "The Sea of Faith" "lay like the folds of a bright girdle furled"
around earth's shore. The bright, mantling folds of faith that once pro-
tected us from the naked silence are like that transfiguring imagination
that once floated "the cliffs of England" on a poetic sea. As metaphor,
however, "The Sea of Faith" is obvious, and the "bright girdle furled" is
clumsy and obscure. Together they seem to signal the poet's loss of confidence in poetic language. And when they are done, nothing is heard
but the expiring breath of a ruined poetics. The night-wind that blows
along the naked shingles of a dreary world is the opposite of the life-
giving wind that inspired Romantic poetry. Its long suspiration is the
sound of death, and the five lines necessary to exhaust it is an auditory
metaphor that consigns the tremulous cadence of poetic language to the
immemorial beating of empty time.

The poem's conclusion is a last stand against a world of broken faiths.
The metaphoric structures of the first stanza are in collapse in the last
stanza as the poet recants his Romantic delusion. The enchanted night
that seemed a land of dreams is a metaphoric deception, its evocative
language stripped of the faith in poetry that sustained its claim to give
us reality. The only words that remain to hold back this dark night are
the vows of lovers. But the call to "be true" is built on the ceremonial
language of "I do." Without the faith that words can make a land of
dreams, the poet's appeal to his love is a frail hope. The answering
words that are necessary to seal the vow are not heard, an absence that
leaves the poet without a concurring voice to strengthen words against
the violence that threatens to obliterate language in confused alarms.
The loss of confidence in metaphor to create mental realities is sounded
one last time when the poet signals that his new vision is *only* metaphor:
"we are here *as on* a darkling plain" (*Poems,* line 35 –emphasis mine).
This last uncertainty that poetic language can give us reality undercuts

even the small hope that the rhetoric of love can arrange a different world from the one in the poem's last lines.

The discursive thought of "Dover Beach" follows the speaker's idea of theme, but the metaphors express the poet's struggle to sustain the life of poetic language. The two modes of expression are epistemological as well as stylistic since the logic of thought and the logic of metaphor shape different kinds of knowledge and different experiences of reality. For Arnold, the sadness at Dover Beach is also at the loss of belief in a poetic language in which the cliffs of England can stand *as* "glimmering and vast."

Gypsy Scholars

The contrasts between Arnold's use of logic in narrative to argue a theme and in metaphor to capture emotions is apparent if we compare "Stanzas from the Grande Chartreuse" and "The Scholar-Gipsy." Both poems may date from 1852, but the first was published in 1855 and the other in 1853. On his honeymoon Arnold visited the monastery of the Carthusians. The poem tells of his visit to their spectral realm where they retire from the changing world to live out their faith in a religion the world derides. "Stanzas from the Grande Chartreuse" reiterates some of the themes of *Empedocles on Etna* without the guise of ancient legend to distance the speaker from the poet. The poem is memorable for its emotional statement of alienation from modern times, but the poem bases these emotions on a logic of thought that pretends that cause and effect will reveal that his responses are reasonable and right, not extreme and damaging. The text is a typically Arnoldian blend of discursive thought whose careful logic is upstaged by moments of singular metaphoric "making" that move outside the logic of thought to capture profound emotion.

In contrast, "The Scholar-Gipsy" rehearses the story of the Oxford scholar who left behind the ways of the world to roam with the gypsies to learn the secret wisdom of life. The logic of argument fails to deliver the poem, which relies at the end on an obscure metaphor ill-designed to bear the poem's conclusion. Between the mystical quest and the collapse of time from Arnold's present and 200 years earlier when the story began, the role of logic in the poem is tenuous. The poem's meaning is explicitly wrapped up in difficult metaphors of the scholar-gypsy and the Tyrian traders that close the poem. The layers of metaphoric association between the speaker's concern with the modern world, the scholar-gypsy's quest, and the ancient Greeks' trading manners must tie the poem together without the unity of argument, narrative, or theme. In "Stanzas from the Grand Chartreuse" Arnold describes the step-by-step ascent up the mountain to the silent courts of the Grande Chartreuse as though the climb itself was part of the illuminating logic. *"Strike leftward!* cries our guide," as though the direction had some meaning intrinsic to the spiritual journey. Once arrived, the poet unifies the "world-famed home" of the monks with a set of insistent images of cold, death, ghostliness, and silence. They are "death in life," and his question is "what am I, that I am here" (*Poems,* line 54, 66). This is the right question since he is not there as a believer, "not as their friend, or child" (*Poems,* line 79). He is there in order to interject himself actively into the metaphor of the ancient Greek who once looked on an even more ancient dead religion:

> But as, on some far northern strand,
> Thinking of his own Gods, a Greek
> In pity and mournful awe might stand
> Before some fallen Runic stone—
> For both were faiths, and both are gone.
>   (*Poems,* lines 80–84)

The "but as" grammar signals Arnold's self-conscious situating of himself within a metaphoric distance from the Carthusians. Of course, the monks have not chosen their seclusion for reasons like those that guide Arnold, and they no doubt do not look on their monastery as like a living tomb in which they are the walking dead.[12] He feels the world derides his belief, and he in turn is there because implicitly he derides theirs, thus linking them to himself as both victims of the world's scorn. Their faith is not his faith, their world is not his world, but, like them, he has lost the belief of his youth and would withdraw from the world he knows. He pities them in order to pity himself, just as he will draw on their retreat from the world to justify metaphorically his own desire to retreat from the claims of life. Despite the logic that tries to tie the speaker to the monks, his problems are distinctly Empedoclean and not religious. He is a man, educated in another mode, out of joint with his times and suffering from his sense of alienation. The central and most famous metaphor in the poem is "Wandering between two worlds, one dead, / The other powerless to be born, / With nowhere yet to rest my head" (*Poems,* lines 85–87). To be between worlds is to be in a void between past and future. The "other" world to which Arnold alludes is not, in fact, powerless to be born, but has already been thrust upon his consciousness as an alien place. He is instead "powerless" to stop the arrival of the future he does not welcome. The "rigorous teachers" of his youth taught him other ways, and he cannot change to accommodate a present peopled by lesser minds, dead faiths, and timid heroes. Even worse is that the meanness of the present has destroyed the beauty of the past since the accomplishments of his old teachers did not prevail. "For what availed it, all the noise / And outcry of the former men?" (*Poems,* lines 127–28). Heroes such as Obermann and Romantic authors who filled his youth cannot sustain him when their "distress" is dismissed by an indifferent present that belittles their tragic passion as tiresome "fret" and complaint.

From the moment the speaker asks the monks to "hide me in your gloom profound," he moves from the first person singular pronoun to the plural "we." As the poem nears its conclusion and the speaker makes his choice to let life pass him by, the use of the plural "we" becomes increasingly prominent. This "we" is bound by the logic of the journey to the monks among whom he has sought refuge, but it does not actually refer to them or any choices they have made. It is a more abstract "we" who once had the same teachers and read the same authors and now are unfit for a changing world. Increasingly the poem divides into "you" and "yours" and "we" and "ours," climaxing with "We are like children reared in shade / Beneath some old-world abbey wall" (*Poems,* lines 169–70). The rhetorical logic of the pronoun anchors this very personal poem in a spiritual crisis common to the best minds of many generations. The poem's appeal lies in the fact that many readers have felt a similar alienation from their own time and culture, but the poem's logic of the journey to the Carthusians has not made that argument, though its metaphoric associations of those lost in time have. The metaphor of "children reared in shade / Beneath some old-world abbey wall" prepares the ground on which the poet will choose his "desert" instead of the world.

The world calls to the poet to "*follow too,*" but the metaphoric attractions are certain to fail to appeal to him. To this man educated on Romantic beauty and rigorous teachers of the mind such as Goethe, Heine, and others who had helped shape the intellectual sensibility of Europe in the nineteenth century, the world calls in the metaphors of medieval life and warfare. Having wrapped his emotional crisis in the metaphor of the archaic way of life of the Carthusians, Arnold can disguise the real claims of his world by figuring them in metaphors of another archaic world. The price of this strategy is that he cannot resolve his Victorian crisis with metaphors that do not confront it. First comes the call to action of the troops with "Pennon, and plume, and flashing lance" who journey forth "To life, to cities, and to war" (*Poems,* lines 178, 180). Then come the hunters with the hounds and "gay dames" who call him to pleasure. Neither action nor pleasure can lure him from the metaphoric space between two worlds that he has created for himself in the spectral grounds of the Grande Chartreuse. Metaphorically he sees himself as " 'fenced early in this cloistral round / Of reverie, of shade, of prayer' " and unable to "flower in foreign air" (*Poems,* lines 205–8). Arnold (not the speaker, if one wants to separate the poem's persona from the poet) was not in fact fenced in any "cloistral round" of reveries, shade, and prayer, but his embrace of the metaphor of the Carthusians and their "dead faith" displaces the ways in which his crisis is different from theirs. Their withdrawal from the world is appropriate for their faith, and Arnold's acceptance of metaphors from their way of life disguises from himself that a similar withdrawal may not be appropriate for him.

The conclusion to this poem is a fascinating example of how Arnold's poetic imagination leads him through metaphors into emotional and intellectual places that he otherwise chooses not to inhabit. This 1855 poem, published after his marriage and work as a school inspector and on the eve of his further social engagement as a critic, chooses the "peace" of a "desert" cloistral ground that is the opposite turf from where he will actually stand for the rest of his quite public life. A similar process of following the logic of his metaphors led Empedocles to jump in the cone of Etna, though Arnold so disapproved of this poem that he withdrew it. Ironically, a poet's willingness to be faithful to metaphor may be one of the best measures of the artist; it is the surest sign that the poet understands and honors the power of language to create a new reality. His best poems are faithful to his metaphors, which may or may not reveal his inner life since what they most clearly reveal is his sensitivity to the way in which words have meanings that control the artist, not that the artist has complete control of language.

"The Scholar-Gipsy" and "Thyrsis" are two major poems in which the logic of metaphor never quite controls the poem. "The Scholar-Gipsy" comes out of the 1852–1853 period, and "Thyrsis," ostensibly an elegy for Clough, comes out of the 1864–1865 period. The scholar-gypsy, the Oxford student who sought the secret of how to rule the "workings of men's brains," is meant as a symbol of the quester after a higher truth than society reveals. Though the original scholar-gypsy intended to return to the world with the knowledge he gained, Arnold fears the world will "spoil" his spirit and urges him to flee "the infection of our mental strife" (*Poems*, line 222). If the scholar-gypsy had any wisdom to share, he should, according to his own ends, return to the world, and if Arnold thought the scholar-gypsy had such knowledge, he should eagerly urge that he share his secrets with an anxious and unhappy world. The metaphor is muddled, however, as the scholar is "tongue-tied" and never has anything to say. At one point Arnold calls him "a truant boy," and his pensive look suggests an unease with himself and his own quest.[13] If he left the world "with powers / Fresh, undiverted to the world without" (*Poems*, lines 161–62), he seems not to have found "the spark from heaven" for which he waited. His chief virtue over those who also wait for the "spark from heaven" in the infected modern world is that he acted on his impulse, unlike "we"

> Light half-believers of our casual creeds,
>   Who never deeply felt, nor clearly willed,
> Whose insight never has borne fruit in deeds,
>   Whose vague resolves never have been fulfilled;
>   For whom each year we see
> Breeds new beginnings, disappointments new;
>   Who hesitate and falter life away,
>   And lose to-morrow the ground won to-day—
>   (*Poems*, lines 172–79)

T. S. Eliot might say that, as "objective correlative," the scholar-gypsy is not an adequate metaphor for the poetic task. The gypsy seems more like than unlike the narrator in his unfulfilled desire for revelation. One flees society and the other counsels him to flee society. The metaphor is not sharply enough drawn to make the contrast Arnold wants to make, and the weakness of the scholar-gypsy as metaphor leads Arnold into the awkward metaphor that closes the poem.

Some critics have said the metaphor of the Tyrian trader who flees the merry Greeks with their freight of "amber grapes, and Chian wine, / Green, bursting figs, and tunnies steeped in brine" (*Poems*, lines 238–39) is so obscure that no parallels can be adequately worked out.[14] Others, such as E. K. Brown, see the Greek traders as like the residents of Arnold's infected modern world, and the Tyrian who flees them to trade instead with the "shy" Iberians as like the scholar who joins the elusive gypsies.[15] Certainly there is a rough parallel such as Brown outlines, but the metaphor is wonderfully obscure and limited in its power. The preference of the Tyrian trader for one set of manners in trade over another one seems hardly worth the endnotes needed to explain it. The metaphor of commerce does not resonate on the exalted plane of the metaphor of the scholar-gypsy as a seeker of overarching wisdom. One reason the metaphors of the scholar-gypsy and the Tyrian trader do not work more gracefully or powerfully is that their flight is not the heart of Arnold's poem. Instead, he uses their flight as a way of commenting on the infected modern world, which is his primary emotional interest. His own frustration and "sad patience" look for no "anodynes," and thus his interest in the scholar-gypsy is more a baleful commentary than a hope for that "spark" that redeems. The metaphor that emotionally leads Arnold in this poem is that of the infected world, and he intensifies his sense of the plague of modern life by his insistence that the scholar-gypsy "fly our paths."

Arnold's awkwardness with metaphors is especially unsettling when he uses a traditional poetic form. His "Thyrsis" is the most ambivalent major "elegy" written for a lost personal friend. Aside from *In Memoriam,* most elegies of the last two centuries that departed from the tradition of praising the dead were usually by poets who were not personally close to the departed. Yeats's "In Memory of Major Robert Gregory," for example, was written out of Yeats's friendship with Robert's mother. In Auden's great elegy to Yeats, one poet addresses another on the basis of their work as poets, not as friends. But Arnold and Clough were old and dear friends, and the poet's oddly diffident attitude toward his friend makes it especially hard to achieve the metaphoric clarity we see in Arnold's best poems.

Arnold aligns himself and Clough in their youth as followers in the quest symbolized by the scholar-gypsy. Instead of remaining true to the scholar-gypsy's quest and keeping away from the troubled clamor of the modern world, Clough was "irked" by the pastoral world and entered the life of "men unblest." Arnold reduces Clough's social altruism to something that "filled his head" but wasted his life and ruined his poetry: "He went; his piping took a troubled sound / Of storms that rage outside our happy ground; / He could not wait their passing, he is dead" (*Poems,* lines 48–50). Instead of being a scholar-gypsy, Clough as Thyrsis becomes the defeated poet and the impatient shepherd. The classical setting works against Clough who as Thyrsis is fated to be defeated. Arnold removes himself from this classical world, however, by contrasting the proficiency of Sicilian shepherd-poets with that of himself as a poet of "our poor Thames." Classical poets could ease the passage of their dead mates into the underworld, but as a poet of "our poor Thames," Arnold will never win Propserpine's ear or "relax Pluto's brow" on behalf of his friend. The metaphoric separation of Clough from the scholar-gypsy and the elegist places him outside the poem's ideal in ways that will be impossible to heal at the end when Arnold tries to reaffirm Clough's essential spirit of kinship with the scholar-gypsy and himself.

Perhaps the most poisonous metaphor tied to Clough is that of the cuckoo. The traditional symbolism of the cuckoo connects it to the ridiculous and amusing. Clough's troubled song and involvement with the world are drawn into a simile with the "cuckoo's parting cry." The cuckoo is called a "too quick despairer" because he mistakes a June storm as the sign that the bloom is gone when in fact all the rich flowers of summer are still to come. Unlike the "light comer" who flies too soon but will return next year, Clough flew too soon and wasted himself forever. He is defeated by "Time," and the signal elm and the quest "are not for him." Time is later associated with the "sickle to the perilous grain," a metaphor that deepens the sense that a foolish Clough was mowed down by the "times."

The power of time to change is implicitly the power to destroy more than to create in Arnold's poetry. "Thyrsis" opens with the exclamation, "How changed is here each spot man makes or fills" (*Poems,* line 1). The signal elm is the symbol of unchanging truth, the essential "tree of life." When Clough submitted himself to time, he was conquered by it, choosing the ephemeral fever and fret of the diseased world instead of the eternal truth of the quest for beauty and wisdom. The world of nature is the setting for the tree and thus embodies eternal beauty. Arnold casts himself as the one who knows the world of nature and Clough as the one silenced in the "town's harsh, heart-wearying roar" (*Poems,* line 234). "I know the Fyfield tree, / I know . . . the grassy harvest . . . I know these slopes; who knows them if not I?" Arnold proclaims in self-validation (*Poems,* lines 106–8, 111). As the one who "knows" nature and finds the elm again, he is both the true quester and the better poet. Clough, in contrast, had only a "rustic flute" that lost its "country tone" and "learnt a stormy note." Having gone among "men who groan," he ruined himself as poet and "tasked thy pipe too sore, and tired thy throat" until "it failed, and thou wast mute" (*Poems,* lines 221–26). Ironically, this fate assigned to Clough was Arnold's future, except that he was not "mute" altogether. He silenced his poet's "pipe" and turned to the pen of prose, specifically to comment on "men who groan."

It is difficult to know if Arnold meant to be so ungenerous to his dead friend, or if an unfortunate choice of metaphors led him into a poetic statement that was more derisive than grieving. He had always been a harsh critic of Clough's poetry, but the poem extends a lack of enthusiasm for his poetry to a condescending dismissal of his friend's life as an ill-chosen path of waste and infidelity to higher truths. The covert argument is that "he failed and I haven't," that "I know" and "he didn't." The severity of the judgments is unkind and inaccurate, both about Clough and his accomplishments and about Arnold and his success. The "grief" in this elegy is replaced by self-assertion and rededication to the quest that Arnold was wise enough not to abandon. He affirms his identity with the scholar-gypsy by indicting the vagaries of Clough and his ruined life.

At the end of the poem Arnold attempts to reintegrate Clough into the metaphors that he has used to separate him out. He includes Clough among those who had always "visions of our light" that made him restless and discontent in the tainted world with "men of care." The "our" in "our light" may include Clough, but it may also refer to Arnold and the scholar-gypsy. Granting that Clough was perhaps more complex and divided in his sensibility than he appeared, Arnold concedes that he, too, has compromised: "Too rare, too rare, grow now my visits here! / 'Mid city-noise, not, as with thee of yore, / Thyrsis! in reach of sheep-bells is my home" (*Poems,* lines 231–33). Moving in among the first Victorian suburbanites, Arnold has chosen his own space "between two worlds" where the fret of city noise is imaginatively eased by having a home within reach of the countryside. The degree to which his own compromise makes him more like Clough than the scholar-gypsy is muted for Arnold by the "last words" assigned to Clough in the poem.

Although Clough remains the example of failure, Arnold gives him one last whisper of a voice. That voice urges Arnold to continue his quest and hold faithful to the ideal:

> *Why faintest thou? I wandered till I died.*
> *Roam on! The light we sought is shining still.*
> *Dost thou ask proof? Our tree yet crowns the hill,*
> *Our Scholar travels yet the loved hill-side.*
> (*Poems,* lines 237–40)

Although the poem's metaphors affirm the example of the scholar-gypsy and the validity of his quest, the history behind this metaphor that we know from "The Scholar-Gipsy" interrogates the poetic statement in "Thyrsis." The scholar-gypsy is also dead and roams the hillside only as a symbol of a time and aspiration that has gone by for both Arnold and Clough. The change proclaimed in the opening line of "Thyrsis" has sent even Arnold into the city, and Clough, whatever the weaknesses of his poetry, did not die because his throat was tired. The scholar-gypsy, we were told, became "pensive and tongue-tied" with no word of wisdom ever to impart. Clough did not resign his part in the metaphor of the scholar-gypsy because he was one of those "light half-believers" of some "casual creeds, / Who never deeply felt, nor clearly willed" (*Poems,* lines 172–73), and Arnold has not been hit by the proverbial "spark from heaven" that never came to the scholar-gypsy either. Arnold wants from his metaphors a clarity that they do not have and that the poems themselves undermine. A tongue-tied scholar-gypsy who is aloof from the world is as silent as a dead Clough, and his value to art, life, or himself is in question. In earlier poems such as "Resignation" Arnold had said that the artist must "from some high station" "look down" on life, but it was necessary that he *see* with the comprehending "sad lucidity of soul." The scholar-gypsy, like the poet, "flees the common life of men," but, unlike the poet, he possesses neither wisdom nor voice as a result. The self-assurances at the end of "Thyrsis" that *"our tree yet crowns the hill, / Our Scholar travels yet the loved hill-side"* are a license to pretend that a strained and compromised metaphor still has power to inspire.

When Arnold subjugates language to idea, he is inclined to vitiate his poem with compromised or hackneyed metaphors. The notion of the scholar-gypsy is stronger as an ideological statement than as a rich metaphor, but as metaphor it is at least fresh in its terms and appropriately related to Arnold's experience. "Rugby Chapel," published in 1867 as a tribute to his father who had died in 1842, relies on overly familiar figures of speech based in a religious ideology that Arnold does not otherwise believe. The poem was in part inspired by some negative comments in print about his father, comments he characterized as suggesting "Papa's being a narrow bustling fanatic" (*Letters,* 3:168).[16] In this letter to his mother, he added, "I think I have done something to fix the true legend about Papa, as those who knew him best feel it ought to run; and this is much." This curious statement refers to the true legend of his father instead of his true character, and to how those who knew him best feel "it ought to run" instead of how he really was. "Rugby Chapel" is indeed an effort to fix a legend in such a way as to praise the father and comfort the mother. Although the poem expresses Arnold's affection for and fond memories of his father, the staleness of his metaphors implicitly suggests his lack of interest in his father's intellectual and spiritual life.

This "legend about Papa" brings him to metaphoric life as a cross between Christ who redeems others and a St. Bernard dog who pulls them from the snow. More than a servant, he is a son of God whose work on earth was to "reviv'st," "Succourest," and "save." The poem sets up three categories of men: those who "eddy about" and do "nothing," those who strive through action to advance "a clear-purposed goal" but fail to do more than survive the storm, and those like his father who also have ideal goals but manage to save many others as they advance mankind toward "the City of God." The structuring metaphors are of the journey through the snowstorm, the shepherd bringing in his sheep, and the rocky desert that must be crossed to get to the Promised Land. If only there were water in this metaphoric wasteland, but there is not even a drop drip drop drop drop to make the poem bloom.[17]

"Rugby Chapel" and "Thyrsis" mark the end of Arnold's poetry because they represent his consuming distrust of the poetic process. He is unwilling to yield himself to the poetic language that so often took him where the metaphors might lead, and frequently into emotional and intellectual turmoil. These poems draw on familiar metaphors where meaning has been rehearsed by other tellings. They lack the spirit of discovery that poetic language embodies when it is making something new. "Rugby Chapel" especially repudiates the emotions and beliefs that were at the center of his poetic thinking. Here, the hero is the man of action who struggles in and for the world. The "languor," "weakness," and "weariness" that earlier resulted in "panic, despair," and flight are now banished by the presence of noble—even angelic— "helpers and friends of mankind" (*Poems*, 1:161). The "furnace of the world" is replaced by the mountain snowstorm whose avalanche strips away the human train of "friends, companions." Arnold's pettiness about Clough, whose life was more devoted to goals Arnold's father would approve of than Arnold's was, seems particularly unpleasant when placed against the excesses of praise for his father.

In defining the three kinds of men in the world of "Rugby Chapel," Arnold eliminated the poet as he had earlier defined him. The central characters or speakers in all of Arnold's poems after *Empedocles on Etna* are revisions on the poet figure in such earlier works as "The Strayed Reveller," "Resignation," and "In Memory of the Author of 'Obermann.' " The narrator in "Tristram and Iseult" and Iseult of Brittany are indirect embodiments of the poet, as is Tristram the harper, but they make no case for poetry or themselves as poets. In "Stanzas from the Grande Chartreuse" the speaker is concerned with poetry but denies the lasting power of poets of his youth. "The kings of modern thought are dumb" in that space between two worlds. "The Scholar-Gipsy" and "Thyrsis" uphold the ideal of the quester, but each is silent. Clough's poetry is corrupted by the modern world, which has become a place where poets cannot survive. The heroic figures in the later poems are not poets in any form. Sohrab and Rustum and Arnold's father in "Rugby Chapel" are men of action who lead others. Sohrab's loss of his son is measured by his worthiness as a great leader who should have had a son to follow him. Rustum is heroic in his youthful courage and potential to be as great as his father. Arnold's father is the ultimate great man whose example leads Arnold to believe that there have been "others like thee in the past," though he remains skeptical that any such are to be found in "the men of the crowd / Who all round me to-day / Bluster or cringe" (*Poems*, lines 154–57).

The pattern in the poems of eliding the figure of the poet and replacing him with the kinds of heroes that Arnold earlier had disavowed is part of the process whereby Arnold brings his own career as poet to a halting conclusion. Arnold never officially or firmly decided not to write poetry, and he seems to have thought of his poetry as his truest work. Part of the problem was that he could not find a model of the poet he could, in good conscience, be. The idealization of the father who saved others was deeply at odds with the poet of "Resignation" who withdrew from the world and watched it from a distance. The harpers—Mycerinus, Empedocles, the Reveller, Tristram—were all figures whose choices were morally ambiguous and whose fates did not offer an avenue by which to live. For Arnold the abiding question was "how to live," and though he would claim that poetry will replace religion in our modern lives, he could not reconcile his belief in the power of poetry with his own life and work as poet. In the prose works that dominate the latter part of his career, Arnold found in the role of critic a way to combine his writing with the social and ethical concerns that his poetry could not, in his mind, adequately serve.

Chapter Six

Culture against Anarchy

Children of the future, whose day has not yet dawned, you, when that day arrives,
will hardly believe what obstructions were long suffered to prevent its coming!

Matthew Arnold, *A French Eton*

Looking back on Arnold's career from the perspective of more than a
century, the break between the poet and the critic appears more sharply
defined than it really was. As the poetry waned, the critical essay
bloomed, but the ideas and concerns that marked his later work grew
out of themes that were lifelong interests. Poems such as "The New
Sirens," "The Strayed Reveller," "Resignation," "The Scholar-Gipsy"—
even those early school poems on Alaric and Cromwell—reveal an intellect that linked poetry, criticism, education, and civic life to creating a
society in which the moral, intellectual, and political life reflected a general commitment to knowledge and truth. In *Culture and Anarchy*
(1869) Arnold would invent such catch phrases as "sweetness and light"
that expressed that ideal of a society striving to become its "best self."
Many of the rhetorical labels Arnold used to describe his ideal of an educated and democratic society are clichés today, but their very familiarity
is evidence of the lasting influence of his ideas. *Culture and Anarchy* is the
most extended prose consideration of Arnold's concerns, but the ideas
represented there are best seen as part of a constellation of ideas that
appear in his best known essays on literature and culture.

Although his frequent mention of the word "culture" has sometimes
been used to slap at Arnold as an elitist in the arts or as an apologist for
the ascendancy of the Western tradition in politics, Arnold's use of the
term "culture" has little relationship to the most common current definitions. For Arnold, "culture" is more a habit of mind than a list of the
arts or a description of societal organization. The "cultured" mind in
Arnold's vocabulary is one that seeks a wide range of knowledge and,
most important, subjects knowledge to a disinterested critical evaluation. The purpose of such a critical perspective is to create the free flow
of ideas out of which we may create a society prepared to discover its
"best self." The object of Arnoldian culture is the perfection of morals,

conduct, and spiritual and aesthetic beauty. Poetry is for Arnold a form of knowledge that encourages critical engagement and enhances our sense of beauty and conduct, rather than a sign of elite education or refined aesthetic sensibilities. Our contemporary definitions of "culture" as high-brow, low-brow, or "popular" refer to tastes and interests associated with social class and level of education. To Arnold "culture" cannot be discussed in these ways; he uses the term to describe a form of freedom of thought or mental life and not any particular social or artistic interests.

Aside from the immeasurable influence of growing up as his remarkable father's son, two other experiences seem to have had the greatest influence on Arnold's definition of "culture." One influence was the long and painful debate he carried on in his poetry about the role of the poet and poetry; the other was his work in the field of education. Poetry itself was of "like spirit," of "one law" with "sweetness and light."[1] In defining the poet Arnold was also implicitly defining many of the chief characteristics of the critic. The poet has knowledge, subdues his own heart to see into that of humanity generally, and looks on life as "a placid and continuous whole" with a "sad lucidity of soul" ("Resignation" in *Poems*, lines 190, 198). The poet's "quiet, and . . . fearless mind" sees into the life of things and, like the Scholar-Gypsy, faithfully pursues the truth that outlasts the troubled sounds of contemporary times. The poet should know life and the world and is nourished by the criticism that provides that knowledge. The Arnoldian critic, with his disinterested mind that seeks to know the best that has been thought and said and to instruct others in the value of culture, is another face of the poet. In *Culture and Anarchy* he writes, "In thus making sweetness and light to be characters of perfection, culture is of like spirit with poetry, follows one law with poetry" (*Culture,* 5:99). Like the ancient poets who were his model, Arnold's poet and critic "want to educe and cultivate what is best and noblest in themselves," "to think clearly, to feel nobly, and to delineate firmly" ("Preface" 1853, 1:13, 15).

His experience in the schools was the second major influence in shaping Arnold as social critic. As Russell Jacoby observes in *The End of Utopia,* "A commitment to public education in service of national cultivation informed all his work" (91). Arnold's job as school inspector, which he took in 1851 in order to marry Frances Lucy Wightman, became a central experience in his life that affected his most important ideas about the effect of social class, the power of education, and the value of democracy. This position gave him day-to-day contact with the harsh world of the powerless. The lower- and middle-class children he saw, in their economic need and their ignorance, were part of England's future, and for that future to be better than the troubled present, England needed greater equality of education for its citizens so that they could move forward with the society as a whole. A large and dissatisfied body of working-class people would only be a force for disorder if they could not feel themselves to be part of the state. Arnold did not imagine an equality that would eliminate the class differences or distribute the wealth, but he did envision an equality before the law in which the state would provide an opportunity for education and for participation in government. Arnold distrusted the fullness of wisdom of any of the three classes but believed that good education could create a society in which all classes might embrace a broad concept of its cultural "best self." If a society did recognize a collective "best self," then the limits of class attitudes could be transcended. His prose became the critic's form of action to move society "towards man's best perfection—the adorning and ennobling of his spirit."[2]

Related Essays

As early as 1860, before his ambitions as a poet had played out, Arnold wrote a striking study of education, social values, and democracy in the form of a report on the state of education on the continent. In 1859 Arnold was asked to take a post with a Royal Commission under the Duke of Newcastle that had been appointed to see what "Measures" might be "required for the Extension of sound and cheap elementary Instruction to all Classes of the People" (Super in *Prose*, 2:327–28). The Commission studied education in other European countries, and Arnold was abroad from March 15 to August 26 visiting schools in France, Switzerland, and the Netherlands. Arnold enjoyed this work and hoped to write "a very interesting report" (*Letters*, 1:492). By January of 1860 he was at work on his report, which he published in May 1861.[3] He expended great care on writing the introduction. The report was published as *The Popular Education of France*, and in the next few years it was followed by other essays on related topics. Arnold's study of continental education, and the introductory essay to the volume, connected the need for mass education, democracy, and culture in ways that would emerge again in the 1869 publication of *Culture and Anarchy*.

The introduction to *The Popular Education of France*, reprinted in 1879 as "Democracy," sees the movement toward democracy as an "effort *to affirm one's own essence;* meaning by this, to develop one's own existence fully and freely, to have ample light and air, to be neither cramped nor overshadowed" ("Democracy," 2:7). "Light and air" is not yet "sweetness and light," but this early essay begins to describe a state of the spirit that Arnold will elaborate on as "culture." Democracy is repeatedly linked in the essay with equality, but Arnold's use of these terms is more abstract than political. Democracy is a way of thinking in which all citizens should have the opportunity to develop their best self, an opportunity for which access to education is essential. Democracy and education are necessary to find that "essence" that becomes one's "best self." His arguments for equality eloquently explain it as more a matter of freeing spirits to be their best selves than of reorganizing government:

> Can it be denied, that to live in a society of equals tends in general to make a man's spirits expand, and his faculties work easily and actively; while, to live in a society of superiors, although it may occasionally be a very good discipline, yet in general tends to tame the spirits and to make the play of the faculties less secure and active? Can it be denied, that to be heavily overshadowed, to be profoundly insignificant, has, on the whole, a depressing and benumbing effect on the character? I know that some individuals react against the strongest impediments, and owe success and greatness to the efforts which they are thus forced to make. But the question is not about individuals. The question is about the common bulk of mankind, persons without extraordinary gifts or exceptional energy, and who will ever require, in order to make the best of themselves, encouragement and directly favouring circumstances. ("Democracy," 2:8–9)

Equality under the law and as a member of the state is "the best condition of improvement and culture attainable" and salvages the lives of the people from its opposite degradations of brutality and servility ("Democracy," 2:9). Its danger was that it encouraged the individual to do as one likes, and doing as one likes without the education to know what best to do is for Arnold the making of social chaos. Arnold argues directly against aristocracy because it possesses less "openness to ideas and ardour for them" than democracy, and such openness to ideas is one of the most important aspects of culture ("Democracy," 2:12). Arnold, who sometimes described himself as a Transcendentalist, praises "a very strong, self-reliant people" who "neither easily learns to act in concert, nor easily brings itself to regard any middling good, any good short of the best, as an object ardently to be coveted and striven for" ("Democracy," 2:13). Taken to its extreme within the individual, this very strong self-reliance becomes "doing as one likes," but as a common trait it may lead a society to become its collective best self.

"Democracy" also argued for the importance of societal values to the creation of character and of the potential deterioration of society if the middle classes "go on exaggerating their spirit of individualism" ("Democracy," 2:25). In *Culture and Anarchy* Arnold will single out for critical comment the nonconformists, or Protestant dissenters, for their "mechanical" and provincial ways of thinking. In "Democracy" he argues that "Protestant Dissent" has had a negative effect on "liberty of thought," that the "social action" of the dissenters "has not been civilizing." Their extreme defense of "liberty of conscience and the right of free opinion" ignore the need for the opinion to be educated if it is to be socially valuable. Arnold had little use for the liberty of conscience when it led the individual to oppose the established state or church. He believed in the innate value of each individual but not necessarily in the equal social or political value of each voice. In fact, the best self he hopes education and democracy can bring into being is one who puts aside the interests of the personal self for the collective good of the whole. He writes:

> It is a very great thing to be able to think as you like; but, after all, an important question remains: *what* you think. It is a fine thing to secure a free stage and no favour; but, after all, the part which you play on that stage will have to be criticised. Now, all the liberty and industry in the world will not ensure these two things: a high reason and a fine culture. ("Democracy," 2:24)

High reason and a fine culture are essential to becoming "a *great* nation," and the British middle classes will "give a decisive turn" to the national history in the next 50 years in shaping the nature of society ("Democracy," 2:25). Arnold says in this early essay that the middle class "will certainly *Americanise*" their country and fail to "mould or assimilate the masses below them" if they remain in their "narrow, harsh, unintelligent, and unattractive spirit and culture" ("Democracy," 2:26). The sympathies of the lower classes are "wider and more liberal" than those of the middle class, and if the middle class cannot win the sympathy or give direction to the lower classes, "society is in danger of falling into anarchy" ("Democracy," 2:26). Arnold urges the classes, especially the middle class, to make a government of "the State" that is "equitable and rational" and can put aside the worship of the individual and represent in actions the nation's best collective character.

Arnold is not blind to the potential limitations of "the State," nor to the opposition the concept stirs in many. He sees the modern State as the necessary form of democracy, of those "free to control the choice" of government and its actions. In a democracy, however "hesitating, blundering, unintelligent, inefficacious, the action of the State may be," the conclusion is, nevertheless, inescapable: "Nothing can free us from this responsibility. The conduct of our affairs is in our own power" ("Democracy," 2:28). To build a State "which really represents its best self, and whose action its intelligence and justice can heartily avow and adopt" ("Democracy," 2:28) is sounder than "to give a more prominent part to the individual." The State that acts with "openness and flexibility of mind," "honestly and rationally" by its laws, is "perhaps the nearest approach to perfection of which men and nations are capable" ("Democracy," 2:29).

This 1859 introduction to a report on education is in some ways clearer and more direct about culture, democracy, and the State than Arnold will be in *Culture and Anarchy* where the style is much more literary and rhetorical. The rhetorical genius of *Culture and Anarchy,* with its catch phrases and its illustrations from the popular culture, for example, won it a wide readership and a place in literary history. "Democracy" was without irony, written to accompany the language of an official report. Still, its eloquence and forthright defense of democracy in the interest of equality and society earns this essay its own place in Arnold's body of work. Arnold's concern for equality under the law and in educational opportunity is a practical matter of the stability of the state and the cohesiveness of society. Within his own time, Arnold's defense of the state as a unified whole to which all classes give allegiance was an unpopular idea. As Lionel Trilling points out, "Liberalism means many things, but to a member of the British middle class of Arnold's time liberalism meant one thing primarily: a State that could not control him except when he indulged in common law crime."[4] Arnold's belief in equality under the law, democracy in government, liberalism in politics, education for the masses, and that reasonable and flexible spirit of mind Arnold calls "culture" was in part a recognition of how the society had already changed under the force of industrialization. It also represented his best hopes for how that change could be made into a positive social good. "Culture" preserves openness and flexibility and holds as its goal becoming the best collective self that its society has imagined.

Arnold's view of the individual as a product of society and a part of
the state is one key way in which his liberalism departs from that of the
influential John Stuart Mill, author of *On Liberty*. In many ways the two
men were complementary spirits. Trilling has aptly described their simi-
larities:

> They shared an assumption of human progress: to both Arnold and Mill
> it seemed clear that the destiny and duty of man was to improve morally
> and spiritually; for both men the idea of development of the full person-
> ality was precious and both looked to Periclean Athens as the ideal condi-
> tion for it; both had read Tocqueville and caught his fear that personal
> development would be prevented by democracy's dull sameness; and
> finally, both shared a profound reliance upon reason. (Trilling 1939, 260)

The crucial defining difference was in their view of the rights of the individual when the interest of the state was concerned. When doing as one
likes unsettled the state, Arnold was willing to subdue the individual's
self-expression, but Mill, who shared Arnold's sense that the individual's
self-expression could be stupid and vulgar, was unwilling to grant the
state authority over the individual. Trilling casts the distinction as Mill
seeing "the individual, full-grown, fully endowed, *joining* an aggregation
of other individuals," and Arnold's "more organic conception of society"
in which the individual does not join society but "springs from it, is
endowed by it; therefore it is difficult, if not impossible, to conceive of
his rights as against or apart from the rights of society as a whole"
(Trilling 1939, 261). The tension between the individual and the Establishment that Arnold resolves in the interest of the state is consistent
throughout his work. It is part of his impatience with dissent in every
form that results in his indifference to the sense of oppression felt by
those for whom the act of dissent is something more principled than
merely "doing as one likes."

The functions of democracy, education, and culture that Arnold drew
up in 1859 are extended to the role of criticism in his 1865 essay, "The
Function of Criticism at the Present Time." Arnold begins this essay
with a reference to a comment about criticism in an earlier essay, "On
Translating Homer." There he had defined the main intellect of Europe
as "a *critical* effort . . . to see the object as in itself it really is."[5] Criticism
must avoid the "eccentric and arbitrary spirit . . . some individual
fancy" that was the tendency of English writers ("Homer," 1:140). The
linking of critical power with creative power in "The Function of Criticism at the Present Time" revises the Romantic ideal of the poet and

moves forward the contemporary theoretical view that writing criticism is essentially the same kind of creative process as writing "literary" works.

Arnold argues that free creative activity may produce great works of literature, but that the critical power creates the atmosphere of ideas, the "power of the moment," in which the creative power is best exercised. If great works of literature are "inspired by a certain intellectual and spiritual atmosphere," then the role of the intellectual is to create a climate in which creative power can flourish and to see clearly and speak for the "best ideas" it can disinterestedly determine. By arguing that the creation of a modern poet "implies a great critical effort behind it," Arnold implicitly explains literary work as in part a social construct.

Arnold saw himself as "a soldier in the war of liberation of humanity."[6] Like Goethe and Heine, he took up the pen in "a life and death battle with Philistinism" ("Heine," 3:111). Contemporary critics who want to deride Arnold's work often point to his discussion of "the best that has been thought and said" or of a nation's "best self" as evidence of an implicit acceptance of cultural values that make "disinterested" criticism impossible. Arnold is careful on many occasions to place words like "truth" and "best" in a relative context. He speaks of "true by comparison," for example,[7] and the power he accords critics relies on a definition of truth that is always malleable and incomplete. If, in criticism, the attention should be given to the most judicious minds, Arnold is very much aware that "Unhappily, in most cases, no two persons agree as to who 'the judicious' are" ("Homer," 1:99). Arnold offers no formulas for determining who or what is the best that we should study. Instead, he sets up principles, such as the effort to be disinterested, by which to make such judgments.

Only a critical intelligence that seeks to judge by keeping a distance from political, social, and practical considerations can create a current of fresh ideas. Criticism that becomes polemical and practical narrows thought and sustains self-satisfaction, but the role of criticism is to refuse to lend itself to pressures that are merely political and practical. Arnold's belief that criticism must express dissatisfaction makes it a force in opposition to the status quo:

> Criticism must maintain its independence of the practical spirit and its aims. Even with well-meant efforts of the practical spirit it must express dissatisfaction, if in the sphere of the ideal they seem impoverishing and limiting. It must not hurry on to the goal because of its practical impor-

tance. It must be patient, and know how to wait; and flexible, and know how to attach itself to things and how to withdraw from them. ("Function," 3:280)

Such a criticism will, Arnold knows, never be popular nor much followed, but the effort "to learn and propagate the best that is known and thought in the world" is the only way in which criticism can serve the world of ideas.

The persistent association in Arnold's thinking between the functions of culture, criticism, and literature is evident in two of his late essays, "The Study of Poetry," written in 1879 and published in 1881, and "Literature and Science," delivered as the Rede lecture at Cambridge in June 1882. Literature is important to Arnold "in proportion to the power of the criticism of life" it offers. As in criticism, in poetry "the idea is everything."[8] Arnold contrasted the future of poetry, which he thought was "immense," to the failure of religion that had "attached its emotion to the fact," which was itself failing ("Study," 9:161). "The fact" to which religion has materialized is not defined in this essay, but Arnold apparently means religion's insistence on its literal truth rather than its metaphoric meaning, a subject he will take up in other essays on religion. In "Literature and Science" he will separate scientific "fact" from the human need for conduct and beauty. In search of these needs, the intellect has a tendency to relate things to one another in diverse ways. This process, which he does not label as making metaphors but which resonates with definitions of metaphor, is the "strength" of the hold of letters on the human mind ("Science," 10:62). Poetry above other kinds of knowledge interprets life for us and will console and sustain us ("Study," 9:161). As the union of thought and art, poetry will resist the confusion between the excellent and the inferior, which he calls "charlatanism."

Much of the rest of "Literature and Science" tries to illustrate the power of poetry as a criticism of life by citing lines from various artists. These "touchstones" of memorable lines are in the minds of most critics one of Arnold's weaker critical methods and vaguest critical explanations. Although he has argued that literature comes out of a moment that criticism helps to create, Arnold's confidence in "touchstones" suggests that isolated lines can exist both outside the moment and outside knowledge of the moment to guide us to knowing the best. In other essays, however, he suggests that study is critical to the soundness of knowledge. Arnold in fact argues for the emotional power of language to separate the excellent from the inferior in art, but he offers little by way of an aesthetic theory to explain why one word charms and another only explicates. He thinks of the great artists as having "high seriousness," but his use of isolated lines bases the case more wholly on the sounds of language than on the character of ideas, seriousness, and moral beauty that can console and sustain us. In the wake of this essay critics have quarreled with Arnold about the poets he included, the poets he left out, and the poets he appreciated too much or too little. The essay's defense of poetry is abstract except for the specifics of quotations whose charm is often not apparent. Its contribution is its strong statements that the strength of literature is as a criticism of life, a defense that neglects poetry's inherent aesthetic qualities, which are indeed crucial to Arnold's sense of the beauty of poetry.[9]

Arnold's confidence in the power of poetry and criticism led him to advocate an education in the humanities and some constraints on the growing belief that science must be the center of our knowledge. In 1865 Arnold again participated in a commission that examined education on the continent and again wrote a long report, which appeared in book form in March of 1868.[10] The first of two "General Conclusions" chapters argued eloquently for the humanist education over the scientific or moralist education. Arnold takes on the popular notions that education's chief purpose is to create good citizens or good Christians or enable one to do his duty or to get on in the world.[11] Such aims are at best secondary and indirect goals of education since the primary aim of instruction "is to enable a man *to know himself and the world.*"[12] Education's aims thus overlap those of criticism and poetry. "To know himself, a man must know the capabilities and performances of the human spirit," and the study of the humanities "greatly feeds and quickens our own activity" (*Schools,* 4:290).

Although Arnold is most associated with justifying the study of classical literature, his views about the best education were actually much broader. Arnold strongly recommends the study of classical literature, but he also acknowledges that the study of "nature" is necessary. Not to know the literature of ancient Greece and Rome is to be imperfectly educated, "but it is also a vital and formative knowledge to know the world, the laws which govern nature, and man as a part of nature" (*Schools,* 4:290). He uses the metaphor of a "circle of knowledge" in which no part of the circle is "common or unclean, none is to be cried up at the expense of another" (*Schools,* 4:292). Arnold's extensive experience observing schools and students has taught him that different kinds of students have different kinds of aptitudes, and he argues for pursuing the kind of education—humanist or realist, as he labels them—most suited to one's aptitudes. He writes:

> Every man is born with aptitudes which give him access to vital and for-mative knowledge by one of these roads; either by the road of studying man and his works, or by the road of studying nature and her works. The business of instruction is to seize and develope these aptitudes. (*Schools,* 4:290–91)

Since both humanists and realists should have knowledge of each other's areas, the basic secondary education should begin with "a liberal culture" that includes languages, history, math, geography, and nature. At the next stage, however, Arnold argues for "a *bifurcation*" according to one's aptitudes but encourages students to continue studying some aspects of both humanities and naturalistic studies. The ideal is a school in which both humanities and sciences are taught and pupils can select the aspects of each that are most related to their own individual apti-tude:

> There should, after a certain point, be no cast-iron course for all scholars, either in humanistic or naturalistic studies. According to his aptitude, the pupil should be suffered to follow principally one branch of either of the two great lines of study; and, above all, to interchange the lines occasion-ally, following, on the line which is not his own line, such lessons as have yet some connection with his own line, or, from any cause whatever, some attraction for him. (*Schools,* 4:301–2)

Humanists and realists are both inclined to be "unjust" to the value of the other's share of knowledge. The humanists believe the most vital thing is to know oneself, and the realists believe it is to know the world. To be trained in letters is to know "the operation of human force, of human freedom and activity" (*Schools,* 4:292). Arnold argues that those educated in the humanities are more prominent in the "government of human affairs" than the realists, but the conduct of human affairs suffers from "the ignorance of physical facts and laws, and from the inadequate conception of nature, and of man as a part of nature" (*Schools,* 4:292). His own education and aptitude had favored letters, but Arnold is clear about the values of both arts and sciences in an education that aims to know the self and the world.

Arnold's interest in good teaching seems especially modern. He fre-quently comments on teaching, noting especially several problems. One is the insistence on Greek and Latin composition and philological study. His esteem for the classics does not blind him to the educational folly of forcing young minds into the rigors of Greek and Latin grammar rather than the beauty of great literature. Not many students are like "Wolf," "who used to sit up the whole night with his feet in a tub of cold water and one of his eyes bound up to rest while he read with the other" in order to get through all the Greek and Latin classics (*Schools*, 4:294).[13] Of the others, many never get "through the philological vestibule at all" and thus never arrive at the enjoyment of literature or the knowledge of self that comes from reading great works of human force. Arnold openly disputes the claim that only through such philological study can students really know the literature, citing as his evidence the study of other literatures such as French that are enhanced by reading instead of grammatical study. For "nine cases out of ten," grammatical studies will take so much of a student's time that he will end his studies with no sense of literature at all:

> His verbal scholarship and his composition he is pretty sure in after life to drop, and then all his Greek and Latin is lost. Greek and Latin *literature*, if he had ever caught the notion of them, would have been far more likely to stick by him. (*Schools*, 4:296)

Since literature is essential to learning about the human spirit and education's aim is to know oneself and the world, instructional practices that fence off the appreciation of literature's power and beauty with grammatical exercises defeats the aim of education.

Arnold also puts limits on the appropriateness of the study of mathematics and modern foreign languages taught for speaking purposes. Mathematics and grammar are, he concedes, excellent for training "exact habits of mind," but "a Latin grammar of thirty pages, and the most elementary treatise of arithmetic and of geometry" will suffice for the preparatory discipline. Only those whose "genuine intellectual life" lies in the study of grammar and mathematics should go beyond a basic training. The teaching of modern foreign languages for speaking "belongs to what I have called the commercial theory of education, and not the liberal theory" (*Schools*, 4:299). The mere ability to speak another language is not for Arnold "vital knowledge," and his suspicion is that "speaking several languages tends to make the thought thin and shallow" (*Schools*, 4:299). "Useful" as it may sometimes be to speak other languages, teaching them is "quite secondary and subordinate" as an aim of education. Education's goal is to teach languages in order to read the literature; those who want to speak modern foreign languages are recommended to live in the country rather than practice in a classroom (*Schools*, 4:300).

Arnold's "General Conclusion. School Studies" anticipates many of the ideas he will consider in "Literature and Science." His conclusions are strikingly familiar as the basic rationale and curriculum for colleges of arts and sciences today. Arnold's justification of liberal education in this essay is not as famous as those of John Stuart Mill and Cardinal Newman, but it has the virtue of being more concrete and conceptualized in terms of the realities of students, teachers, and institutions. The years of inspecting schools and the two studies of European educational systems made Arnold the most thoughtful and thoroughly informed of Victorians writing about directions in modern education. His proposals for curricular innovation are humane and balanced. In reading the essay one is struck by Arnold's articulation of the ideal teacher who is well trained in the subject area, whose aim is to find and develop the individual's aptitude, and whose faith is that everyone has some special aptitude.[14] Although this essay is not part of the anthologized Arnold whom most students today study, its influence was deeply felt in his time and in the history of education.

Arnold again took up the claims of humanities and naturalistic studies in 1882 under the heading of "Literature and Science," terms that reflect a sharper opposition than he had earlier been willing to draw. By 1882 an open debate had emerged between science and the humanities in an effort to claim the curricular future. T. H. Huxley in an 1880 address had cited Arnold's views and made a stronger case for science, largely by repudiating Arnold's ideal of the liberal education as the essential learning of the educated man. "Literature and Science" was Arnold's attempt to reply in a major address that would pull together a number of his ideas in other essays. The lecture was very successful, and on his tour of the United States in 1883 he was so often asked to give this lecture that he wrote home that "I get as sick of the lecture myself as Lord Hartington is said to get of his own speeches before he is through with them."[15]

The terms Arnold engages in this essay are the familiar claims of practical or vocational education over those of the liberal arts. Rhetorically he begins by a clever evoking of Plato as the embodiment of an impractical education that was well enough for those who have leisure for philosophy. He then acknowledges the historical difference created by the emerging of a "great industrial community" that "must and will shape its education to suit its own needs" ("Science," 10:55). The question is which education is in fact "practically the best now."

> I am going to ask whether the present movement for ousting letters from their old predominance in education, and for transferring the predominance in education to the natural sciences, whether this brisk and flourishing movement ought to prevail, and whether it is likely that in the end it really will prevail. ("Science," 10:55)

In characterizing Huxley's "enlarged" restatement of Arnold's arguments for humanities, Arnold notes that Huxley seems to understand "letters" as *belles lettres*, a narrowing of Arnold's original category that he will use to counter the validity of Huxley's general argument against the humanities.

Arnold reasserts that by studying the best that has been thought and said in the world he means to include the history and cultural contributions in all fields:

> by knowing ancient Greece, I understand knowing her as the giver of Greek art, and the guide to a free and right use of reason and to scientific method, and the founder of our mathematics and physics and astronomy and biology,—I understand knowing her as all this, and not merely knowing certain Greek poems, and histories, and treatises, and speeches,— so as to the knowledge of modern nations also. ("Science," 10:58–59)

By claiming as part of the liberal education the range of contributions of a society, including its science, Arnold tries to defeat Huxley's arguments by carving away the ground of real difference between them. His definition of "literature" was not, in fact, so clearly inclusive in "General Conclusion" as it has become in "Literature and Science." Subjects like math, physics, astronomy, and biology had earlier been defined as the "naturalist studies" of the "realists" in contrast to the literary studies of the humanists.

Arnold's purpose in redefining the vocabulary of the debate is to capture the curriculum from the claims of too much science and too little literature. While allowing that the major findings of science are a critical part of what we need to know about the world, he questions whether the study of the "processes by which those results are reached" is a necessary part. It is one thing to know that when the candle burns "the wax is converted into carbonic acid and water"; it is another that "we are made to see that the conversion into carbonic acid and water does actu-

ally happen" ("Science," 10:60). The history of the five-credit-hour lab
course in chemistry and biology would indicate that Arnold substantially lost this part of the argument.

The force of Arnold's essay is that the study of letters, now broadly
defined as "humane letters," serves the major factors in the "building up
of human life, and say that they are the power of conduct, the power of
intellect and knowledge, the power of beauty, and the power of social
life and manners" ("Science," 10:61–62). Though all knowledge is
"interesting," Arnold is concerned with those kinds of knowledge that
serve best the human intellect's desire to relate facts to principles, the
"need of relating what we have learnt and known to the sense which we
have in us for conduct, to the sense which we have in us for beauty"
("Science," 10:63). The impulse for relating what we know to our sense
of conduct and beauty is no less than the desire for good, and the desire
for good is the human "instinct of self-preservation" ("Science," 10:63).
With this language Arnold connects the study of the humanities with
the ends of religion and the thrust of Victorian science itself.

The desire for the good, to relate what we know to our sense of conduct and beauty, returns the argument to the special value of poetry.
The eloquence and emotions in poetry offer a criticism of life that
refreshes and delights. Poetry will even help us "to relate the results of
modern science to our need for conduct, our need for beauty," he claims
("Science," 10:68). Poetry is really "the criticism of life by gifted men," a
conclusion that pulls the ideas of "Literature and Science" into harmony
with Arnold's other essays on society, poetry, democracy, and education.

The Victorian debate about the place of letters and science in the curriculum has continued into the present day with only slight variations in
the pattern. Arnold ends his essay stating his belief that the study of
humane letters is not in "much actual danger of being thrust out from
their leading place in education, in spite of the array of authorities
against them at this moment" ("Science," 10:72). Even periods of "confusion and false tendency" will correct themselves because letters are
too basic to human nature to long yield ground. He concludes of the
humanities:

> We shall be brought back to them by our wants and aspirations. And a
> poor humanist may possess his soul in patience, neither strive nor cry,
> admit the energy and brilliancy of the partisans of physical science, and
> their present favour with the public, to be far greater than his own, and
> still have a happy faith that the nature of things works silently on behalf
> of the studies which he loves, and that, while we shall all have to

acquaint ourselves with the great results reached by modern science, and to give ourselves as much training in its disciplines as we can conveniently carry, yet the majority of men will always require humane letters; and so much the more, as they have the more and the greater results of science to relate to the need in man for conduct, and to the need in him for beauty. ("Science," 10:72–73)

Arnold's critics in his day thought his belief in the value of studying classical literature and humane letters was too impractical for an industrial society and too indifferent to the importance of science in reshaping reality. Arnold's critics today argue that his defense of classical literature is too elitist and too centered on the Western tradition. The criticism of both ages has its point, but both sets of critics somewhat distort his arguments to advance their own. Given the long-standing competition between humanities and sciences that has been fought out over 100 years of school curriculums, Arnold's acceptance of the importance of naturalistic studies and hard sciences is more flexible and balanced than has often been the case in the ensuing debates. Displacing the study of literature with the study of theory in today's universities would no doubt trouble Arnold deeply, and his name has often been invoked to counter the emphasis on theory. He would no doubt argue that literature's power "of engaging the emotions" will win back its place with students against the "false tendency" of the scholars. Arnold often cites his own education in classical literature and the value it has for him, but in his era he was more liberal than elitist. He argued for the inclusion of English literature, which was not taught in school at the time, and for the merits of many European authors, some of them contemporary and radical, such as George Sand. His education was almost wholly in classical and European literatures, but his belief in the value of humane letters did not exclude other literatures. He sought to study the best that has been known and said in the world. Our contemporary sense of the world has expanded, but the efforts to retrieve women writers and to acquaint ourselves with a wider range of literatures from diverse cultures is only another form of discovering and knowing a larger view of the best that has been thought and said in a vastly redrawn world.

Culture and Anarchy

Culture and Anarchy has been the most influential and recently the most controversial of Arnold's writings. This set of six essays published together in 1869 contains most of the phrases and ideas that have in contemporary times resulted in the dismissive attacks on Arnold and the pervasive misreadings of his ideas when reduced to a handful of textual snippets taken out of context. Those wishing to either subvert the power of Western cultural hegemony or lament the decline of the cultural hegemony of the West have found Arnold's ideas of use to their own agendas. "Culture" itself has become a meaning-laden word in every context from anthropology to literature to politics and is "high," "low," "popular," and "counter." As Jacoby reminds us, "culture" in the twentieth century has often been used to show contempt for liberalism and the Enlightenment (35).[16] Those on the left in the third world often disdain "culture" because of the deceit and hypocrisy of its promises, and those on the right, such as the Nazis, hate culture for itself (Jacoby, 35). Jacoby quotes the famous lines from Nazi playwright Hanns Johst, "When I hear the word culture, I reach for my gun" (34). "Culture" has become the battleground between opposing ideologies in the post–World War II world.

Those who assume that Arnold's use of the term is static and refers only to classical art and English literature interpret his use to mean the elite learning of those in power who use their influence to oppress and deny other groups. If "culture" means to open up knowledge and create free thinking and the flow of ideas of all sorts, then "culture" acts to leaven the existing power and open new avenues of thinking. There has, however, been no consensus in recent years on Arnold's use of the term.

The critical discourse about *Culture and Anarchy* is well illustrated by the 1994 edition edited by Samuel Lipman as part of Yale University's Rethinking the Western Tradition series. In addition to Arnold's 1869 text, this edition includes essays by several critics from varying positions. Among the things they most criticize is his belief in the efficacy of the State to help bring about a more unified culture. Steven Marcus especially points to Arnold's advocacy of the role of the State in public education, which he dismisses as "the national wasteland of secondary education in America."[17] The blame he assigns to "bodies" of state governments and teachers ignores the role of the state in funding for public school buildings, the founding of the land grant universities, national research funds for the sciences and humanities, scholarship programs and hot lunches for the needy, and federal enforcement of civil rights legislation and guidelines in the areas of integration, discrimination, affirmative action, and sexual harassment. Still, he concludes, "to lose belief in education, to cease to hope that education is the means to light, would be to admit that the cause of light is itself lost" (Marcus, 185).

Gerald Graff, best known for his method of "teaching the conflicts" in a multicultural society, concludes that Arnold's culture and anarchy argument "is a dead end. If we are sincere about creating a common culture under democratic conditions, that kind of argument won't get us there."[18] Graff sees Arnold as only committed to the free play of reason when "its dictates coincide with those of unreflective custom, tradition, and consensus" (188). Arnold's appeal is not, he says, to the rationality of his readers, "but to their emotional loyalty to common traditions, what Arnold calls 'the main current of national life' and 'the main stream of human life' " (Graff, 189). Maurice Cowling notes that conservatives like William Bennett find Arnold of limited use since his idea of culture erodes the traditional role of religion.[19] Russell Jacoby's 1999 book, *The End of Utopia,* makes one of the strongest contemporary defenses of Arnold, this time from the left. Jacoby writes of Arnold, "His criticism of the coarseness of culture is driven by his egalitarian sympathies. An impoverished life and circumstances do not allow cultivation and growth. To put this differently, Arnold's criticism of mass culture is grounded in his democratic ethos" (Jacoby, 93–94). These critics give us some indication of the current controversy surrounding *Culture and Anarchy,* a controversy that does not segment itself clearly into right and left political or theoretical camps.

Arnold's own definition of culture comes early in the book and has little to do with established power or literary masters. He defines culture as

> being a pursuit of our total perfection by means of getting to know, on all the matters which most concern us, the best which has been thought and said in the world, and, through this knowledge, turning a stream of fresh and free thought upon our stock notions and habits, which we now follow staunchly but mechanically, vainly imagining that there is a virtue in following them staunchly which makes up for the mischief of following them mechanically.[20]

Like criticism, culture questions tradition and the status quo for purposes of creating fresh and free thought. Arnold directly repudiates the "notion of something bookish, pedantic, and futile" that has become connected with the word culture (Lipman, 5). He believes that reading enhances one's "solidity and value," but "culture" is more a state of mind than the acquisition of particular knowledge:

> If a man without books or reading, or reading nothing but his letters and the newspapers, gets nevertheless a fresh and free play of the best

thoughts upon his stock notions and habits, he has got culture. He has got that for which we prize and recommend culture; he has got that which at the present moment we seek culture that it may give us. This inward operation is the very life and essence of culture, as we conceive it. (Lipman, 5–6)

Arnold's stress on the inward nature of culture defines it as something more like the life of the mind than a body of knowledge. The purpose of this mental life is to question, to reason, and to further the free flow of ideas.

Perhaps it is less Arnold's definition of "culture" than the nature of his fears about anarchy that excite controversy. He argues that "doing as one likes" will dissolve a national identity by substituting the vagaries of individualistic action. His most telling examples of the dangers of doing as one likes are often taken from the social unrest of the working class. "Outbreaks of rowdyism" follow the dissolving of "feudal habits of sub-ordination and deference," and the lack of "the idea of public duty and of discipline, superior to the individual's self-will" place the assertion of personal liberty over the "State" (*Culture*, 5:118–21). Arnold is not opposed to revolutionary change if it can come in an orderly fashion, but he has no sympathy for disorder in the streets:

So whatever brings risk of tumult and disorder, . . . multitudinous meet-ings in their public places and parks,—demonstrations perfectly unnec-essary in the present course of our affairs,—our best self, or right reason, plainly enjoins us to set our faces against. It enjoins us to encourage and uphold the occupants of the executive power, whoever they may be, in firmly prohibiting them. (*Culture*, 5:136)

Arnold's obvious distaste for the working class has drawn critical fire. Raymond Williams says Arnold's "tone" is evidence of his "priggishness and spiritual pride" (Williams, 116). Prejudice outweighs reason, and Williams notes that "a deep emotional fear darkens the light. It is there in his words: *hoot, bawl, threaten, rough, smash*" (Williams, 125). Arnold's responses may seem more reasonable then than now. Arnold's England was especially fearful of violence connected with revolutions on the continent and disorder in its own cities by masses of workers displaced from rural life by an emerging industrial capitalism. The pattern of capitalist exploitation of the working class in the intervening century makes Arnold's sense of threat seem to be a misshapen response to conflicts of power between those who rule and those who seek fair treatment from them.

For contemporary American readers who recall the march on Washington for civil rights or the demonstrations against the war in Vietnam, Arnold's hard impatience with disorder in the streets seemingly aligns him with the forces of repression. Readers who know the Victorian history of labor organizing, Irish rebellion, and expansion of the franchise may also cast Arnold among the ruling elite who used power to keep the poor in their place.

Arnold's sense of "conduct" is, he confesses, "hereditary," and in his harshest comment on working-class dissent, he recalls his father's remark: " 'As for rioting, the old Roman way of dealing with *that* is always the right one; flog the rank and file, and fling the ringleaders from the Tarpeian Rock.' "[21] Arnold himself concludes, "Monster-processions in the street and forcible irruptions into the parks, even in professed support of this good design, ought to be unflinchingly forbidden and repressed" (*Culture*, 5:223). Social violence essentially undoes Arnold's hopes that culture can build a humane and unified nation. His anger and concern are evident in the strong rhetoric he uses to advance the State and subdue dissent, but even when his anxieties overcome his liberalism, the fullness of his ideas about culture and disorder are more complex than his rant.

In fairness, Arnold's harsh statements about the working class need to be put in the context of his description of other classes. *Culture and Anarchy* is famous for the labels he applies to the three classes: the "Barbarians" who are the aristocrats, the "Philistines" who are the middle class, and the "Populace" who are the working class. No class is seen as fully appropriate to dominate the society or wield the authority that he thinks the State must finally have to guarantee an orderly and humane democracy. The aristocratic class are Barbarians because, like their namesakes, theirs is "an exterior culture mainly," gifted in looks, manners, field sports, and individualism, but whose young men are unintelligent. Their lack of an intellectual or spiritual inner life is a sharp drawback in governing a nation. In times of expansion, their "haughty resistance" to ideas makes of their serenity only "futility and sterility" (*Culture*, 5:125). Inherited "wealth, power, and consideration" are in Arnold's mind "trying and dangerous things" (*Culture*, 5:202). To honor the aristocratic class is to honor a "false ideal" of pleasure and ease, and the effect of aristocratic leadership cannot be "salutary" to the community as a whole. Arnold opposes the inheritance rights of children of the wealthy and would break up the estates of the aristocracy.

Identifying himself as a man from the great middle class who may well illustrate their defects, Arnold nevertheless reserves his harshest criticism for this group, which he labels "the Philistines." Arnold's first use of the term "Philistinism" to characterize the narrow interests of a materialist middle class occurred in his 1863 essay on the popular German literary figure, Heinrich Heine. His definition in this essay is perhaps an important clarification of his later use of the term in *Culture and Anarchy*. Heine, who was both German and Jewish, uses the label to express his preference for the French, whose Paris is "the new Jerusalem." *Philistia* in Heine's context is associated with Germany, and Arnold extends it to the English middle class. Arnold defines "Philistine" originally as "a strong, dogged, unenlightened opponent of the chosen people, of the children of the light . . . humdrum people, slaves to routine, enemies to light; stupid and oppressive, but at the same time very strong"("Heine," 3:112). Arnold extends this usage to the British who have suppressed the "practically inconvenient" when principles were in the way of purpose, making them "of all people the most inaccessible to ideas and the most impatient of them" ("Heine," 3:113).

In *Culture and Anarchy* Arnold adds that the middle class "seeks to affirm—its ordinary self, not its best self; and it is a machinery, an industrial machinery" (*Culture*, 5:143). Philistines like "business, and money-making," tea meetings or trade unions (*Culture*, 5:145). As a class their energy makes them natural leaders though their materialistic vision limits their greatness. He is especially disappointed with the middle class because their abilities and energy give them more potential to create a humane society.

Arnold divides the lower class into two segments. One is the energetic and inventive working class whose goals make them properly part of the middle class. The remaining "vast residuum" of the working class he labels the Populace. This group,

> raw and half-developed, has long lain half-hidden amidst its poverty and squalor, and is now issuing from its hiding-place to assert an Englishman's heaven-born privilege of doing as he likes, and is beginning to perplex us by marching where it likes, meeting where it likes, bawling what it likes, breaking what it likes. (*Culture*, 5:143)

Although Arnold sees a basic common humanity in all the classes, when any one of them looks at ideas without sympathy, they are fundamentally of the Populace:

every time that we snatch up a vehement opinion in ignorance and passion, every time that we long to crush an adversary by sheer violence, every time that we are envious, every time that we are brutal, every time that we adore mere power or success, every time that we add our voice to swell a blind clamour against some unpopular personage, every time that we trample savagely on the fallen,—he has found in his own bosom the eternal spirit of the Populace. (*Culture*, 5:144–45)

Instead of an actual social class, Arnold describes under this label the mob mentality, much as it is presented by other writers such as Mark Twain.

Arnold's equally famous, and controversial, use of the terms "Hebraism" and "Hellenism" further subdivides the classes. Both groups share with culture the goal of man's perfection, but Hebraism stresses conduct and obedience, or "strictness of conscience," and Hellenism stresses seeing things as they really are, of "spontaneity of consciousness" (*Culture*, 5:165). In one of his most explicit definitions Arnold writes:

Hebraism,—the insisting on perfection in one part of our nature and not in all; the singling out the moral side, the side of obedience and action, for such intent regard; making strictness of the moral conscience so far the principal thing, and putting off for hereafter and for another world the care for being complete at all points, the full and harmonious development of our humanity. (*Culture*, 5:185)

Arnold associates Hebraism with Christianity and Hellenism with, obviously, Greek art and thought.[22] His chief objection to the spirit of Hebraism is its narrowness in what it seeks to know and in what it appreciates. Obedience constrains and controls, and Arnold wants culture to open and create. The difference in the vision is the question of whether "man is indeed a gentle and simple being, showing the traces of a noble and divine nature; or an unhappy chained captive, labouring with groanings that cannot be uttered to free himself from the body of this death" (*Culture*, 5:169). In another irreverent metaphor he contrasts the "Saviour" who "banished joy" with the "alma Venus" (*Culture*, 5:169).

Although he draws his contrasts sharply, Arnold's position is that both Hebraism and Hellenism are "contributions to human development," and that different eras in history rightfully call forth more of one than the other. In Arnold's time, the narrow ambitions of the middle class, the resistance to ideas by the aristocrats, the general impoverishment of the working class, in tandem with the insistence of science on its laws and a sectarian Protestant dissent movement, had unbalanced society in the direction of the meanest and most provincial forms of Hebraism. He sees a similarity between religion as a mechanical law and middle-class concern for making money: "What havoc do the united conceptions make of our lives!" His plea is for enlarging the view of life.

Arnold uses the term "machinery" to characterize any order of values that has become an unexamined rule of practice instead of a living form of thought subject to criticism. Philistinism is social machinery; religious zealotry is spiritual machinery. "Faith in machinery" is England's "besetting danger," he says. His use of this word may parallel the contemporary use of "ideology" or "ideological thinking." In its extreme form, machinery becomes fanaticism. Arnold especially applies this word to mindless political rhetoric about freedom, England's greatness, wealth, and the contributions of the workers. "Machinery" is the dogmatic and hackneyed wisdom of slogans and popular rhetoric that is the opposite of "sweetness and light."

The nature of culture is sweetness and light, but readers have often found this phrase annoyingly abstract. "Sweetness and light" are "characters of perfection" (*Culture*, 5:99), but Arnold goes to considerable effort to describe the kinds of objectives and traits he believes that such perfection, or culture, would include. One trait is, of course, "desire after the things of the mind simply for their own sakes and for the pleasure of seeing them as they are," but culture also means

> the love of our neighbour, the impulses towards action, help, and benefi-
> cence, the desire for removing human error, clearing human confusion,
> and diminishing human misery, the noble aspiration to leave the world
> better and happier than we found it,—motives eminently such as are
> called social,—come in as part of the grounds of culture, and the main
> and pre-eminent part. Culture is then properly described not as having
> its origin in curiosity, but as having its origin in the love of perfection; it
> is *a study of perfection*. (*Culture*, 5:91)

In its ultimate manifestation, culture represents for Arnold "the will of God" (*Culture*, 5:93). Beauty in art, perfection in human social and moral conduct, and the free play of ideas in intellectual life are the components of "sweetness and light."

The powerful and popular Protestant dissenters, also known as the nonconformists, that bloomed in Arnold's day were in his mind major forces in opposition to his ideal of culture. They were dogmatic in their beliefs, narrow in their interests, preoccupied with conduct, and outside the established Anglican church. He dismissively labeled them as "*hole-and-corner* forms of religion" who "favour provincialism" (Lipman, 12). Neither Arnold's distaste for the Christian fundamentalists of his day nor his defense of the uses of the established church have much to do with any religious belief about God.[23] Instead, he measures them in terms of their utility in advancing culture.

Arnold places an uncomfortably high value on being in the mainstream of society's establishments. Unlike Protestant dissenters, who cannot affirm the unity and harmony necessary for culture to become the national identity, the Anglican church, because it is the established state church, is "in contact with the main current of national life" (Lipman, 11). Arnold's enthusiasm for the Establishment (the capitalization is his) may seem naive or even oppressive to contemporary readers, but we need to understand his rationale for the merits of being within the mainstream of established institutions. Since extremes of "doing as one likes" break down the harmony of society, being a member of "an Establishment" is a corrective disciple:

> One may say that to be reared a member of an Establishment is in itself a lesson of religious moderation, and a help towards culture and harmonious perfection. Instead of battling for his own private forms for expressing the inexpressible and defining the undefinable, a man takes those which have commended themselves most to the religious life of his nation; and while he may be sure that within those forms the religious side of his own nature may find its satisfaction, he has leisure and composure to satisfy other sides of his nature as well. (Lipman, 11)

This attitude reveals the essential lack of deep religious feeling in Arnold. For him the Anglican church's forms will satisfy his religious needs, and, being thus settled, he can devote his thought to other, more interesting, kinds of knowledge.

As a part of his notion of culture, the emphasis on being within the mainstream strengthens the State but excludes those who were not reared as members of the Establishment. Arnold mentions in his discussion of the religious Establishment the Roman Catholic and Jewish faiths as being outside the English Establishment. Both religions, however, rest on establishments of their own that are not national, he notes, but "cosmopolitan." Arnold believes that any of these religious establishments can produce "men of national mark" and "highest spiritual significance," unlike the Puritans and dissenters who, "a generation or two outside the Establishment" no longer do (Lipman, 10). Arnold does not fully work through the ways in which the Establishment can become inflexible, and thus opposed to culture as he has defined it, and inequitable, and thus opposed to the democracy he advocates. Arnold's ideal of culture would have no place for bigotry or discrimination, but his insistence on the virtues of being in the mainstream leads directly to attitudes that embody such thinking. The following passage illustrates the direction of this idea:

> it would still have been better for a man, through the last eighteen hundred years, to have been a Christian, and a member of one of the great Christian communions, than to have been a Jew or a Socinian; because the being in contact with the main stream of human life is of more moment for a man's total spiritual growth, and for his bringing to perfection the gifts committed to him, which is his business on earth, than any speculative opinion which he may hold or think he holds. (Lipman, 21)

Ideas such as this one raise doubts about the means necessary to achieve Arnold's end of culture.

In other places Arnold goes out of his way to condemn attitudes he considers biased and unfair. He writes, with intense irony, for example, "it never was any part of our creed that the great right and blessedness of an Irishman, or, indeed, of anybody on earth except an Englishman, is to do as he likes" (*Culture*, 5:121). He goes on to contrast the Fenian, who "remains cold" to "our symbolical Truss Manufactory," with the English rough rioting in Hyde Park:

> He is our own flesh and blood; he is a Protestant; he is framed by nature to do as we do, hate what we hate, love what we love; his is capable of feeling the symbolical force of the Truss Manufactory; the question of questions, for him, is a wages question. (*Culture*, 5:122).

He concludes by recasting in the Populace's terms the quest for perfection as "Mrs. Gooch's Golden Rule," or the divine injunction, *"Ever remember, my dear Dan, that you should look forward to being some day manager of that concern!"*

The Establishment and the State are part of Arnold's organization of authority in a nation where the community's interest outweighs the individual's right to do as one likes. The only basis of authority he recognizes is "right reason of the community," but the problem is determining the organization for rule. None of the classes is to be trusted as an adequate center to determine right reason. Although he uses words like "authority," Arnold essentially envisions a capable democracy as the voice of right reason. The State represents the community as a "working power" above the wishes and ideas of any one class. Established institutions such as the church provide value systems across class lines that will give the "community" an identity not absorbed in class consciousness. Arnold imagines the State to be the "best self" of the community and trustworthy as a center of authority.

In "The Function of Criticism" Arnold uses one of his most inflammatory and misunderstood phrases: *"Force till right is ready"* ("Function," 3:266). He is translating a line from Joubert, and his explanation helps clarify the nature of authority he envisions. "Force" is "the existing order of things" and is justified as the legitimate ruler until we have given "free assent of the will" to "right." Authority, or force, changes when society can see "right" and will it:

> The way in which for us it may change and transform force, the existing order of things, and become, in its turn, the legitimate ruler of the world, should depend on the way in which, when our time comes, we see it and will it. Therefore for other people enamoured of their own newly discerned right, to attempt to impose it upon us as ours, and violently to substitute their right for our force, is an act of tyranny, and to be resisted. ("Function," 3:266)

If one interprets "we" to mean an elite ruling class, *"force till right is ready"* may itself sound tyrannical. Arnold's attachment to the concept of State, however, modifies the meaning of "force" in the context of his belief in the rule of democracy. As Jacoby puts it, "Arnold believed that everyone in a democracy could be part of the elite. He rejected the private or individualist solution" (Jacoby, 98).

The tension between Arnold's vocabulary, which has often taken on different connotations for today's readers, and the basic humaneness of his social vision is one reason for the confusion about his ideas. His language in discussing the Populace can be devastatingly dismissive, but he wants to educate them and bring them into the functioning democracy. He stereotypes the middle class as Philistines but also sees in them the potential for English greatness. He ridicules narrow and provincial minds but wants to educate them to be flexible and enlightened. He praises the Establishment and calls for an organization of authority to keep the social order but wants this to happen by a democratic voice of the community's best self. Arnold writes out of his classical education, his ironic and deflating sense of humor, and his place as a public intellectual. If his language and his examples often brand him with the limits of his own experience, his ideas never lose the vision of an enlightened democratic society in which rational intelligence and a quest for perfection would define our best selves and the ideal community.

Chapter Seven

Religion, Poetry, and the Culture of Righteousness

"He fables, yet speaks truth!"
Matthew Arnold, *Empedocles on Etna*

In his essay, "The Study of Poetry," Matthew Arnold had written that "most of what now passes with us for religion and philosophy will be replaced by poetry" ("Study," 9:162). In his own career, Arnold passed from writing poetry to writing about religion. From 1869 until 1877 books and essays about religion dominated Arnold's work. Three major books, *St. Paul and Protestantism* in 1870, *Literature and Dogma* in 1873, and *God and the Bible* in 1875, were designed to salvage religious belief and the words of the Bible from what Arnold saw as a narrow literalism of interpretation and perversion of meaning that he believed would eventually destroy the power of religious faith. Arnold addressed the question of "why meddle with religion at all?" and answered it in terms of human need. "At the present moment two things about the Christian religion must surely be clear to anybody with eyes in his head. One is, that men cannot do without it; the other, that they cannot do with it as it is."[1]

Arnold's ideas about Christianity and his way of reading the Bible were controversial at the time among both conservatives and radicals, and they remain so in some quarters today. Among modern liberal theologians, who see in Christ a moral model based in love rather than a supernatural being sent to save us for eternity, Arnold's work resonates with the main currents of thought, just as he had hoped it would.[2] For many who know him primarily as a poet or critic, however, Arnold as biblical exegete is little known or much appreciated. In fact, Arnold's writings about religion are significant to the general student of his work because they provide a foundation for his beliefs about the importance of poetry, culture, language, and conduct. His late writings reflect that interest in religion, but they also make clear the continuity of his think-

ing about the power of language, the function of poetry, and the importance of criticism and culture.

Arnold spoke of God sparingly and aslant. God was "some unknown
power," an "eternal not ourselves which makes for righteousness," or
"that stream of tendency by which all things seek to fulfil the law of
their being."[3] As indirectly as he spoke of God, Arnold nevertheless
spoke often of an eternal power beyond ourselves. When he defined
"culture" as perfection he anchored his definition in an ideal that was
not the product of institutions, education, or the state. The "beauty" of
poetry was not a scientific phenomenon nor a skill one learned in school.
Implicitly, God is the perfection of sweetness and light. The pursuit of
perfection that was the task of culture was a process with no end in
sight. Arnold was not comfortable saying what God was—and he was
sure God was not a "person"—but his thinking never fully departed
from the belief in an eternal dimension to human experience. As Arnold
aged and faced the tragedy of three of his sons' deaths, the Christianity
of his mother and father became a central element in his thinking about
social ethics and moral development.

Although Arnold frequently references an eternal power, he is not a
metaphysician. He saw, looking back on the history of Christianity's
development, that "It was inevitable that the speculative metaphysics
should come, but they were not the foundation" (*Dogma*, 6:94). Arnold's
primary concern is conduct, and the power of religion is its ability to
translate into human behavior the principles of love and righteousness.
His books on religion grow partly out of an impatience with the dissenters, or Puritans, who read the Bible literally and presumed to know
how God thinks, and then turned their understanding of God into
dogma. Such minds are the antithesis of the rational and disinterested
critical intelligence that Arnold sees as crucial to finding our best selves
and creating the state as society's collective best self. He writes, "The
mental habit of him who imagines that Balaam's ass spoke, in no
respects differs from the mental habit of him who imagines that a
Madonna of wood or stone winked; and the one, who says that God's
Church makes him believe what he believes, and the other, who says
that God's Word makes him believe what he believes, are for the
philosopher perfectly alike in not really and truly knowing, when they
say *God's Church* and *God's Word,* what it is they say, or whereof they
affirm" (*Culture*, 5:173).

Arnold's concern with literal readings of the Bible and narrow dogmatic interpretations of doctrine grows out of his sense that such think-

ing is "mechanical" and "Hebraistic." Since the ideal of culture required flexibility of mind and "sweetness and light," dogmatic religious practices undermine the fundamentals of effective ethical behavior and human happiness. He sees the fairy tale of miracles that has invaded religion as a kind of clap-trap that will undermine the credibility of all religion. Arnold undertakes this extended effort to reinterpret religion and the Bible because Christianity, through the translation of Jesus' life, is the ultimate model of what perfection of conduct might be. The triumph of Puritanism for Arnold would mean the triumph of our ordinary self, not our best self.

Believing that science had disproved the Bible as factual, Arnold had to convince his educated audience that biblical texts could still be read for great moral wisdom. The Bible for Arnold is a form of poetry and must be read in the same metaphoric way as poetry to find its essential "truth." That "truth" for Arnold is not the account of miracles or the supernatural beliefs in incarnation or virgin birth; it is the poetic expression of human ethical realities and emotional desires for good as expressed in metaphors. He describes Paul's language as "figured speech" that "has its own beauty and propriety. His language is, much of it, eastern language, imaginative language; there is no need for turning it, as Puritanism has done, into the positive language of the schools" (*St. Paul,* 6:69). In a turnaround of emphasis from his earlier statement, Arnold seems to decide that instead of poetry replacing what passes for religion, he must teach us to see that most of what passes for religion is a form of poetry.

At the same time that Arnold argues that the Bible is essentially literary language, he insists paradoxically that one can prove the scientific value of the truth of religion. Many readers will be puzzled by the distinctions Arnold sees between literary language, which must not be interpreted as if it were the language of science, and his insistence that biblical statements of truth can be scientifically verified with the facts of human experience. In Arnold's view, the metaphysical trappings of Christianity are falsehoods that cannot be sustained, but the essence of Christianity is proven by experience. He writes, "What essentially characterises a religious teacher, and gives him his permanent worth and vitality, is, after all, just the scientific value of his teaching, its correspondence with important facts and the light it throws on them" (*St. Paul,* 6:8). As Basil Willey notes, "Arnold was sufficiently a child of his own time to revere 'science' as knowledge which could be *verified.*"[4] In the matter of conduct, Arnold felt that human experience could verify the rightness of moral teachings. The nature of the eternal remained un-knowable, but the *effect* of righteousness in human life was demonstrable from history and experience. His pursuit of religion was to find truths from human conduct that could be verified and thus relied upon to guide our lives, not theories about the nature of God, which was the realm of poetry.

For Arnold the common characteristic of poetry, culture, and religion is the importance of language as the vehicle for creating orders of knowledge that can enlighten our understanding of human reality and tutor our sense of the righteous and good. Ruth apRoberts says that Arnold's writing about religion "is an extensive piece of literary criti-cism, perhaps, after all, his finest" (apRoberts, 200). Few would disagree that books such as *St. Paul and Protestantism* or *Literature and Dogma* are forms of literary criticism: the disagreement has been whether there is any religious foundation behind it and, if not, whether Arnold's work can be called Christian writing. As James C. Livingston notes, critics from Arnold's contemporary, J. C. Shairp, to modernists such as T. S. Eliot "have asserted that Arnold does subsume religion within culture—i.e., that 'literature, or Culture, tended with Arnold to usurp the place of Religion' " (Livingston, 66). apRoberts and Livingston are contempo-rary embodiments of the debate about the degree and kind of Arnold's Christianity and the linguistic nature of his writing about it. apRoberts stresses Arnold's use of metaphor and links him to the modern poet Wallace Stevens and the creation of linguistic "fictions"—that is, the structures of thought that cultures create as their beliefs and value sys-tem. Livingston argues that it is a misreading to attribute to Arnold "a noncognitivist, non-referential employment of language" (12). Their debate is not whether Arnold is a Christian of some kind, but about whether the basis for his belief is foundational or linguistic.

Others, however, notably T. S. Eliot, have argued that Arnold's putting aside of the metaphysical side of religion empties his thinking of spiritual understanding and makes his critical reading of the Bible not only useless as religious commentary but actually hostile to the essence of religion. For Eliot, for whom the fundamental Christian truth is "Incarnation," Arnold's disbelief in the miracles and the supernatural aspects of Jesus' birth and death began the modern degradation of reli-gion.[5] The unity of religious belief in a Christian community is impor-tant to Eliot, and he sees that Arnold's distaste for theology and dogma dismisses doctrinal differences upon which individual Christian religions base their identity. In his view, Arnold is indifferent to the niceties of theological and ecclesiastical distinctions (386). Eliot's religious thinking is sectarian and Arnold's is ecumenical. Arnold's stress on the emotional value of religion rather than its spiritual revelation provokes Eliot to an ill-tempered dismissal of Arnold's advice as merely getting an emotional kick from Christianity without needing to believe it (385).

Eliot's intemperate essay grows out of his sense that Arnold's argument about the nature and power of religion attacks the spiritual reality essential to a metaphysical religion whose truths are based in revelation. Basil Willey observed that those, and he cites C. S. Lewis among others, who hold "that Christianity is nothing if not supernatural and miraculous, would dismiss Arnold's religious writings as futile attempts to water down 'unacceptable' dogmas and to replace orthodoxy by a non-miraculous, minimal religion based on moral precepts" (Willey 1975, 236). For a Christian such as Eliot, the central concerns would be the state of the soul or the design of God in history, not "conduct" or happiness, as Arnold defines it. As apRoberts observes, the question of whether Arnold is "a Christian" does enter into the importance one may assign to his writing on religion. If, as she argues, one assumes "that Christianity must be supernaturalist, the answer would have been simply no" (apRoberts, 200). Much of contemporary liberal moral theology has followed the direction of Arnold's thought away from metaphysics, however, and his approach to the Bible and definition of religion as conduct are part of the recognized dialogue within modern Christianity. Nevertheless, the arguments over miracle and doctrine within modern Christianity have not subsided, and Arnold's religious writings remain both important and controversial.

Arnold clearly hoped that his work on religion would salvage the ethical and moral power of religion at a moment in which the scientific evidence that the Bible could not be literal truth had undermined the credibility of the Bible as God's literal revelations to the world. In his new preface to *St. Paul and Protestantism* in 1887, some 16 years after its initial publication, Arnold could ask of the "doctrines of unscriptural Protestantism" and the "Dissidence of Dissent," "what open mind does not now perceive its narrowness, poverty, and sterility?" (*St. Paul,* 6:3). Dissenters did not, of course, take Arnold's lessons to heart, abandon their literal views of the Bible, re-enter the established church, and concentrate on interpreting metaphors for ethical conduct. Arnold, who was always an interested but critical observer of the United States of America, would perhaps be dismayed at the vitality of contemporary fundamentalism and the conflict about religious dogma that has entered so deeply into the political realm and marred the exercise of tolerance in domestic and international life. "Politics are," he said, "a good thing, and religion is a good thing; but they make a fractious mixture" (*St. Paul*, 6:104).

St. Paul and Protestantism

The apostle Paul became the focus of Arnold's first extended commentary on the Bible because Paul for so long had been widely recognized as the authority on doctrines central to Protestantism. Arnold concentrates on Paul's Epistle to the Romans. From Arnold's perspective, Paul's *Letters* in the New Testament had been abused by Protestantism and Puritanism in particular. Arnold's contention is that Protestantism has for three centuries missed Paul's essential doctrine through its preoccupation with predestination, original sin, and justification (*St. Paul*, 6:72). For Arnold, the issue was the mistaken reading of Paul, whose literary style worked on a different level from that of a literal reading. The literal readings were a "monstrous and grotesque caricature" that lost his meaning (*Culture*, 5:182). The Calvinists talk "about God just as if he were a man in the next street," but Arnold wants to show that it is Calvinism, not Paul, who "professes this exact acquaintance with God and his doings" (*St. Paul*, 6:9). Paul's text must be read more figuratively to learn its essential truth.

Arnold distinguishes between the figurative language of Paul and the literal and sometimes legalistic language of church doctrine.[6] Paul was educated in the literary modes of Jewish writing, which were more metaphoric and allegorical than literal. Thus, Paul possessed "a much juster sense of the true scope and limits of diction in religious deliverances than we have," Arnold explains (*St Paul*, 6:20). His figurative writing is appropriately read as "religious emotion" expressed in language that is eloquent but not that of "formal scientific propositions." Those who read Paul literally confound the character of his work and thus "abuse" his meaning. Since he has used the term "Hebraise" in another context in *Culture and Anarchy*, Arnold says that Paul "Orientalises," a term that seems to mean to speak figuratively. "Prosaic and unintelligent Western readers" often lack the necessary "tact for style" to understand Paul's text as talismanic (*St. Paul*, 6:22). Such language may be richly evocative of emotions and translatable as true to experience, but it can be an "interruption to the argument" (*St. Paul*, 6:22). The "tact for style" needed to read a writer like Paul requires an understanding of how figurative language works and an education sufficient to interpret metaphors correctly. "In short," he argues, "no man, we said, who knows nothing else, knows even his Bible. And we showed how readers of the Bible attached to essential words and ideas of the Bible a sense which was not the writer's"(*St. Paul*, 6:7).

Unlike the Calvinist whose desire is "to flee from the wrath to come" or the Methodist whose desire is "for eternal bliss," Paul as writer is set in motion by "the master-impulse of Hebraism,—*the desire for righteousness*" (*St. Paul*, 6:23). The aim of all religion is *"access to God,"* which meant for the Hebrew, according to Arnold, "access to the source of the *moral* order in especial, and harmony with it" (*St. Paul*, 6:24). Paul's virtues are the specifics that he provides of the moral law and his desire to establish them as effective in our lives. Arnold notes the mystical side of Paul but values the practical moral principles.

The two central characteristics Arnold sees in Paul are "his mercies," that is, his insistence on gentleness, humbleness, forbearance, charity, and his *"solidarity"* with humankind, by which Arnold means his respect for the interests that bind together humanity (*St. Paul*, 6:26). For Arnold these characteristics are the basis for conduct that is the foundation of personal morality and the collective best self that is the state. Paul's solidarity with humanity is based in his understanding of Christ's solidarity of men in which humankind is conceived as one body (*St. Paul*, 6:49). This solidarity is the basis for loving others as one's self.

Paul's religious vision revolves around harmony with the moral order of the universe and solidarity with humanity. This is a fundamentally different kind of religious vision whose center is *not* "the desire to flee from eternal wrath" or "the desire to obtain eternal bliss" (*St. Paul*, 6:28). Arnold's earlier work had expressed his concern for an enlightened and humane democratic society where citizen and state alike could pursue the realization of their best self. His reading of Paul sees in his teachings the appropriate gospel for such a society. The "grotesque distortion" Arnold sees in Puritan interpretations of Paul aligns him with a supernatural world and focuses on individual redemption instead of the social good.

Like poetry, Paul's writing represents metaphoric orders of meaning that reveal the truth of human experience. For Arnold the moral law is found in actual experience, and the path to righteousness is through "right reason and duty," virtues familiar to us from Arnold's earlier prose work. Arnold never fully defines righteousness as explicitly as he indexes the variety of sins. As Basil Willey notes, Arnold wrote in a time during which it was believed that "everybody knew perfectly well what was the right thing to do on any occasion, and what was wrong" (Willey 1975, 256). Arnold clearly placed denial of selfish will and a loving regard for one's fellow human beings at the center of his concept of righteousness, and in general his definition of the righteous seems to track traditional middle-class moral values of the time. Through righteousness, not commands, taboos, nor Mosaic law, we can harmonize our actions, the flow of our spirits, and the desires of the flesh with the universal moral order. The result is "our peace and happiness" (*St. Paul*, 6:32). The essence of Christianity for Arnold is *"Grace and peace by the annulment of our ordinary self through the mildness and sweet reasonableness of Jesus Christ"* (*St. Paul*, 6:121).

The heart of Arnold's quarrel with the "wrong" readings of Paul is what he sees as "the three essential terms of Pauline theology." He identifies these terms as *"calling, justification, sanctification."* In his revision they are more properly phrased as *"dying with Christ, resurrection from the dead, growing into Christ"* (*St. Paul*, 6:50). Arnold's revision of meaning strips the terms of their metaphysical dimensions. Arnold defines Paul's mature idea of resurrection as having no connection "with physical death." Further, he sees the popular interpretation of resurrection as "a miracle which guarantees the promised future miracle of our own resurrection" as inconsistent with Paul's later writing. Instead, Arnold defines Paul's central doctrine as *"to die with Christ to the law of the flesh, to live with Christ to the law of the mind"* (*St. Paul*, 6:47). Dying with Christ means to follow Christ's example in subduing appetite and self-will, *"all impulses of selfishness,"* through faith and love when reason and conscience cannot govern. When the law of Christ's life becomes the law of one's own life, one is a "new creature." One is "transformed by the renewing of your mind, and rise with him." This "resurrection" is not to eternal life but to "that harmonious conformity with the real and eternal order, that sense of pleasing God who trieth the hearts, which is life and peace, and which grows more and more till it becomes glory" (*St. Paul*, 6:48). It is not a resurrection from physical death.

Arnold's definitions of dying and rising in Christ need no metaphysical realities behind them. Paul's idea of resurrection was for now, and to righteousness. Arnold sees Christ as the ideal of conduct but not as part of a Trinity in which he is the Son of God. Arnold rejects that Christ's birth was a "Messianic advent." Unlike the Puritans, Arnold has little interest in sin, which he defines as "an impotence to be got rid of," and not worth thinking about "beyond what is indispensable for the firm effort to get rid of it"(*St. Paul,* 6:35). With the idea of the importance of "dying" in Christ in order to conquer selfishness and appetites, Arnold translates into personal moral behavior his objections to a citizen "doing as one likes." The collective act of "rising" in Christ would create in a society the ideal of the state. Although some have argued that this is morality but not religion, Arnold has given his social ideals a foundation in his beliefs in the concept of an eternal harmony made manifest in the life and words of Christ. This "infinite element" for Arnold reaches "beyond the strictly moral element" to give us "an impulsion outside ourselves which is at once awful and beneficent," a phrase that is another slanting way in which Arnold seems to say God (*St. Paul,* 6:37).

Arnold's antagonism to Puritanism is that its beliefs not only have little to do with Paul's teachings but even deter Christ's meaning from shaping a more moral world. Puritan tenets are "in the main, at present, an obstacle to progress and to true civilization" (*St. Paul,* 6:74). The Puritan preoccupation with sin, atonement, and resurrection into a New Jerusalem of a heavenly world deflects potential energy and goodness away from realizing in this life Christ's actual teachings. Arnold finds objectionable the Puritan emphasis on the "elect," a label for those "called" or "chosen" for salvation. Holding a conception of God that "has blinded and reprobated other men, so that they shall not reach this blessing, is to quit the ground of personal experience, and to begin employing the magnified and non-natural man in the next street" (*St. Paul,* 6:60). He finds this idea "extraneous" to Paul and repellent as a "notion of God" (*St. Paul,* 6:63). The Puritan idea of sacrifice is merely one of "buying off the wrath of a powerful being," a notion Arnold finds "merely superstitious" (*St. Paul,* 6:65). In summary, the Puritan beliefs in "ransom, redemption, propitiation, blood, offering," are all subordinate to Paul's "central idea of *identification with Christ through dying with him*" (*St. Paul,* 6:69).

Puritan self-righteousness assumes the truth of its interpretation of gospel, an attitude that Arnold believes prevents the Puritans from growing toward better insight. By setting themselves apart from the national church, the Puritans prevent the growth of the collective life, a charge Arnold had raised against the dissenters in *Culture and Anarchy.* Arnold sees the development of the Church of England as proceeding gradually from ideas and traditions, while the dissenting groups focus on the revelation of special opinions. In contrast to the new sects, the established church possesses much greater "freedom of mind" because of its history of progressive development that has been critically examined.

Arnold's hope is that his work will show the Puritans that their beliefs are not the gospel and will further the unification of the Protestant dissenters to the Church of England.

Arnold's hope that *St. Paul and Protestantism* might further the unification of the wrongheaded Puritan dissenters with the right-thinking established church is naive if it is not disingenuous. His interpretation of Paul's writing is brilliant and moving if one is willing to find spiritual wisdom in a religious tradition that has yielded its metaphysical foundation. For Christians such as Eliot or C. S. Lewis, or the evangelical Christians of our own day, Arnold's interpretation of Christianity does not address their need for a religion of miracle or eternal salvation. Arnold's lack of interest in sin eliminates fear of punishment, and his imaginative reasoning is a frame of mind blind to the emotional religious needs that rely on miracle and metaphysics for validation. His critical reading of Paul's text, though well informed, lacks the kind of exegetical thoroughness of a biblical scholar. Arnold was indeed suspicious of the elaborate scholarship that reduced the Bible to a kind of mechanical interpretation. The insensitivity to dissent that we saw in his contempt for the rowdy workers disrupting the streets also weakens his ability to understand religious dissent. Arnold seems unable to imagine that the Puritan dissenters are no more likely to drop their complaint and re-enter the establishment than the workers are to stop their strikes. The strength of this work is the rational and humane pattern of moral behavior that Arnold finds in the example of Christ as presented by Paul. Traditional ideas of faith, love, sacrifice, and resurrection are given a secular reality in human experience whose end is a better world in the here and now.

Literature and Dogma

The book that appeared as *Literature and Dogma* in 1873 comprises essays written in 1871 and 1872. The essays reflect the controversies about religion that were part of Victorian intellectual life, but they also attempt to respond to the ongoing debate sparked by Arnold's own writing. The book was popular, and Arnold regarded it as the most useful and comforting of his works. The essays grew out of his desire to answer a crisis in religion that he felt was robbing the masses of their ability to believe in the Bible. One factor contributing to the crisis was, of course, the new science of geology and evolution; another was the sustained "Higher Criticism" of the Bible from German scholars and their English followers who regarded the Bible as a historical document that should be approached in a scientific manner of study. Yet another position in the Victorian debate was that of the Utilitarians, who, on the whole, questioned the usefulness of religion. Arnold was very much aware of these currents, but in *Literature and Dogma* he focused on what Protestant sects, such as the Methodists and Presbyterians, and their teachings were doing to destroy the Bible's credibility. He aimed the book at the educated reading public, not at the specialized audiences of theologians and scholars.

Instead of attacking religion, Arnold sees himself as defending what he calls its "natural" truth. The "natural," or true to the scientific reality, is in contrast with the supernatural. Since science has destroyed the credibility of religion based on the supernatural, he seeks to revalidate it in terms of its relevance to the "natural" world. His language in this set of essays is direct, and he rewords his central points from chapter to chapter for clarity and emphasis. More than in *St. Paul and Protestantism,* Arnold draws heavily in *Literature and Dogma* on quotations from the Bible to convince readers that his interpretations are sound in terms of scriptural sources. Many of the ideas in *St. Paul and Protestantism* reappear in *Literature and Dogma,* but the focus on developing a rationale for a new religion of the Bible for the masses gives *Literature and Dogma* a wider scope and a more general application. For readers of his earlier literary criticism and *Culture and Anarchy,* it links his conceptions of the value of literary study and the role of culture to his emphasis on Christianity in the final stages of his career.

Arnold's central premise in *Literature and Dogma,* as in *St. Paul and Protestantism,* is that the Bible must be read as literature, not as science, and that dogma based on a narrow and overly precise reading of biblical texts distorts the essential meaning of Jesus' teachings. In a wider context than in his commentary on the writings of Paul, Arnold seeks to show how religious dogma has been invaded by the fairy tale of miracles, what he calls in the German, *Aberglaube.* Instead of miracle, Arnold argues that Jesus is the ideal natural man whose message of righteousness contains both the method and secret for peace and happiness. The dogma of the learned religions is not only mistaken but "mischievous as well as vain" (*Dogma,* 6:383). Since the masses are increasingly unable to trust the supernatural accounts of the churches, Arnold wants to put a new ground of verifiable experience beneath the meaning of Jesus and to define God as *"the best one knows"* (*Dogma,* 6:372). Arnold rejected the common definition of God as "the Supreme Personal First Cause." He worried that when this definition of God was exposed as "*not* the order of nature," as merely "an assumption, and not a fact," then "our whole superstructure falls to pieces like a house of cards. And this is just what is happening at present" (*Dogma,* 6:366).

One of Arnold's strongest arguments is of the danger of basing religious belief on apocalyptic predictions and miracles such as resurrection. Dealing with religion and conduct on the basis of "extra-belief" (*Aberglaube*) or superstition is costly since the time comes when we discover that the supernatural is "*not* certain; and then the whole certainty of religion seems discredited, and the basis of conduct gone" (*Dogma,* 6:232). Arnold understands that the tendency of people is to attribute to miracle a source of authority above reason and evidence, but he is aware how little scrutiny the accounts of miracles can really bear. He is also aware of the errors and contradictions in biblical accounts. The reporters of Jesus' words, he argues, were unable fully to understand his teachings, which were often over their heads. He notes repeatedly that the sayings of Jesus often do not support the literal reading of the recorders who wrote the books of the Bible. The reporters, living in a dim time and often limited in wisdom and experience, made many mistakes in fact, argument, and philosophy. "It is not surprising, certainly," he writes, "that men with the mental range of their time . . . stuck hopelessly fast in the literal meaning of the words" (*Dogma,* 6:262). He cites in particular their obviously erroneous prophecies of an immediate return of Christ as evidence of the mistakes made by the writers of the books of the New Testament. The new biblical criticism, especially from German scholars, has added to the shakiness of belief in miracle by showing how such beliefs arise and become myths (*Dogma,* 6:246). For Arnold, if what Christians believe on the basis of miracle is valuable, he must make its value independent of miracles.

For Arnold, an essential part of a proper understanding of religion is a wide experience of what he calls "culture." In *Literature and Dogma* Arnold defines culture now as "*reading;* but *reading* with a purpose to guide it, and with system" (*Dogma,* 6:162). Such reading means "acquainting ourselves with the best that has been known and said in the world," and reading the Bible without culture will lead the masses to dispose of it as "a priestly imposture" (*Dogma,* 6:151). Through reading, or culture, one realizes that the "language of the Bible is fluid, passing, and literary, not rigid, fixed, and scientific." He defends the opacity of biblical language as a form of literary language "*thrown out* at an object of consciousness not fully grasped, which inspired emotion"

(*Dogma*, 6:189). Reading literary language requires more skill and more "tact" than reading scientific language does. In order to read it well, we need first to have read broadly. Culture gives us *"the power, through reading, to estimate the proportion and relation in what we read"* (*Dogma*, 6:152–53). Those educated by a great deal of reading learn to interpret through "the criterion of *reason*" (*Dogma*, 6:156). He contrasts this kind of reading with the scholarly work in history and mythology of the German critics. Their fallacy of reading the Bible is their reliance on the facts but without the "justness of perception"; as mere "specialists," they lack the fullness of understanding that culture teaches (*Dogma*, 6:158). They can read as scholars but not as poets. For Arnold, reading and the study of letters educates beyond the power of logic or scholarship; sound judgment and an understanding of how literary language works outweigh abstruse reasoning.

Arnold takes the definition of God as one of his central examples of the mistaken effort by theologians to employ literary terms "as if they were *scientific* terms" (*Dogma*, 6:170). "God" is, he argues, a literary term, and we can only define it in terms of *"the best that man knows or can know."* Theologians who define God as "A Great Personal First Cause" whose son is Jesus and whose attributes are described in the detail of the Athanasian Creed "cannot possibly be verified" (*Dogma*, 6:171, 374). Arnold believes that his definition of God as "the enduring Power, not ourselves, that makes for righteousness" can be verified by the experience of righteousness in history (*Dogma*, 6:373). He does not problematize "righteousness." A contemporary skeptic schooled in post-structuralist theory may question whether Arnold's definition is more verifiable than the one he attacks since the interpretation of righteousness in history has itself become historically determined. For Arnold, however, the difference between morality as "a thoroughly definite and ascertained idea" and God as "a term of poetry and eloquence" is clear and important. The desire for righteousness is the essence of Jesus' teachings, the primary effect of Jesus' example is on conduct, and righteousness in conduct can be verified.

Arnold defines the object of religion as conduct, which he rather literally tallies up as *three-fourths* of human life (the remaining fourth is the study of arts and sciences, he says). Conduct refers to "one or other of man's two elementary instincts,—the instinct of self-preservation and the reproductive instinct" (*Dogma*, 6:287). The faults of conduct also break into two categories—"faults of temper and faults of sensuality" (*Dogma*, 6:287). Arnold lists what some of these faults are—pride, folly, adultery, murder, greed, etc.—and notes that Jesus was explicit in giving commandments about them. Misconduct results from self-assertion over the will of God and indulging the desires of the flesh. Religion is mistaken, however, in interpreting Jesus' call for "repentance" as lamenting one's sins; for Arnold the proper understanding of repentance is a *"new inward movement"* for *"a change of the inner man"* (*Dogma,* 6:288–89).

The crux of Arnold's interpretation of Christianity lies in how the life of Jesus becomes an influence on conduct that can translate the "Eternal Power, not ourselves, which makes for righteousness" into actions that bring peace and happiness in this world. To this end, "the work of Jesus Christ" was "that he came *to restore the intuition*" (*Dogma,* 6:284). This strange and perhaps unexpected phrase seems to describe an emotional state in which the heart and mind are in harmony with the desire for righteousness. To accomplish this restoration of "the intuition," Jesus brought a method and a secret that, according to Arnold, was the real essence of his mystery. As in *St. Paul and Protestantism,* Arnold recasts the traditional Christian ideas of sacrifice, death, and resurrection through Christ to mean conquering one's selfish desires, living in the model of Christ, and arising with Christ to a realization of our real and best self. The method is to live in Christ's example and the secret is that when one does that, one finds peace and harmony with the eternal order of righteousness. Repentance "attaches itself" to method, and peace attaches itself to his secret. Perhaps clearer is Arnold's association of Christ's method with his influence on conscience. Through examination of our inner selves, we find "two selves" or two lives pulling in different directions—one toward "the lower and transient self" and the other toward "the higher and permanent self" (*Dogma,* 6:292). The renouncing of the lower self is the path to happiness. "Peace through Jesus Christ" means finding the harmony of one's best self with the moral order of the universe and translating it as conduct.

Arnold's definition of Jesus' work and the transformation it brings recalls the influence of Wordsworth in his life. A Christ whose goal is "to restore the intuition" is a Romantic inspiration. The inward movement of the heart toward the realization of a self in harmony with the universal order resonates with the lessons Wordsworth teaches Dorothy in "Lines Composed a Few Miles Above Tintern Abbey." In his poem on Wordsworth's death, "Memorial Verses," Arnold portrays the gift of Wordsworth to his generation as not unlike Arnold's conception of Jesus. Wordsworth, too, brought the heart and mind into a unity and made dead spirits fresh through his "healing power."

He laid us as we lay at birth
On the cool flowery lap of earth,
Smiles broke from us and we had ease;
The hills were round us, and the breeze
Went o'er the sun-lit fields again;
Our foreheads felt the wind and rain.
Our youth returned; for there was shed
On spirits that had long been dead,
Spirits dried up and closely furled,
The freshness of the early world.

(Poems, lines 48–57)

In Romanticism, this sense of becoming one's best self in harmony with an eternal power not ourselves is expressed in metaphors of oneness with nature. The state of peace and happiness Arnold knew in his youthful Romanticism is not unlike that the older Arnold attributes to the influence of Christ.

Arnold is troubled by the opposition Protestant doctrines draw between "faith" and reason, and one of his most interesting contributions is his redefinition of faith. The essence of what mainstream Christianity means by faith is "to take on trust what perplexes the reason" (*Dogma*, 6:312). Arnold charged that religion's insistence that one believe what is patently unbelievable serves the institution of the established church because it provides a way to defend statements of doctrine such as the Athanasian Creed. The substitution of abstruse and "worthless" creeds for the simple teachings of Christ destroy real faith by insisting on superstition. The notion that the purest faith is to believe "as a little child" leads to a disdain for study, reading, and reason. Such anti-intellectual "possessors of *gospel-truth*" extend their disdain for reason to "art, and literature, and science" (*Dogma*, 6:312). Instead of relying on accepting what cannot be made reasonable, Arnold argues throughout that we can with study and reason understand the teachings of Jesus, and that his truths are verifiable from human experience.

Rejecting the definition of faith as believing what is not reasonable, Arnold instead defines faith as a positive and reasoned act of attaching ourselves to what we can know of the truth of Jesus' life. In the Christian context, the truth is the example of righteousness in the life of Christ. True faith is fidelity to that example, not a blind acceptance as truth that which is patently unbelievable. We must, he says, "attend" to what is perfectly clear. *"Cleaving, attaching oneself fast"* to what we can understand of Jesus' life is the true wisdom, not "submission of the reason to what puzzles" (*Dogma*, 6:313). The work of Jesus in fact provides sureness and understanding, and by cleaving to his example, we may transform our lives through His influence. Thus, Arnold's formal definition of faith is: *"the being able to cleave to a power of goodness appealing to our higher and real self, not to our lower and apparent self"* (*Dogma*, 6:315).

Much of *Literature and Dogma* is devoted to some broad historical generalizations about the periodic "re-invasions" of *Aberglaube*, or superstitious belief in miracles. One such invasion came about 600 years after the golden era of King David, when the Chosen People of Israel began to ask why their enemies prospered and they did not.[7] "With difficulties pressing the Jewish community on all sides," Israel was confused since they believed themselves favored by God. They "were perplexed and indignant when the privileged seed became unprosperous" (*Dogma*, 6:208). Their disappointed expectations bred anger that their enemies prospered instead. Skepticism about Israel's covenant with God grew, which Arnold sees expressed in the Book of Ecclesiastes. "Many there were, no doubt," Arnold writes, "who had lost all living sense that the promises were made to *righteousness;* who took them mechanically, as made to them and assured to them because they were the seed of Abraham" (*Dogma*, 6: 208). The unfulfilled present created an expectation that the future would somehow bring some great and redressing change, such as the coming of the Messiah. It also produced a sharper sense of the ways Israel had itself broken its covenant with the Eternal, a consciousness that strengthened the need for repentance against the day of the Messianic advent. In the climate of such hopes, Arnold notes, Jesus was "the very last sort of Messiah that the Jews expected" (*Dogma*, 6:214). They looked for glory and power, not humility and weakness, and Arnold traces Christianity's definition of God as a "magnified and non-natural man" to Jewish beliefs in the Old Testament (*Dogma*, 6:215).

A second major period of *Aberglaube* came after the death of Jesus. Jesus himself directed his teachings toward a more inward religion in which happiness would be restored by "re-applying emotion" to righteousness (*Dogma*, 6:218). The example of "sweet reasonableness" (Arnold's translation of *epiekeia*) Jesus brought to feelings and conduct did not satisfy the expectation of grandeur that was the climate into which he came. "The mild, inward, self-renouncing and sacrificed Servant of the Eternal, the new and better Messiah, was yet, before the present generation passed, to come on the clouds of heaven in power and glory like the Messiah of Daniel, to gather by trumpet-call his elect from the four winds, and to set his apostles on twelve thrones judging the twelve tribes of Israel" (*Dogma*, 6:230). The *Aberglaube* that soon surrounded Christ in time surpassed with the masses the original attractiveness of Jesus. The Christian church also found prophecy and miracle useful in building its power. The result was that popular Christianity created "a phantasmagorical advent of Jesus Christ, a resurrection and judgment, Christ's adherents glorified, his rejectors punished everlastingly" (*Dogma*, 6:231).

Arnold understands that "the spirit of man should entertain hopes and anticipations, beyond what it actually knows and can verify," but he deeply believed that fairy tales ultimately deprive religion of its credibility (*Dogma*, 6:212). These myths of "extra-belief" are a kind of poetry, but they are not science and cannot be verified. The modern "masses," Arnold notes, "with their rude practical instinct, go straight to the heart of the matter," and they will ask for proof that is clear and certain (*Dogma*, 6:366). His worry, and the motive for writing, was that if Christianity is not made "verifiable" by experience and based on moral truth rather than metaphysics, the masses will "pitch the whole Bible to the winds" (*Dogma*, 6:367).

Arnold closes *Literature and Dogma* with the prediction that there will be less religion in the future. In some sweeping generalizations he characterizes Catholicism as having laid hold of the "secret" of Jesus; and Protestantism, in a similar way, "laid hold on his 'method' " (*Dogma*, 6:351). Protestantism stressed Jesus' method "of inwardness and sincerity," and Catholicism his self-renouncement. "The chief word with Protestantism is the word of the method: *repentance, conversion;* the chief word with Catholicism is the word of the secret: *peace, joy*" (*Dogma*, 6:352). As religion based on miracles begins to dissolve, Arnold believes that Catholicism will grow in the time of transition because it rests more on authority as against reason. Arnold essentially sees both Catholicism and Protestantism as reduced to "thaumaturgy," a word that means "miracles" but also simply "magic." In an apparent reference to some of the Higher Criticism, Arnold labels "learned pseudo-science" applied to the Bible as an "utter blunder" that should be thrown aside (*Dogma*, 6:384). Despite his sense that religion will wane and become irrelevant, Arnold strongly believes that people, even the "masses," will return to the Bible "because they cannot do without it. Because happiness is our being's end and aim, and happiness belongs to righteousness, and righteousness is revealed in the Bible" (*Dogma*, 6:380). To give up the Bible is like giving up food or sleep, and when a time of "reconstruction" of religion comes, Arnold hopes that his criticism of the Bible will be in the "main lines" of that construction (*Dogma,* 6:381).

God and the Bible

If the "main lines" of liberal moral theology that became Christian humanism have indeed reflected Arnold's effort to see in Christ's life a model for humane and ethical living instead of an agent for eternal salvation, many theologians and biblical scholars of his time did not find him so persuasive. The publication of *God and the Bible* in the fall of 1875 was in direct response to the criticism his earlier work had excited, particularly *Literature and Dogma.* Much of the content of *God and the Bible* revisits controversial ideas that Arnold had discussed in his earlier writing on religion. Arnold sought in this new book to turn back negative critical attacks on the "truth" of the Bible. The attacks included those he was accused of and those of the German critics, whom he characterized as "extremely fanciful and untrustworthy" (*God,* 7:374). He believed that his criticism was a positive force that would strengthen the importance of the Bible, not a critique that debunked its value or its fundamental message. Still, there are in *God and the Bible* many passages with an even stronger tone of disdain for those who defend the religion of miracles than in the earlier work. His language, instead of being defensive or conciliatory, is blunt and occasionally ridiculing. *God and the Bible* makes a barbed attack on his critics that recalls the rhetoric of *Culture and Anarchy* more than the deliberative style of his other writing about religion.

Arnold sees the critics as objecting especially to his conclusions about the meaning of the term "God," man's knowledge of God, biblical documents in general, his account of the Canon of the Gospels, and his estimate of the New Testament book of John (*God,* 7:150). He reasserts his aim to address those who question the truth of the Bible in order to lead them to a deeper understanding of Christianity. Several chapters elaborate on the derivation of the canon of the gospels and the validity of his belief in John as the major author of the fourth book of the New Testament. These chapters are perhaps Arnold's most scholarly exegesis of biblical texts, though today they seem primarily interesting as insight on the nineteenth-century debate between the German critics on one side and the conservative theologians on the other. These chapters are more aimed at specific biblical scholars and critics of his work than at the generally educated reading public that Arnold saw as his major audience.

One criticism of his style more than his scholarship that Arnold addresses is "the reproach of irreverent language, of improper and offensive personalities" (*God*, 7:150). Arnold denies being guilty of ridiculing religious faith or making personal attacks on the clergy, and in the broad sense of his best intentions, he is right about the general thrust of his work. Arnold was, however, always a wit, and a sharp-tongued one at times. He begins this book, for example, with the "martyrdom" of "Polycarp" who labeled the disfigured religion of his day as atheism. Arnold then promptly insists that "popular Christianity at present is so wide of the truth, is such a disfigurement of the truth, that it fairly deserves" to be charged with atheism itself, but that he has refrained from doing so. Instead of speaking tactfully about "*aberglaube* invading," as he had done in *Literature and Dogma*, Arnold irreverently says that the God of popular religion is a "fairy-tale . . . dressed . . . metaphysically," a fairy tale it is impossible to treat with "solemnity" (*God*, 7:151). The concept of the Trinity he dismisses as "a trio of magnified and nonnatural men" (*God*, 7:152). He accuses the late Bishop of Winchester of rhetorical "clap-trap" and argues, "The use of clap-trap to such a public by such a man ought at least to be always severely treated before the tribunal of letters and science" (*God* 7:153–54). At one point he compares the report of water turning to wine at the marriage feast at Cana as like the "extravagance of supposing Cinderella's fairy godmother to have actually changed the pumpkin into a coach and six" (*God*, 7:170). By using demeaning language that reduces the miracles of religious belief to ridiculous fairy tales, Arnold often acts out the irreverence he hopes to deny. From a literary perspective, the form of the book as a reply to critics sets up a spirited interchange that unleashes Arnold's cleverness. The language often gives *God and the Bible* a lively and humorous style more like the style of *Culture and Anarchy* than the earnestness of *St. Paul and Protestantism* and *Literature and Dogma*.

Although most of the ideas in *God and the Bible* are familiar since the book was conceived as a rebuttal to criticism of his earlier work, Arnold makes several interesting new points that deserve mention. His somewhat torturous discussion of "*being*" is reductive but interesting in light of the importance this term has had in modern religious and philosophical discussions. Arnold impatiently questions the soundness of Descartes' axiom, "*Cogito, ergo sum;* I think, therefore I am" (*God*, 7:176). Arnold confesses "without shame" that he has never derived the light from this saying that others claim for it because "the philosopher omits to tell us what he exactly means by to *be*, to *exist*" (*God*, 7:177). In order to bring Descartes' axiom into some context that is not abstrusely philosophical, Arnold translates it as "I think, therefore I feel that I am alive," a restatement that makes consciousness the measure of existence, or being (*God*, 7:177). Arnold, who acknowledges that Descartes might not really have meant this, notes that he also uses phrases such as "infinite substance" that suggest that substances are measured by the degree of reality, or being, they have (*God*, 7:178). Being, then, is not a metaphysical entity but a material thing.

After a lengthy etymological tracing of related words Arnold concludes that the roots of "*is*, *be*, and *exist*" were "these harmless concretes, *breathe*, *grow*, and *stand*" (*God*, 7:184). Breathing, growing, and standing forth are thus the substance of being, and being is more a subject for physiology than metaphysics (*God*, 7:188–89). Being expressed not metaphysics but his sense of a living, developing thing that operates or acts in nature. Having arrived at this deflating sense of Descartes, Arnold points his ridicule at the philosophers and metaphysicians who have attached such flights of abstract thought to the "essence" of being only to wind up in the "animal." He ends this discussion with strained humor that may not be the highest mark of his cleverness:

> So perfidiously do these words *is* and *be*,—on which we embarked our hopes because we fancied they would bring us to a thinking and a loving, independent of all material organisation,—so perfidiously do they land us in mere creature-worship of the grossest kind. Nay, and perhaps the one man who uses that wonderful abstract word, *essence*, with propriety, will turn out to be, not the metaphysician or the theologian, but the perfumer. For while nothing but perplexity can come from speaking of the essence or *breathing* of the Divine Nature, there is really much felicity in speaking of the essence or *breathing* of roses. (*God*, 7:189)

A second new and daring discussion is Arnold's argument that Darwin's theories do not affect religion. The discussion is a response to the criticism that Darwin assigns the origin of the moral perception "to a social instinct, [which] arise[s] out of evolution and inheritance" (*God*, 7:222). To Arnold, the origin of moral perceptions "does not matter two straws" (*God*, 7:222). He is "astonished" that some interpret Darwinian moral origins as meaning that all that has been said about an enduring power that makes for righteousness must "fall to the ground" (*God*, 7:223). The discussion that follows, one of Arnold's boldest and most imaginative, links Darwin's theories of reproductive instinct and self-preservation with the Ten Commandments. He traces how evolving human society in its earliest period may have initially acted on the instinct of reproduction, but that in time the family bond grew out of this instinct. From this "twilight ante-natal life of humanity, almost as much as the life which each man passes in the womb before he is born," man passes into the known history of institutions and civilizations. As his "real history" begins, the human race carries with it the "habit" acquired by nature:

> he gives effect to it in fixed customs, rules, laws, and institutions. His religion consists in acknowledging and reverencing the awful sanctions with which this right way for man has, he believes, been invested by the mighty *not ourselves* which surrounds us; and the more emphatically he places a feeling under the guardianship of these sanctions, the more impressive is his testimony to the hold it has upon him. (*God,* 7:225)

This habit of nature, growing out of the reproductive instinct, becomes in Jewish ancient history the commandment, "Honor thy father and mother," Arnold argues. He then makes a similar argument for the relationship of the instinct for self-preservation with the commandment, "Thou shalt not commit adultery."

The substance of Arnold's discussion about the "innocence" of Darwin's doctrines to religion is that moral ideas evolved before religion touched them with emotion, a thesis about the genealogy of religion that is not likely to satisfy his or Darwin's critics. Defining religion as "morality touched by emotion," Arnold argues that the habits developed from instincts became more powerful when touched by emotion and refigured as religion (*God,* 7:227). The evolution of habits and then morals and finally religion is a process that Arnold, taking his term from Goethe, describes as what culture has won of nature. Christianity is a "culture-conquest" in which the rawness of nature is, through moral habits and religious and social rules, brought into the control of the "unnatural" (*God,* 7:229).

Arnold describes his effort to write about religion as "an attempt conservative, and an attempt religious" (*God,* 7:398). The depth of knowledge he brings to this work and the reverence Arnold always expresses for the ideal of Jesus leaves little doubt of his belief that religion is a positive moral force in the lives of humanity. His fear that new ways of thinking could lead people away from the Bible, and thus away from the essence of Christianity, sustained him in his efforts to show the masses that religion needed no metaphysics. In the context of preserving Christianity's vitality to the masses, his efforts to illuminate the continuing importance of the Bible were considered "conservative" by radicals who had hoped that religion was fast going to ruin (Willey 1975, 255). His argument against the metaphysical base to religion was not a conservative one, however, and even today in the range of popular religious beliefs his definition of religion as morality touched by emotion would be considered a liberal form of Humanist Christianity. Asking whether Arnold believed in God in order to settle questions about the depth of his religious conviction is the kind of reductive and narrow theological approach that he hoped to change. Arnold believed in moral conduct in an ethical world. For Arnold, the evident power of righteousness in the world was the "incarnation" of God. The evidence that Arnold believed in the reality of this God was his optimism that humanity could learn, that a state could rule wisely, and that the conduct of human life could indeed reflect reasoned thought, effective action, and loving hearts.

Chapter Eight

Arnoldian Conclusions in
a Postmodern Time

> To know how others stand, that we may know how we ourselves stand; and to know
> how we ourselves stand, that we may correct our mistakes and achieve our deliver-
> ance—that is our problem.
>
> Matthew Arnold, "On the Modern Element in Literature"

From his earliest poems to his last published words, Matthew Arnold addressed himself to questions of how one was to live in the world as a moral and social being. Ideally, life should, he thought, bring happiness, and his struggle was to find for himself and for his culture the ethical and effective ways to achieve that. The youthful experiences of his own heart and temperament taught him that it was not easy to be happy; the deprivation and ignorance he saw in his career as a school inspector taught him that life could be so hard and so limited that the development of one's best self was almost impossible. His own love of poetry taught him the sustaining beauty and wisdom of "the best that has been thought and said," and his work in education gave him an opportunity to extend that kind of enrichment to the masses. Seldom has a man's education, morality, and vocation come together more effectively to allow him to translate his life into one of public work than the one Arnold created for himself. As Basil Willey said some 50 years ago, Arnold was not the most representative man of his age, but he was the most intelligent because he understood the main movements of his time.[1]

The power of Arnold's efforts to answer his abiding question, how to live, resides in part in his understanding of how and why sustaining answers could be so difficult to find. The task was more challenging because Arnold saw many tensions that had to be balanced or reconciled. Arnold did not believe that there was no private life separate from the public life, nor that everything was political. Neither did he believe that there was no basis for making cultural and moral judgments about what was good or how one might be better. He believed that the right to do as one likes or say what one thinks was inscribed with the responsibility to act in the interest of the general good and to have something informed and thoughtful to say when one spoke out. He did not believe, as many others did, that dogma or metaphysics could provide the answers. For Arnold dogma was too inflexible to allow critical thinking, and metaphysics was too anchored in fairy tale to order reality.

For Arnold the balance of personal and public, political and moral, social and religious was not easily achieved and could not be held without constant critical examination. Arnold rejected the personal God of popular religion and drew his knowledge of God from the verifiable effect in this world of the idea of God. From within this definition, to see the will of God one had to know the world and critically examine it. Poetry and criticism became in one sense the modernist intellectual's path of pilgrimage. Trilling, and many others since, have characterized Arnold's way of thinking as dialectical or Hegelian because he constantly tried to translate emotion into action, aesthetic beauty into cultural harmony, and religion into righteousness. For Trilling, "Arnold's eclectic and dialectical method has its vitality exactly because it is the method of history."[2]

Arnold's criticism is an effort to affect the dialectic of history, a motivation that we see acted out in the many essays and books he wrote to reply to reviews of previous work. Arnold's public voice was not a conciliatory one, but it did not evade the confusing relations of class and society or, as Arac argues, stand "passive before a future" in which he relied on prophecy to "validate him" (Arac, 117). Although the melancholy part of Arnold was tempted to remain in the "desert" of a ruined historical, aesthetic, and religious faith, he did not do so. He looked hard at France after the Revolution and tried to articulate for his countrymen a concept of democracy in which the people became the state instead of positioning themselves in opposition to it. He studied rigorously the education systems of Europe and sought reform of public schools in England. Arnold's poetry is the site of his struggle to make emotion *do* something that could animate and ennoble. In fidelity to his beliefs, when he could not make his poetry fulfill that expectation, he withdrew it or turned away from writing it. His prose is the dialectical effort to influence history and belief.

Although Arnold was in many ways a man of convention, his life and work, as Russell Jacoby observes, "explode conventional political categories" (Jacoby, 90). The same might also be said of religious categories. The son of Thomas Arnold of Rugby Chapel wrote more about religion than any other major Victorian writer of the age. He wrote in order to show the essential and lasting meaning in the Bible, but his method of doing so was to take all the metaphysics out of belief. Religion translated as conduct in the world of human relations. Despite his obvious earnestness, in his time he was considered by many to be religion's most cleverly hostile critic. He also wrote more about public education than any other major Victorian writer, but his topic was not the grandeur of "the idea of a university" so much as the idea of appropriate elementary and secondary school curricula for the masses. In politics, he believed in democracy, not as a traditional liberal who opposed the power of the state over the individual, but as one who, distrusting the wisdom of each class to lead, nevertheless felt that a strong democratic state was the only form of government one could defend.

In his day and in ours Arnold has been an easy target for critics because his ideas, complex and contextualized by experience and critical observation, do not follow clear ideological lines. Yet the connecting lines of the main currents of his thought about literature, democracy, and religion are essentially consistent. Anchored in the practical realities of experience, Arnold always looked to the metaphoric language he called poetry to construct the harmony that could give the multitextured and confusing surface of life an inner sense of beauty and peace. In his early work he thought of the poet as one who had to be above the fray of life in order to see and know, but in time he looked to the fray as the source of experience that could verify the truth of the poet, or of the religious teacher. No truth too abstract to help us know how to live was worth his consideration. No religious belief about other worlds or miracles could seduce his commitment to practiced morality. No poetry that did not "do" something for us was worth writing.

Arnold was not without his prejudices and insensitivities, and these were primarily directed to those who aggressively challenged the established order. Many would label him an elitist, but his desire to educate, to bring the masses along with the progress of the society, was a stronger, more consistent motivation than his occasional haughty and dismissive attitudes toward the rowdy or the Puritan dissenter. The primary targets of his concern were the working class that sought to organize labor and change political order and the religious dissenters who would disestablish the Church of England. Arnold's criticism makes it clear that he, too, had strong disagreements and critical observations about politics, the state, and the church, but he valued tradition and reasonableness in reform above radical alternatives. The source of much of his criticism of dissent was his belief that "doing as one likes" would undo the need to build collectively amid the chaos of an individualist agenda. Arnold's belief in the State as the best vehicle for overcoming the limits of any one class, limits he had scathingly outlined in *Culture and Anarchy*, represents the practical application he tried to make of his beliefs in such values as equality and democracy. His blindness was, of course, that he did not understand that others might not be able to share his confidence that the State, or the church, was in the end the best way to represent the whole.

Reading Matthew Arnold after the events of the twentieth century, one sees in his practical idealism a kind of innocence of the possibilities of murderous evil and oppression that have stunned the consciousness of his inheritors of European culture. If it is hard to displace Arnold's solutions with ideas that are better, it is also difficult fully to trust them. Arnold's criticism was from within the value system of the society and religion he knew, but it was not a genuinely deconstructive criticism. It did not open up those systems of belief to a profound revaluation of values such as Nietzsche began and others have continued. Arnold gives us a genealogy of miracles, but not of morals. One of the lessons of the twentieth century is that it is dangerous to accept received values without probing them further than Arnold did.

The question that underlies all of Arnold's work—how to live—remains the central and increasingly desperate question of modern times. His answers were characteristically more pragmatic than idealistic or ideological. Arnold insisted that he was not a philosopher, but his philosophical inclinations resonate with the thinking of other nineteenth-century pragmatists. His concern was that morals be enacted, not just described, and that the measure of good was how effectively one could translate morality into a way of living. Jesus could be called a son of God because his life was a translation into conduct of principles of righteousness, not because he had divine origins. Conduct, not one's inner life or ideological or moral intent, was how the individual and the state made goodness a reality in the world.

Perhaps more important to us today than his actual ideas about the state, or culture, or poetry, or Jesus, is the method of critical thought Arnold espoused. Sweetness and light have dimmed in our politicized world, but the need for a disinterested criticism is greater than ever when the claims of ideology and the seductions of an invasive media play insistently on our consciousness. The inescapable cultural construction of values makes a genuinely disinterested criticism an ideal beyond full realization, but an increasingly diverse culture of competing claims and opposing values makes it an ever more desirable way of trying to think.

Writing in 1949 in a new preface just 10 years after the original publication of his landmark study of Arnold, and one year before the publication of *The Liberal Imagination,* Lionel Trilling observes that, though "the Third Reich has fallen," the "assault on mind which the Nazis made has not failed," only its voices have changed.[3] Further, he warns, it is dangerous to assume that only those on the opposite side are the source of absolutism. "Our liberals and intellectuals," Trilling writes, "have become even less eager than ten years ago to see the object as it really is, less willing to believe that in a time of change and danger openness and flexibility of mind are, as Arnold said, the first of virtues" (Trilling 1949, n.p.). The dangers Trilling saw in 1949 have taken many different forms but have not lessened. In what Louis Menand has called the philosophical "patrolling" of the academy by those outside it, the struggle to defend intellectual ideas that undermined the established Western tradition politicized the humanities.[4] These quarrels, often bitter and rigid on both sides, were known in the media as "political correctness," a phrase the Right associated with the Communist Party and that the Left associated with McCarthyism. Those on the right who often cited Arnold in their defense of culture did not recall his insistence on the free play of thought. The embrace of a post-structuralist critique of values should have waved the academy away from ideological certainties with which the Left often responded. The process of revaluation of values by postmodern theory became, in the absence of an Arnoldian critical tact, culture *wars.* The liberating insights and revitalization of scholarship that came in the wake of new theoretical directions were bloodied by ideological attacks from both the Left and the Right that have damaged the public standing of our disciplines and our profession as a whole. Arnold's effort to reason objectively, to see things whole, to distance himself from emotionally blinding involvement, offers us a useful model of critical and analytical thinking that criticism needs and our profession is again tentatively embracing. If it is not a model we can fully realize or absolutely believe, it nevertheless remains one that is worth pursuing.

Notes

Chapter One

1. This quotation appears in a note in *The Complete Prose Works of Matthew Arnold*, 11 vols., ed. R. H. Super (Ann Arbor: University of Michigan Press, 1960–77), 10:464; *Complete Prose Works* hereafter cited in text as *Prose* by volume and page number.

2. Letter to his mother on June 5, 1869, in *The Letters of Matthew Arnold*, 3 vols., ed. Cecil Y. Lang (Charlottesville: University Press of Virginia, 1996–98), 3:347; quotations from the *Letters* hereafter cited in text as *Letters* by volume and page number.

3. Jonathan Arac, *Critical Genealogies: Historical Situations for Postmodern Literary Studies* (New York: Columbia University Press, 1987), 121; hereafter cited in text.

4. Gertrude Himmelfarb, "Dissent and Dogma," *The New Republic* June 13, 1994, 45–48; reprinted as review essay of *Culture and Anarchy*, ed. Samuel Lipman, in *Nineteenth Century Prose* 21, no. 2 (1994): 47.

5. Raymond Williams, *Culture and Society 1780–1950* (New York: Columbia University Press, 1958), 125; hereafter cited in text.

6. Edward W. Said, *Culture and Imperialism* (New York: Knopf, 1993; reprint, New York: Vintage Books, 1994), 105; hereafter cited in text as Said 1994.

7. Edward W. Said, *Orientalism* (New York: Pantheon Books, 1978; reprint, New York: Vintage Books, 1979), 228.

8. T. S. Eliot, "Francis Herbert Bradley," in *Selected Essays* (New York: Harcourt, Brace & World, 1964), 398.

9. Russell Jacoby, *The End of Utopia* (New York: Basic Books, 1999); hereafter cited in text.

10. Donald D. Stone, *Communications with the Future: Matthew Arnold in Dialogue* (Ann Arbor: University of Michigan Press, 1997), v.

11. Chapter 6 of this study will look at the essays in the Lipman edition in more detail.

12. The "Marguerite" poems are "Meeting," "Parting," "Isolation. To Marguerite," "To Marguerite—Continued," "A Farewell," "Absence," and "The Terrace at Berne."

13. Nicholas Shrimpton, "One Life or Two? What Happened to Arnold After 1853," review of *A Life of Matthew Arnold*, by Nicholas Murray, *Times Literary Supplement*, June 14, 1996, 5; hereafter cited in text.

14. Helen Vendler, "The Unburied Life," *The New Republic* June 21, 1999, 48.

15. Thomas Arnold is the model of the headmaster in Thomas Hughes's *Tom Brown's School Days,* a "novel" published in 1857 that recalls Hughes's years at Rugby.

16. See Nicholas Murray, *A Life of Matthew Arnold* (New York: St. Martin's Press, 1996), 66, for a fuller discussion of Lord Lansdowne. Murray hereafter cited in text.

17. Park Honan, in *Matthew Arnold: A Life* (London: Weidenfeld and Nicolson, 1981; reprint, Cambridge, Mass.: Harvard University Press, 1983), suggests that Arnold's visit of 1848 was a rendezvous with a woman he already knew. Honan hereafter cited in text.

18. This well-known cliché about lost love was originally a heartfelt line from Tennyson's *In Memoriam* spoken about his dear dead friend, Arthur Hallam.

19. A number of parodies of uneven cleverness satirize Arnold's doom and gloom honeymoon poems. The two most famous are "Dover Bitch" and "Chartreuse Blues."

20. Honan (247–60) provides a good overview of not only Arnold's work but the politics of the office that coordinated school inspection.

21. See Murray (348–51) for an account of Arnold's death.

22. Matthew Arnold, "Introduction: Democracy," in *Prose,* 2:7; hereafter cited in text as "Democracy" by volume and page number.

23. Lionel Trilling, *Matthew Arnold* (New York: W. W. Norton, 1939), 179; hereafter cited in text as Trilling 1939.

Chapter Two

1. Murray says that Arnold's brother, Tom, is the source of the characterization as a "social lion" (47).

2. All dates connected with the writing and publication of the poems are from *The Poems of Matthew Arnold,* 2d ed., ed. Kenneth Allott and Miriam Allott (London: Longman, 1979); hereafter cited in text as *Poems,* with citations from the text of the poems identified by line number.

3. J. Hillis Miller, *The Disappearance of God* (Cambridge, Mass.: Harvard University Press, 1963; reprint, New York: Schocken Books, 1965), 226; hereafter cited in text as Miller 1965.

4. The phrase is from Walter Houghton's landmark *The Victorian Frame of Mind* (New Haven, Conn.: Yale University Press, 1957). Though Houghton's study was more complex, later critics tended to see the tension of the Victorian mind as between two opposing views, experiences, voices, landscapes, and so forth. Arnold's habit of posing two views within one poem, for example, Empedocles and Callicles, led critics in particular to pursue this binary structure in describing his state of mind.

5. Nineteenth-century Englishmen used the term "race" broadly to define as "other" a wide range of peoples with dark complexions and non-British origins. In *Wuthering Heights,* for example, Nelly Dean calls Heathcliff a "gipsy" and speculates that he may have come from Spain, Madagascar ("a little Lascar"), America, China, or India, origins that might make him racially Indian, Asian, or Negro. As Deborah Epstein Nord writes in her recent essay, "'Marks of Race': Gypsy Figures and Eccentric Femininity in Nineteenth-Century Women's Writing," *Victorian Studies* 41 (Winter 1998): 189–210, "In nineteenth-century lore, gypsies were considered not merely a distinct group with specific social practices and means of subsistence but a separate race" (189).

6. Trilling 1939, 16; Trilling speculates that Arnold was in part "Byronizing" in his portrait of a ruined Rome (1939, 16).

7. Trilling observes that Cromwell was "an attractive subject for a young man in an age unsure of the future of democracy, especially a young man concerned with the problems of laissez-faire and the Ten Hours' Bill, whose father was a friend of Carlyle and the champion of the non-priestly church for which Cromwell had fought. Nevertheless, the real significance of the poem was neither political nor religious, but profoundly personal; it is young Matthew himself who is aghast at the awfulness of being the moral vessel of truth" (1939, 17).

8. Alaric conquered Rome in A.D. 410 and died later that same year while invading Sicily.

9. Alan Grob, "Arnold's 'Mycerinus': The Fate of Pleasure," *Victorian Poetry* 20 (Spring 1982): 13; hereafter cited in text as Grob 1982.

10. Matthew Arnold to John Duke Coleridge, April 11, 1843 (*Letters,* 1:54).

11. Almost 25 years after his Cromwell poem, the nature of British rule in Jamaica was more likely to have caught Arnold's attention. In 1865 E. J. Eyre, the British Governor of Jamaica, ordered an assault on the black population in retaliation for the killing of some whites. Edward Said argues that Arnold approved of this kind of action as "a deterrent to rampant disorder—colonial, Irish, domestic," and that Arnold's readers, if they look at them at all, regard them "as irrelevant to the more important cultural theory that Arnold appears to be promoting for all the ages" (1994, 130–31). Arnold unquestionably favored force to quell riots, but Said's conclusion that he approved an order to massacre a group of people in retaliation perhaps extends the inferences too far.

12. Christopher Hill, *God's Englishman* (London: Penguin, 1972), 112–13; hereafter cited in text.

13. Not all critics would agree. A. Dwight Culler, in *Imaginative Reason: The Poetry of Matthew Arnold* (New Haven, Conn.: Yale University Press, 1966), sees both Alaric and Cromwell as types of the "madman" (45). Culler hereafter cited in text.

14. The headnote to the poem provides the sources from Herodotus that Arnold used (*Poems,* 26–27).

15. David G. Riede, *Matthew Arnold and the Betrayal of Language* (Charlottesville: University Press of Virginia, 1988), 46; hereafter cited in text.

16. Allan Brick, in "Equilibrium in the Poetry of Matthew Arnold," *University of Toronto Quarterly* 30 (1960): 49, says "His withdrawal is to be neither a retirement nor an escape, but a modest affirmation."

17. To say Arnold resisted sexual attraction and the distraction of women is not to say that he always succeeded. The love poems to "Marguerite" are charged with sexual attraction. In general, however, Arnold considered women a distraction that he did not need, unless, of course, they were his mother or sister, whose intellectual companionship he deeply valued.

18. William E. Buckler, in *On the Poetry of Matthew Arnold* (New York: New York University Press, 1982), argues that the poem returns to an "imaginative solution" and that Arnold's open-ended form frees him "from the moral disposition that a poet may take from his sources or from his own time-frame" (22). Buckler hereafter cited in text.

19. Matthew Arnold, "Literature and Science," in *Prose,* 10:68; hereafter cited in text as "Science" by volume and page number.

20. Alfred Tennyson, *The Poems of Tennyson,* ed. Christopher Ricks (London: Longmans, 1969), 1,671; hereafter cited in text.

Chapter Three

1. The most recent biography of Arnold, Ian Hamilton's *A Gift Imprisoned: The Poetic Life of Matthew Arnold* (New York: Basic Books, 1999), makes accounting for Arnold's turn from poetry the focus of his work.

2. Culler (53–54) gives a sometimes humorous account of the reception of Arnold's first book among friends and family, quoting Edward Quillinan's letter to Henry Crabb Robinson, "To tell you the truth much as I do like the Arnolds, & more than like some of them, Jane & her Mother for example, I never suspected there was any *poetry* in the family till I read M.A.'s."

3. In reality, Arnold's mother also wrote poetry. See Honan (7–8) for a sample of her verse.

4. The exact dating of Arnold's poems continues to be a scholarly problem. As Nicholas Shrimpton remarked, our ignorance of the dates of composition of these poems makes "the attempt to write a narrative history of Arnold's creative life between 1845 and 1853 . . . a high risk process" (4).

5. Alan Roper, in *Arnold's Poetic Landscapes* (Baltimore, Md.: Johns Hopkins University Press, 1969), thinks that "The Strayed Reveller" is a "more likely referent" (122).

6. G. Robert Stange, *Matthew Arnold. The Poet As Humanist.* (Princeton, N.J.: Princeton University Press, 1967), 52; hereafter cited in text.

7. Arnold drafted the synopsis in a letter to Clough in March, 1849. It is printed in *Letters* (1:137–138) and in *Poems* (48–49).

8. W. B. Yeats, *The Collected Poems of W. B. Yeats* (London: Macmillan, 1950), 101.

9. Quoted in the headnote to the poem in Tennyson (400).

10. Critics have occasionally looked at the relationship between Arnold and Clough as more "conflicted" than a close friendship between heterosexual men might be. See Herbert Sussman, *Victorian Masculinities* (Cambridge: Cambridge University Press, 1995), for a study of the conflicts in Victorian male identity. See Joseph Bristow, " 'Love, let us be true to one another': Matthew Arnold, Arthur Hugh Clough, and 'our Aqueous Ages,' " *Literature and History* 4 (1995): 27–49, for a recent essay interested in "the sexual ebbs and flows" of several poems by Arnold and Clough (28). Bristow is not "trying to concoct a previously unknown homoeroticism between Arnold and Clough," but he does stress the "intense intimacy" of an "impassioned attachment" expressed in "amatory declarations." He argues that both men felt a hostility to women, marriage, and reproduction. My own view is that Arnold, taking himself very seriously, resisted women in his early twenties because his sexual attraction to them might derail his earnest search for his poetic identity. Arnold's life contains a series of typically happy and intimate relationships with women, beginning with his mother, his sister, Jane ("K"), and ending with his wife and daughters. Both Arnold and Clough soon enough are caught up in romantic tangles with women, and Arnold had a long, happy, and apparently, intimate marriage. Arnold no doubt had a distaste for, shall we say, unhallowed sex, but he seems no worse about this than other "liberal" Victorian men. Clough's poetry was a bit notorious for a preoccupation (for a Victorian) with sexual relations with women.

11. The footnote in *Poems,* for example, suggests that the pictorial detail "may have been worked up partly to compensate for the lack of rhyme and conventional meter" (68n). My reading is that these details are crucial to defining the vision of the true poet.

12. Stange is one critic who does. See his discussion on pp. 54–70.

13. In a nicely ironic biographical note in *Poems* (90), we learn that the original group leader was a *Captain* Hamilton who apparently organized the trip for the family by means of carriage and walking.

14. Stange (57) says that the poem "displays so complex a use of definition by contrast (of what I have called Arnold's 'this-but-not-that' method) that the reader must exert himself to discriminate its meanings."

15. Arnold supplied a long note to the poem when it was published again in 1868 and 1869. Allott reprints the note in *Poems* (135–36).

16. Aside from Honan's theory that "Marguerite" was really Mary Claude, a summer neighbor to the Arnold family, no one has ever identified who "Marguerite" might have been. Other biographers, such as Murray, have not accepted Honan's explanation, preferring to leave the matter open to speculation. Honan's theory has the strength of explaining how such a deep relation-

ship could have developed and some biographical evidence to suggest that Arnold's friends knew of his interest in her. Honan's case makes "Marguerite" an intelligent and accomplished woman of the literary world, a demystifying explanation that does lack the more familiar, and more misogynist, notions of a pert young miss in a Swiss kerchief with a shady past.

Chapter Four

1. In an 1849 letter to Arnold from his friend, J. C. Shairp. For an account of this correspondence see C. B. Tinker and H. F. Lowry, eds., *The Poetry of Matthew Arnold: A Commentary* (New York: Russell and Russell, 1940), 287.

2. The discussion of *Empedocles on Etna* in this chapter is a revision of my essay, "Empedocles, Suicide, and the Order of Things," *Victorian Poetry* 26 (1988): 75–90. See also Linda Lee Ray [Pratt], "Callicles on Etna: The Other Mask," *Victorian Poetry* 7 (1969): 309–20, for other ideas about the poem that are background for my thinking.

3. Every generation of critics of Arnold's work have given the poem major attention. Among the most notable essays or chapters in books that focus on *Empedocles on Etna* are Walter Houghton, "Arnold's *Empedocles on Etna*," *Victorian Studies* 1 (1958; hereafter cited in text); Culler's chapter in *Imaginative Reasoning* (153–77); Buckler's discussion in *On the Poetry of Matthew Arnold* (119–46); Riede's discussion in *Matthew Arnold and the Betrayal of Language* (78–94); Roper's discussion in *Arnold's Poetic Landscapes* (183–208); and Paul Zietlow's essay "Heard but Unheeded: The Songs of Callicles in Matthew Arnold's *Empedocles on Etna*," *Victorian Poetry* 21, no. 3 (1983): 241–56.

4. Matthew Arnold, "Preface to First Edition of *Poems*," in *Prose* 1:1, 2–3; hereafter cited in text as "Preface" 1853 by volume and page number.

5. J. Hillis Miller, *The Linguistic Moment* (Princeton, N.J.: Princeton University Press, 1985), 30. Hereafter cited in text as Miller 1985.

6. Matthew Arnold, "Wordsworth," in *Prose*, 9:46.

7. Matthew Arnold, "Preface to Second Edition of *Poems*," in *Prose* 1:16; hereafter cited in text as "Preface" 1854 by volume and page number.

8. In 1867 Arnold again reprinted the poem with a note that he did so at the urging of Robert Browning. The poetic and emotional crisis that *Empedocles* captured in the younger Arnold had apparently been resolved by that time. The lyrics of Callicles, which relate stories from classical mythology, were often reprinted separately from the poem.

9. Matthew Arnold, "Spinoza and the Bible," in *Prose*, 3:176.

10. George Rosen, *Madness in Society* (Chicago: University of Chicago Press, 1968), 178.

11. George Burrows, *Commentaries on the Causes, Forms, Symptoms, and Treatment, Moral and Medical, of Insanity* (London: 1828), 18.

12. Henry Romilly Fedden, *Suicide: A Social and Historical Study* (London: Peter Davies, 1938), 247.

13. Emile Durkheim, *Suicide* (Paris: F. Alcan, 1897), 336.

14. The term is from Michel Foucault, *The Order of Things* (New York: Vintage Books, 1973), 323; hereafter cited in text.

15. Matthew Arnold, "On the Modern Element in Literature," in *Prose,* 1:32; hereafter cited in text as "Modern" by volume and page number.

Chapter Five

1. The poem has frequently been interpreted as being about the nature of art. Beverly Taylor, "Imagination and Art in Arnold's 'Tristram and Iseult': The Importance of 'Making,' " *Studies in English Literature 1500–1900* 22, no. 4 (1982): 633–45, argues that "the created form—whether tapestry, poem, or dream—can be accepted and interpreted precisely because it is art rather than life" (634). William A. Ulmer, "Romantic Modernity in Arnold's 'Tristram and Iseult,' " *Texas Studies in Literature and Languages* 27, no. 1 (1985): 62–85, says that the poem is Arnold's "most artfully self-conscious interrogation of art" (62). See also Robert A. Greenberg, "Matthew Arnold's Refuge of Art: 'Tristram and Iseult,' " *Victorian Newsletter,* no. 25 (Spring 1964): 1–4; M. G. Sundell, "The Intellectual Background and Structure of Arnold's 'Tristram and Iseult,' " *Victorian Poetry* 1, no. 4 (1963): 272–83; and Riede, 127–34.

2. J. L. Kendall, "The Unity of Arnold's 'Tristram and Iseult,' " *Victorian Poetry* 1, no. 2 (1963): 140–45, argues that "it is quite possible and indeed much more logical to regard the narrator as a character in his own right" (144).

3. The trope is from Henry James who used it to describe the Jamesian narrative technique.

4. Culler includes the children, who listen attentively to their mother's story as sharing in the process: "Through art they and their mother distanced themselves from their experience, achieved control over it, and transformed it into a thing of beauty" (150).

5. The Allotts do so in their edition of *The Complete Poems.* They also associate the description of Vivian with "Marguerite" (236).

6. See in particular Barbara Fass Leavy, "Iseult of Brittany: A New Interpretation of Matthew Arnold's 'Tristram and Iseult,' " *Victorian Poetry* 18, no. 1 (1980): 1–22. Leavy argues that the poem is an example of "female fantasy" in which Iseult uses the legend of Merlin and Vivian "to project herself imaginatively into the role of her rival and conceive of a relationship in which she is the adventurous and dominating rather than passive and submissive partner" (3). Riede also believes Iseult immerses herself deeply into fantasy as escape from reality (128).

7. Ruth apRoberts, *Arnold and God* (Berkeley: University of California Press, 1983), 8; hereafter cited in text.

8. Culler notes that "the French word for daisy is *marguerite,*" a point he thinks may mean that "Arnold had left his personal signature in one corner of his painting" (151).

9. Buckler notes that in "Dover Beach" the "movement from quiet, well-anchored serenity to torrential despair is lacking in external motivation" (104). Douglas Bush, *Matthew Arnold: A Survey of His Poetry and Prose* (New York: Collier-Macmillan, 1971), observes that the transfer of ebb and flow from human misery to The Sea of Faith is not wholly logical (76).

10. Ruth Ann Pitman, in "On Dover Beach," *Essays in Criticism* 23 (1973): 109–36, argues that the poem "is made up of a series of incomplete sonnets" (129).

11. See in particular Riede, who notes echoes of Wordsworth, Milton, and Shakespeare (199–200).

12. Riede notes that Arnold is not describing the real monastery but "a literary monastery from the tradition of Gothic novels" (122).

13. Alan Grob, in "Arnold's 'The Scholar-Gipsy': The Use and Abuse of History," *Victorian Poetry* 34, no. 2 (1996): 149–74, notes that instead of standing as a beacon of hope, Arnold's scholar-gypsy "express[es] nothing so much as desperation, denial, and despair, with any progressively conceived historical expectations repeatedly undermined and undone by the strategies and tactics of Arnoldian representation" (150–51).

14. George Saintsbury's 1899 commentary in *Matthew Arnold* is the hallmark example of this view.

15. In *Poems* (368), Allott gives a useful summary of Brown's argument, which appeared in the *Revue Anglo-Americaine* 12 (1934–1945): 224–25.

16. See *Poems* (482) for a discussion of the review that sparked the letter.

17. The paraphrase is, of course, from section 5 of T. S. Eliot's *The Waste Land*.

Chapter Six

1. Matthew Arnold, *Culture and Anarchy* in *Prose*, 5:99; hereafter cited in text as *Culture* by volume and page number.

2. Matthew Arnold, *A French Eton*, in *Prose*, 2:325.

3. Super notes that Arnold printed the report "on his own account" and later received from Longmans a bill for more than £80 (in *Prose*, 2:331).

4. See Trilling (1939, 179–89) for a discussion of Arnold's liberalism.

5. Matthew Arnold, "On Translating Homer," in *Prose*, 1:140; hereafter cited in text as "Homer" by volume and page number.

6. Arnold draws the line from Goethe and applies it to Heinrich Heine ("Heinrich Heine" in *Prose*, 3:108; hereafter cited in text as "Heine" by volume and page number).

7. Matthew Arnold, "The Function of Criticism at the Present Time," in *Prose*, 3:261; hereafter cited in text as "Function" by volume and page number.

8. Matthew Arnold, "The Study of Poetry," in *Prose* 9:161; hereafter cited in text as "Study" by volume and page number.

9. The essay ends by affirming that good literature will never lose its supremacy, even if "an era is opening in which we are to see multitudes of a common sort of readers, and masses of a common sort of literature; that such readers do not want and could not relish anything better than such literature, and that to provide it is becoming a vast and profitable industry" ("Study," 9:188). The "momentary appearances" that good literature has "lost currency with the world" has, despite Arnold's efforts, stretched into a very long moment and a vast and profitable industry.

10. This book apparently sold much better than his first report and as he had refused to handle its publication, he was not stuck with unexpected bills! (Super in *Prose*, 4:351).

11. All of Arnold's discussions about education refer to boys and men, who were, at the time, the only sex to go to the universities.

12. Matthew Arnold, *Schools and Universities on the Continent* in *Prose*, 4:290; hereafter cited in text as *Schools* by volume and page number.

13. "F. A. Wolf" [Mark Pattison] in *North British Review*, June 1865, 249, 252–54, according to Super's notes to the text in *Prose*, 4:381. According to Murray, Pattison is thought to have been the model for George Eliot's Casaubon in *Middlemarch* (289).

14. "We are called to this knowledge by special aptitudes which are born with us; the grand thing in teaching is to have faith that some aptitudes of this kind everyone has" (*Schools*, 4:300).

15. Super's notes cite this quotation from Arnold's letter to his younger daughter as part of the account of the 29 times he gave the lecture in the United States in about four months (*Prose*, 10:464–65).

16. Jacoby's use of "liberalism and the Enlightenment" in the context of twentieth-century criticism is somewhat confusing, but he seems to use it to suggest the role of the state in assisting the individual to economic, educational, and legal equality. The liberal state has often been criticized as a paternalistic oppressor whose massive powers actually limit the individual's freedom. In some ways Arnold's focus on the state as the center of power looks forward to modern liberalism in which the state is the vital source of rights and the protector and enforcer of them. In the nineteenth century in the United States, the conflict between "states' rights" or the supremacy of the Union played out in a Civil War the essential debate between Mill and Arnold on doing as one likes.

17. Steven Marcus, "*Culture and Anarchy* Today," in *Culture and Anarchy*, by Matthew Arnold, ed. Samuel Lipman (New Haven, Conn.: Yale University Press, 1994), 179; hereafter cited in text.

18. Gerald Graff, "Arnold, Reason, and Common Culture," in *Culture and Anarchy*, by Matthew Arnold, ed. Samuel Lipman (New Haven, Conn.: Yale University Press, 1994), 187; hereafter cited in text.

19. Maurice Cowling, "One-and-a-half-Cheers for Matthew Arnold," in *Culture and Anarchy,* by Matthew Arnold, ed. Samuel Lipman (New Haven, Conn.: Yale University Press, 1994), 212.

20. The quotations from the preface to *Culture and Anarchy* are taken from Samuel Lipman, ed., *Culture and Anarchy,* by Matthew Arnold, Rethinking the Western Tradition series (New Haven, Conn.: Yale University Press, 1994), 5; hereafter cited in text as Lipman. The Lipman edition uses the preface found in Arnold's 1869 version of *Culture and Anarchy*; this preface is not contained in Super's *Collected Prose Works* of Arnold.

21. This perhaps embarrassing reflection on his father appeared in the first edition of *Culture and Anarchy* and was cut from subsequent editions. It does not appear in the Super edition. This reference is from the Lipman edition, which uses the text of the first edition.

22. Arnold has occasionally been taken to task by contemporary scholars for his pejorative use of a term associated with Jews. He draws the term from the Old Testament discipline of obedience to the law, but he associates it in the essay with Christianity, in particular the zealous Protestants of his day.

23. For a reading that sees *Culture and Anarchy* as more reflective of "a new possibility for Christianity," see apRoberts, chapter 6.

Chapter Seven

1. Matthew Arnold, "Preface" to *God and the Bible* in *Prose,* 7:378; hereafter cited in text as *God.*

2. See James C. Livingston, *Matthew Arnold and Christianity* (Columbia: University of South Carolina Press, 1986), 178–90, for an excellent account of Arnold's place in modern religious thought. Livingston sees Arnold as reflecting ideas from nineteenth-century Protestant liberalism and modernist Catholicism. Livingston hereafter cited in text.

3. These quotations come from line 133 of "Stanzas in Memory of the Author of 'Obermann,'" (*Poems,* 142); Matthew Arnold, *St. Paul and Protestantism* in *Prose,* 6:10 (hereafter cited in text as *St. Paul* by volume and page number); and Matthew Arnold, *Literature and Dogma* in *Prose,* 6:196 (hereafter cited in text as *Dogma* by volume and page number).

4. Basil Willey, "Arnold and Religion," in *Matthew Arnold,* ed. Kenneth Allott (London: G. Bell and Sons, 1975), 245.

5. T. S. Eliot, "Arnold and Pater," in *Selected Essays* (New York: Harcourt, Brace & World, 1964), 388; hereafter cited in text.

6. Arnold's education about Christianity surpassed his expertise in Hebrew studies, a limitation that needs to be weighed when he comments on Judaism.

7. Arnold uses the name "Israel" both in the singular and plural to mean the Jews of the Old Testament.

Chapter Eight

    1. Basil Willey, *Nineteenth Century Studies* (New York: Columbia University Press, 1949), 251.

    2. This quotation is from Trilling's "Introduction"(1939, xiii).

    3. This quotation is from Trilling's "Preface to the Second Edition," which first appeared in the 1949 edition of *Matthew Arnold.* The preface has no pagination; hereafter cited in text as Trilling 1949.

    4. Louis Menand, "The Limits of Academic Freedom," in *The Future of Academic Freedom,* ed. Louis Menand (Chicago: University of Chicago Press, 1996), 3.

Selected Bibliography

PRIMARY WORKS

The Complete Prose Works of Matthew Arnold. Ed. R. H. Super. 11 vols. Ann Arbor: University of Michigan Press, 1960–77.

Essays, Letters, and Reviews. Ed. Fraser Neiman. Cambridge, Mass.: Harvard University Press, 1960.

The Letters of Matthew Arnold. Ed. Cecil Y. Lang. 3 vols. Charlottesville: University Press of Virginia, 1996–98.

The Poems of Matthew Arnold. Ed. Kenneth Allott and Miriam Allott. London: Longman, 1979.

Biographies

Bonnerot, Louis. *Matthew Arnold, poète: Essai de biographie psychologique.* Paris: Didier, 1947. An insightful French interpretation of the psychological life behind many of Arnold's best-known poems.

Chambers, E. K. *Matthew Arnold.* London: Oxford University Press, 1947. A short overview of Arnold's life based on generally known materials.

Hamilton, Ian. *A Gift Imprisoned: The Poetic Life of Matthew Arnold.* New York: Basic Books, 1999. A new account of why Arnold did not continue to write poetry. Hamilton laments that Arnold's shift from poetry to prose was a battle that Arnold unfortunately lost.

Honan, Park. *Matthew Arnold: A Life.* London: Weidenfeld and Nicolson, 1981; reprint, Cambridge, Mass.: Harvard University Press, 1983. A major and lively account of Arnold's life with research not available to the earlier biographers. Honan's study is best known for his thesis that "Marguerite" was Arnold's holiday neighbor, Mary Claude.

Murray, Nicholas. *A Life of Matthew Arnold.* New York: St. Martin's Press, 1996. A comprehensive biographical study that disagrees with Honan that the evidence clearly identifies "Marguerite" as Mary Claude.

Trilling, Lionel. *Matthew Arnold.* New York: W. W. Norton, 1939; reprint, New York: Columbia University Press, 1949. An influential study of Arnold that places him within the context of traditional liberal thought.

Ward, Mrs. Humphry [Mary Augusta Arnold]. *A Writer's Recollections.* 2 vols. New York: Harper & Brothers, 1918. A lively and sometimes humorous account of Arnold's early life written by his niece from within the perspective of the family circle.

SECONDARY WORKS

Books and Sections of Books

Alexander, Edward. *Matthew Arnold and John Stuart Mill.* New York: Columbia University Press, 1968. Contrasts Arnold's and Mill's liberalism.

————. *Matthew Arnold, John Ruskin, and the Modern Temper.* Columbus: Ohio State University Press, 1973. Explores Arnold's use of classical literature to define the "modern" temper and contrasts him with Ruskin's sense of the pervasive melancholy of Victorian modernism.

Allott, Kenneth A. "A Background for *Empedocles on Etna.*" In *Essays and Studies 1968,* ed. Simeon Potter. London: John Murray, 1968.

————, ed. *Matthew Arnold.* London: G. Bell and Sons, 1975. An excellent collection of essays by noted scholars, including David De Laura and Basil Willey.

Allott, Miriam, ed. *Essays and Studies: Matthew Arnold A Centennial Review.* London: John Murray, 1988. Essays, mainly on the poetry of Arnold in the context of his time by such scholars as John Farrell and Nicholas Shrimpton.

Anderson, Warren D. *Matthew Arnold and the Classical Tradition.* Ann Arbor: University of Michigan Press, 1965. Explores Arnold's knowledge of and use of classical literary traditions.

apRoberts, Ruth. *Arnold and God.* Berkeley: University of California Press, 1983. One of the best contemporary studies of Arnold's religious beliefs, especially their relationship to modernist ideas.

Arac, Jonathan. *Critical Genealogies.* New York: Columbia University Press, 1987. Chapter 5 on "Matthew Arnold and English Studies: The Power of Prophecy" examines the influence of Arnold and evaluates his use for contemporary theorists.

Bloom, Harold, ed. *Modern Critical Views: Matthew Arnold.* New York: Chelsea House, 1987. A collection of some of the best known commentaries from such critics as J. Hillis Miller and A. Dwight Culler. Includes one new essay by Sara Suleri on reading *Empedocles on Etna.*

Buckler, William E. *On the Poetry of Matthew Arnold.* New York: New York University Press, 1982. Sound readings of many of the major poems with a special interest in their independence of autobiographical contexts.

Bush, Douglas. *Matthew Arnold: A Survey of His Poetry and Prose.* New York: Macmillan, 1971. A useful introductory survey of Arnold's body of work.

Carroll, Joseph. *The Cultural Theory of Matthew Arnold.* Berkeley: University of California Press, 1982. An important study that examines Arnold's theories about culture in both the poetry and prose to make the case that Arnold's critical value rests primarily in his ideas and reasoning, not on his humane sensibility.

Christ, Carol T. *Victorian and Modern Poetics.* Chicago: University of Chicago Press, 1984. In this important study of the continuities between Victorian and modern poetry, Christ examines the way in which Arnold's poetry represents the tensions Victorian poets expressed about history.

Collini, Stefan. *Arnold*. Oxford: Oxford University Press, 1988. Overview of Arnold's rhetoric in terms of his tone and temper of mind.

Coulling, Sidney. *Matthew Arnold and His Critics: A Study of His Controversies*. Athens: Ohio University Press, 1974. Useful study of the critical attacks on Arnold.

Culler, A. Dwight. *Imaginative Reason: The Poetry of Matthew Arnold*. New Haven, Conn.: Yale University Press, 1966. Influential study of how Arnold's poetry addresses his central problem of how we are to live. Chapters on *Empedocles on Etna*, "The Scholar-Gipsy," and "Tristram and Iseult."

Dale, Peter Allan. *The Victorian Critic and the Idea of History: Carlyle, Arnold, and Pater*. Cambridge, Mass.: Harvard University Press, 1977. Argues that the idea of history informs Arnold's attitude toward literature and the shape of his literary career.

De Laura, David J. "Arnold and Goethe: The One on the Intellectual Throne." In *Essays Presented to Richard D. Altick*, eds. James R. Kincaid and Albert J. Kuhn. Columbus: Ohio State University Press, 1984. Arnold's views of Goethe are unique in his time but not isolated or singular.

————. *Hebrew and Hellene in Victorian England: Newman, Arnold, and Pater*. Austin: University of Texas Press, 1969. Influential study of artistic and cultural context of these terms in Arnold.

————, ed. *Matthew Arnold: A Collection of Critical Essays*. Englewood Cliffs, N.J.: Prentice-Hall, 1973. A sampling of essays on a variety of works for general introduction to Arnold study.

Eliot, T. S. *Selected Essays*. New York: Harcourt, Brace & World, 1964. Contains Eliot's essay on "Arnold and Pater."

Fletcher, Pauline. *Gardens and Grim Ravines*. Princeton, N.J.: Princeton University Press, 1983. Contains a chapter on Arnold's use of the forest glade.

Giddings, Robert, ed. *Matthew Arnold: Between Two Worlds*. Totowa, N.J.: Barnes and Noble, 1986. A collection of essays placing Arnold within the context of issues of his day such as industrialization, the Bishop Colenso controversy, and the fight for Ireland.

Gottfried, Leon. *Matthew Arnold and the Romantics*. Lincoln: University of Nebraska Press, 1963. Arnold's relationship to the Romantic poets.

Houghton, Walter. *The Victorian Frame of Mind*. New Haven, Conn.: Yale University Press, 1957. Influential study of the contours of Victorian thinking.

Jacoby, Russell. *The End of Utopia*. New York: Basic Books, 1999. See chapter on "Mass Culture and Anarchy" for discussion of Arnold's importance as an uncompromising critic of popular culture and democratic commitment.

Johnson, E. D. H. *The Alien Vision of Victorian Poetry*. Princeton, N.J.: Princeton University Press, 1952. Pioneer study of the multiple perspectives and voices of the Victorian poets.

Johnson, W. Stacy. *The Voices of Matthew Arnold*. New Haven, Conn.: Yale University Press, 1961. A study of the poetic voices of ambivalence and self-questioning in Arnold's poetry.

Kaplan, Fred. *The Poet's Sense of Self in Nineteenth-Century Poetry*. Detroit, Mich.: Wayne State University Press, 1972. Chapter 9, "The Banquet of the Muses," is about *Empedocles on Etna*.

Kelleher, John V. "Matthew Arnold and the Celtic Revival." In *Perspectives in Criticism*, ed. Harry Levin. Cambridge, Mass.: Harvard University Press, 1950. Argues that Arnold's moderated enthusiasm for Celtic literature became the standard view.

Kermode, Frank. *Romantic Image*. New York: Viking Press, 1964. In this important study of the function of the image in modern poetry, Kermode stresses the Romantic dialogue in *Empedocles on Etna*.

Langbaum, Robert. *The Mysteries of Identity. A Theme in Modern Literature*. New York: Oxford University Press, 1977. In his chapter, "Arnold: Waning Energy," Langbaum argues that Arnold gives us a more convincing version of modern urban numbness and alienation than the other Victorian poets.

Levenson, Michael H. *A Genealogy of Modernism*. Cambridge: Cambridge University Press, 1984. A section on "Arnold, Huxley, Pater: Toward a small world and a large self," argues that Arnold was willing to change Christianity in order to retain it and to appropriate the scientific world view as a way of looking at religion.

Lipman, Samuel, ed. *Culture and Anarchy*, by Matthew Arnold. Rethinking the Western Tradition series. New Haven, Conn.: Yale University Press, 1994. This reissue of *Culture and Anarchy* contains essays by Lipman, Maurice Cowling, Gerald Graff, and Steven Marcus evaluating the importance of Arnold's work in light of contemporary theory.

Livingston, James C. *Matthew Arnold and Christianity*. Columbia: University of South Carolina Press, 1986. One of the best recent studies of Arnold's religious thought placing him in the liberal Christian tradition of the nineteenth and twentieth centuries.

Machann, Clinton, and Forrest D. Burt, eds. *Matthew Arnold in His Time and Ours: Centenary Essays*. Charlottesville: University Press of Virginia, 1988. Collection of essays given by well-known Arnoldians at the 1988 conference on Arnold at Texas A & M.

McCarthy, Patrick J. *Matthew Arnold and the Three Classes*. New York: Columbia University Press, 1964. A study of Arnold's three classes of the populace, the middle class, and the aristocracy.

Miller, J. Hillis. *The Disappearance of God*. Cambridge, Mass.: Harvard University Press, 1963; reprint, New York: Schocken, 1965. A landmark study of the spiritual history of the Victorians with a chapter on Arnold.

———. *The Linguistic Moment*. Princeton, N.J.: Princeton University Press, 1985. Chapter 1, "From Stevens to Arnold to Wordsworth" offers a deconstructive reading of Arnold's use of language as suspension of reference. Miller argues that Empedocles' suicide is only a "verbal action."

Riede, David. *Matthew Arnold and the Betrayal of Language.* Charlottesville: University Press of Virginia, 1988. A deconstructive reading in the manner of J. Hillis Miller that argues that Arnold's words do not represent what he means and become empty signifiers.

Robbins, William. *The Arnoldian Principle of Flexibility.* English Literary Studies. Victoria, British Columbia: University of Victoria, 1979. Ideas in Arnold that oppose extremism.

―――. *The Ethical Idealisim of Matthew Arnold.* Toronto: University of Toronto Press, 1959. Examines Arnold's religious thought between the 1860s and 1880s and its sources as the foundation for his ethical thinking.

Roper, Alan. *Arnold's Poetic Landscapes.* Baltimore, Md.: Johns Hopkins University Press, 1969. Roper establishes several characteristic landscapes that structure the meaning of many of Arnold's best poems.

Said, Edward W. *Orientalism.* New York: Pantheon Books, 1978; reprint, New York: Vintage Books, 1979.

Schneider, Mary W. *Poetry in the Age of Democracy: The Literary Criticism of Matthew Arnold.* Lawrence: University Press of Kansas, 1989. Explores Arnold's sense of the place of criticism and poetry in democratic culture.

Shaw, W. David. *The Lucid Veil. Poetic Truth in the Victorian Age.* Madison: University of Wisconsin Press, 1987. Chapters on "Agnostic Theories of the Word: Arnold's Deconstruction" (141–47) and "Arnold's Platonism: Analogies of Self and State" (217–24).

Stange, G. Robert. *Matthew Arnold; The Poet as Humanist.* Princeton, N.J.: Princeton University Press, 1967. Study organized around Arnold's ideas, especially his ideas of poetry, nature, self, and love.

Stone, Donald D. *Communications with the Future: Matthew Arnold in Dialogue.* Ann Arbor: University of Michigan Press, 1997. Looks at the dialogic relationship of Arnold's thought to several major modern thinkers, including Nietzsche, Gadamer, Foucault, and Rorty.

Super, Robert H. *The Time Spirit of Matthew Arnold.* Ann Arbor: University of Michigan Press, 1970. Essays from a series of lectures, including commentary on *Empedocles on Etna.*

Sussman, Herbert. *Victorian Masculinities.* Cambridge: Cambridge University Press, 1995. Comments on the desexualized monks in Arnold's "Stanzas from the Grande Chartreuse."

Tinker, C. B. and H. F. Lowry. *The Poetry of Matthew Arnold.* New York: Russell & Russell, 1940. An early and informative commentary on the individual poems.

Willey, Basil. *Nineteenth Century Studies.* New York: Columbia University Press, 1949. An influential study of nineteenth-century cultural context. His chapter on Arnold focuses on *Culture and Anarchy* and the religious writings.

Williams, Raymond. *Culture and Society 1780–1950.* New York: Columbia University Press, 1958. Examines Arnold's sense of culture as influenced by industrialization and the dissent of the working class, which Williams finds Arnold to demean.

Articles in Journals

The Arnoldian. Vols. 1–15. Journal published twice a year with essays about Arnold and reviews of books of interest to Arnold scholars. Name and contents changed in 1988 to *Nineteenth Century Prose.*

Beaty, Jerome. "All Victoria's Horses and All Victoria's Men." *New Literary History* 1 (1970): 271–92.

Berryman, Charles. "Arnold's *Empedocles on Etna.*" *Victorian Newsletter* 29 (1966): 5–9.

Brick, Allan. "Equilibrium in the Poetry of Matthew Arnold." *University of Toronto Quarterly* 30 (1960): 45–56.

Bristow, Joseph. " 'Love, let us be true to one another': Matthew Arnold, Arthur Hugh Clough, and 'our Aqueous Ages.' " *Literature and History* 4 (1995): 27–49.

Buckler, William. "Victorian Modernism: The Arnold-Hardy Succession." *Browning Institute Studies* 11 (1983): 9–21.

Coats, John. "Two Versions of the Problem of the Modern Intellectual: *Empedocles on Etna* and 'Cleon.' " *Modern Language Review* 79 (1984): 769–82.

De Laura, David. "Coleridge, Hamlet, and Arnold's Empedocles." *Papers on Language and Literature* 8 (1972): 17–25.

———. "Matthew Arnold and the Nightmare of History." *Victorian Poetry,* Stratford-upon-Avon Series 15 (London: Edward Arnold, 1972): 37–57.

Dickstein, Morris. "Arnold Then and Now: The Use and Misuse of Criticism." *Critical Inquiry* 9 (1983): 483–507.

Farrell, John P. "Matthew Arnold's Tragic Vision." *PMLA* 85 (1970): 107–17.

Feltes, N. N. "Matthew Arnold and the Modern Spirit: A Reassessment." *University of Toronto Quarterly* 32 (1962): 27–36.

Greenberg, Robert A. "Matthew Arnold's Refuge of Art: 'Tristram and Iseult.' " *Victorian Newsletter* 25 (1964): 1–4

Grob, Alan. "Arnold's 'Mycerinus': The Fate of Pleasure." *Victorian Poetry* 20 (1982): 1–20.

———. "Arnold's 'The Scholar-Gipsy': The Use and Abuse of History." *Victorian Poetry* 34 (1996): 149–74.

———. "The Poetry of Pessimism: Arnold's 'Resignation.' " *Victorian Poetry* 26 (1988): 25–44.

Himmelfarb, Gertrude. "Dissent and Dogma." *The New Republic,* June 13, 1994, 45–48.

Houghton, Walter. "Arnold's *Empedocles on Etna.*" *Victorian Studies* 1 (1958): 311–36.

Kendall, J. L. "The Unity of Arnold's 'Tristram and Iseult.'" *Victorian Poetry* 1 (1963): 140–45.

Knight, G. Wilson. "'The Scholar-Gipsy': An Interpretation." *Review of English Studies* 6 (1955): 53–62.

Leavy, Barbara Fass. "Iseult of Brittany: A New Interpretation of Matthew Arnold's 'Tristram and Iseult.'" *Victorian Poetry* 18 (1980): 1–22.

Longenbach, James. "Arnold and the Modern Apocalypse." *PMLA* 104 (1989): 844–55.

Neff, D. S. "*The Times,* the Crimean War, and 'Stanzas from the Grande Chartreuse.'" *Papers on Language and Literature* 33 (1997): 169–81.

Neiman, Fraser. "The Zeitgeist of Matthew Arnold." *PMLA* 72 (1957): 977–78.

Nineteenth Century Prose. Vols. 16, no. 2 (1989) and 21, no. 2 (1994) devoted to Arnold.

Peltason, Timothy. "The Function of Matthew Arnold at the Present Time." *College English* 56 (1994): 749–65.

Perkins, David. "Arnold and the Function of Literature." *Journal of English Literary History* 18 (1951): 287–309.

Pitman, Ruth Ann. "On Dover Beach." *Essays in Criticism* 23 (1973): 109–36.

Pratt, Linda Ray. "Empedocles, Suicide, and the Order of Things." *Victorian Poetry* 26 (1988): 75–90.

Ray, Linda Lee [Linda Ray Pratt]. "Callicles on Etna: The Other Mask." *Victorian Poetry* 7 (1969): 309–20.

Raymond, Meredith B. "Apollo and Arnold's *Empedocles on Etna.*" *Review of English Studies* 8 (1967): 22–32.

Shrimpton, Nicholas. "One Life or Two? What Happened to Arnold After 1853." Review of *A Life of Matthew Arnold,* by Nicholas Murray. *Times Literary Supplement,* June 14, 1996, 4–5.

Sundell, M. G. "The Intellectual Background and Structure of Arnold's 'Tristram and Iseult.'" *Victorian Poetry* 1 (1963): 272–83.

Taylor, Beverly. "Imagination and Art in Arnold's 'Tristram and Iseult': The Importance of 'Making.'" *Studies in English Literature 1500–1900* 22 (1982): 633–45.

Ulmer, William A. "Romantic Modernity in Arnold's 'Tristram and Iseult.'" *Texas Studies in Literature and Language* 27 (1985): 62–85.

Vendler, Helen. "The Unburied Life." *The New Republic,* June 21, 1999, 48–52.

Victorian Poetry 26 (1988). Fifteen essays in special commemorative issue on the centennial of Arnold's death.

Wallace, Jennifer. "Translation in Arnold's *Empedocles.*" *Essays in Criticism* 45 (1995): 301–23.

Zeitlow, Paul. "Heard But Unheeded: The Songs of Callicles in Matthew Arnold's *Empedocles on Etna.*" *Victorian Poetry* 21 (1983): 241–56.

Index

poetry (*continued*)
  gods and, 28, 29; poet's vision and,
  25; as positive good, 71; power of, 15,
  33, 38, 65, 81, 102, 103; reality of
  human life in, 45, 46, 57; religion as
  form of, 33, 123; society and, 38;
  spiritual crises in, 66; suffering in, 22;
  uses of, 39; value of, 108; "vents" for
  action in, 34, 56; Victorian, 2
"Populace," 113, 114, 115, 118, 119
Popular Education of France, The, 96–97
Postmodernism, literary past and, 4
Poststructuralism, literary past and, 4
Pound, Ezra, 2, 77
power: of beauty, 108; beyond ourselves,
  122; of conduct, 108; creative, 100,
  101; critical, 100, 101; of criticism,
  103; of education, 95; eternal, 122,
  134, 135; of knowledge, 108; of language, 86, 102, 122; of literature,
  105; of poetry, 15, 33, 38, 65, 81,
  102, 103; of religion, 122; of social
  life, 108
predestination, 126
"Preface to Poems 1853," 34, 39, 56, 58,
  71
prose: *Culture and Anarchy,* 1, 3, 5–6, 12,
  13, 15, 17, 35, 94, 95, 96, 98, 99,
  109–20, 126, 129, 131, 138, 139,
  146; "Democracy," 96, 98, 99; *Discourses in America,* 1; *A French Eton,* 94;
  "The Function of Criticism at the Present Time," 71, 100, 119; "General
  Conclusion. School Studies," 103,
  106, 107; *God and the Bible,* 3, 13,
  121, 138–42; *Last Essays on Church
  and Religion,* 13; *Literature and Dogma,*
  1, 3, 13, 121, 124, 130–38, 139;
  "Literature and Science," 33, 34, 102,
  106, 107, 108; "On the Modern Element in Literature," 11, 68, 143; "On
  Translating Homer," 100; *The Popular
  Education of France,* 96–97; "Preface to
  Poems 1853," 34, 39, 56, 58, 71;
  "Spinoza and the Bible," 59; *St. Paul
  and Protestantism,* 13, 121, 124, 125,
  126–30, 131, 134, 139; "The Study
  of Poetry," 33, 102, 121

Protestant Dissent, 98, 116, 117, 122
Protestantism, 13, 98, 116, 125, 135,
  137
provincialism, 117
Puritanism, 27–28, 117, 122, 123, 126,
  127, 128, 129, 130

"A Question," 20

religion, 2; *Aberglaube* and, 131, 132,
  136, 139; Anglican, 117; apocalyptic
  predictions and, 132; Calvinism, 126,
  127; Catholicism, 28, 137; Christianity, 12, 13, 18, 115, 118, 121, 125;
  Church of England, 13; collapse of,
  13; conduct and, 18, 133, 145; controversies about, 130–38; culture
  and, 111, 132; decline of, 124, 137;
  defining, 125, 141; destruction of,
  121; dissent and, 98; emotional value
  of, 125; failure of, 102; faith in, 121;
  God's will, 12, 17, 18, 116, 134;
  Hebraism, 17, 18, 115, 116, 127;
  "Higher Criticism" and, 130, 131;
  "hole-and-corner" forms, 117; Jesus
  Christ, 13, 18, 121, 124, 128, 129,
  134, 136, 137, 138, 141; Judaism,
  117, 118, 136, 141; literal truth in,
  102; metaphoric meaning in, 102;
  need for, 12; as poetry, form of, 123;
  power of, 122; preoccupation with,
  12; Protestantism, 13, 98, 116, 125,
  135, 137; provincial, 117; Puritanism,
  27–28, 117, 122, 123, 126, 127,
  128, 129, 130; replaced by poetry,
  121; righteousness and, 18, 122; sal-
  vaging, 3; science and, 130, 131;
  superstition and, 132; truth of, 123
repentance, 134, 137
"Resignation," 46–52, 62, 91, 92, 93,
  94
Riede, David, 29, 32
righteousness, 12, 18, 128, 131, 133,
  134, 137, 144; desire for, 127; effect
  of, 124; model for, 13; religion and,
  122
rights: of free opinion, 98; individual, 3,
  100; of inheritance, 16, 113

The Author

Linda Ray Pratt received her Ph.D. from Emory University in 1971 and is a professor of English. She has served as chair of the department at the University of Nebraska–Lincoln and interim dean of the College of Arts and Sciences. She is a former national president of the American Association of University Professors and has published in the fields of higher education as well as in Victorian literature and modern poetry.

The Editor

Herbert Sussman is professor of English at Northeastern University. His publications in Victorian literature include *Victorian Masculinities: Manhood and Masculine Poetics in Early Victorian Literature and Art; Fact into Figure: Typology in Carlyle, Ruskin, and the Pre-Raphaelite Brotherhood;* and *Victorians and the Machine: The Literary Response to Technology.*

ADZ - 7341